Martin Oppermann
Editor

Geography and Tourism Marketing

"**T**he collection of papers assembled by Martin Oppermann provides a timely reminder of the nexus between geography and tourism. In particular, it emphasises that, despite innovations in tourism market segmentation which have resulted in more emphasis being placed on psychographics, geography remains a fundamental distinguishing variable in planning by public and private sector tourism marketing organisations. The superiority of geographic segmentation in terms of access to, and targettability of, markets is highlighted and it is suggested that the application of Geographic Information Systems (GIS) in tourism marketing will bring about a resurgence of this approach.

This volume brings together contributions from well known authors, who emphasize the relevance of the geographic perspective to various facets of the tourism marketing process. It will provide a valuable case study resource to tourism marketing and management students and practitioners alike."

Bill Faulkner, PhD
Director
Centre for Tourism
and Hotel Management Research
Griffith University
Gold Coast, Australia

"**W**ith the rediscovery of geography as a vital basis for market segmentation, Martin Oppermann's collection is a timely and invaluable contribution to the field. The book includes both practical and theoretical contributions from many of the world's leading tourism researchers, and case studies are offered from destinations as diverse as Barbados, Australia, and Sarawak. Of particular relevance are investigations of the Internet and Geographic Information Systems as applied marketing tools."

Dr. David Weaver
Faculty of Business and Hotel Management
Griffith University
Queensland, Australia

Geography and Tourism Marketing

The *Travel & Tourism Marketing* series:

Communication and Channel Systems in Tourism Marketing, edited by Muzaffer Uysal and Daniel R. Fesenmaier

Economic Psychology of Travel and Tourism, edited by John C. Crotts and W. Fred van Raaij

Recent Advances in Tourism Marketing Research, edited by Daniel R. Fesenmaier, Joseph T. O'Leary, and Muzaffer Uysal

Marketing Issues in Pacific Area Tourism, edited by John C. Crotts and Chris A. Ryan

Geography and Tourism Marketing, edited by Martin Oppermann

These books were published simultaneously as special thematic issues of the *Journal of Travel & Tourism Marketing* and are available bound separately. For further information, call 1-800-HAWORTH (outside US/Canada: 607-722-5857), Fax 1-800-895-0582 (outside US/Canada: 607-771-0012) or e-mail getinfo@haworth.com

Geography and Tourism Marketing

Martin Oppermann
Editor

The Haworth Press, Inc.
New York • London

Geography and Tourism Marketing has also been published as *Journal of Travel & Tourism Marketing*, Volume 6, Numbers 3/4 1997.

The development, preparation, and publication of this work has been undertaken with great care. However, the publisher, employees, editors, and agents of The Haworth Press and all imprints of The Haworth Press, Inc., including The Haworth Medical Press and Pharmaceutical Products Press, are not responsible for any errors contained herein or for consequences that may ensue from use of materials or information contained in this work. Opinions expressed by the author(s) are not necessarily those of The Haworth Press, Inc.

The Haworth Press, Inc., 10 Alice Street, Binghamton, NY 13904-1580 USA

Cover design by Thomas J. Mayshock Jr.

Library of Congress Cataloging-in-Publication Data

Geography and tourism marketing / Martin Oppermann, editor.
     p. cm.
     "Has also been published as Journal of travel & tourism marketing, volume 6, numbers 3/4, 1997"–T.p. verso.
     Includes bibliographical references and index.
     ISBN 0-7890-0335-X (alk. paper). – ISBN 0-7890-0336-8 (alk. paper)
     1. Tourist trade–Marketing. I. Oppermann, Martin
G155.A1G424 1997   97-26368
338.4′791–dc21   CIP

INDEXING & ABSTRACTING

Contributions to this publication are selectively indexed or abstracted in print, electronic, online, or CD-ROM version(s) of the reference tools and information services listed below. This list is current as of the copyright date of this publication. See the end of this section for additional notes.

- *ABSCAN, Inc.,* P. O. Box 2384, Monroe, LA 71207-2384

- *Cabell's Directory of Publishing Opportunities in Business & Economics (comprehensive & descriptive bibliographic listing with editorial criteria and publication production data for selected business & economics journals),* Cabell Publishing Company, Box 5428, Tobe Hahn Station, Beaumont, TX 77726-5428

- *Centre des Hautes Etudes Touristiques (CHET),* IMMEUBLE EUROFFICE, 38 av. de l'Europe B.P. 661, 13094 Aix-en-Provence Cedex 2, France

- *CNPIEC Reference Guide: Chinese National Directory of Foreign Periodicals,* P.O. Box 88, Beijing, Peoples Republic of China

- *IBZ International Bibliography of Periodical Literature,* Zeller Verlag GmbH & Co., P.O.B. 1949, d-49009 Osnabruck, Germany

- *International Hospitality and Tourism Database, The,* John Wiley & Sons, Inc., 605 Third Avenue, New York, NY 10158-0012

- *INTERNET ACCESS (& additional networks) Bulletin Board for Libraries ("BUBL"), coverage of information resources on INTERNET, JANET, and other networks.*
  - <URL:http://bubl.ac.uk/>
  - The new locations will be found under <URL:http://bubl.ac. uk/link/>.
  - Any existing BUBL users who have problems finding information on the new service should contact the BUBL help line by sending e-mail to <bubl@bubl.ac.uk>.
  The Andersonian Library, Curran Building, 101 St. James Road, Glasgow G4 0NS, Scotland

(continued)

- *Journal of Health Care Marketing (abstracts section)*, Georgia Tech-School of Management, Ivan Allen College-225 North Avenue NW, Atlanta, GA 30332

- *Journal of Travel Research,* Business Research Division, University of Colorado, Boulder, CO 80309-0420

- *Leisure, Recreation & Tourism Abstracts, c/o CAB International/CAB ACCESS . . . available in print, diskettes updated weekly, and on INTERNET. Providing full bibliographic listings, author affiliation, augmented keyword searching,* CAB International, P.O. Box 100, Wallingford Oxon OX10 8DE, United Kingdom

- *Lodging & Restaurant Index,* Purdue University, Stone Hall Room 220, West Lafayette, IN 47907-1002

- *Management & Marketing Abstracts,* Pira International, Randalls Road, Leatherhead, Surrey KT22 7RU, England

- *Sage Urban Studies Abstracts (SUSA),* Sage Publications, Inc., 2455 Teller Road, Newbury Park, CA 91320

- *Social Planning/Policy & Development Abstracts (SOPODA),* Sociological Abstracts, Inc., P. O. Box 22206, San Diego, CA 92192-0206

- *Sociological Abstracts (SA),* Sociological Abstracts, Inc., P. O. Box 22206, San Diego, CA 92192-0206

- *Sport Database/Discus,* Sport Information Resource Center, 1600 James Naismith Drive, Suite 107, Gloucester, Ontario K1B 5N4, Canada

- *Worldwide Hospitality & Tourism Trends Database ("WHATT" Database), International CD-ROM research database for hospitality students, researchers, and planners with 3 international editorial bases, and functions with support of the Hotel & Catering International Management Association (HCIMA),* William F. Harrah College of Hotel Administration, Box 456023, 4505 Maryland Parkway, Las Vegas, NV 89154-6023

(continued)

SPECIAL BIBLIOGRAPHIC NOTES

related to special journal issues (separates)
and indexing/abstracting

☐ indexing/abstracting services in this list will also cover material in any "separate" that is co-published simultaneously with Haworth's special thematic journal issue or DocuSerial. Indexing/abstracting usually covers material at the article/chapter level.

☐ monographic co-editions are intended for either non-subscribers or libraries which intend to purchase a second copy for their circulating collections.

☐ monographic co-editions are reported to all jobbers/wholesalers/approval plans. The source journal is listed as the "series" to assist the prevention of duplicate purchasing in the same manner utilized for books-in-series.

☐ to facilitate user/access services all indexing/abstracting services are encouraged to utilize the co-indexing entry note indicated at the bottom of the first page of each article/chapter/contribution.

☐ this is intended to assist a library user of any reference tool (whether print, electronic, online, or CD-ROM) to locate the monographic version if the library has purchased this version but not a subscription to the source journal.

☐ individual articles/chapters in any Haworth publication are also available through the Haworth Document Delivery Services (HDDS).

Geography and Tourism Marketing

CONTENTS

ABOUT THE EDITOR

Martin Oppermann, PhD, is Senior Lecturer in Tourism Management at Waiariki Polytechnic in Rotorua, New Zealand. Prior to this position, he taught at the University of Nevada, Las Vegas and the University of Tübingen. Having also worked as a consultant, marketing manager, and tour guide, he knows the tourism industry from both an academic perspective and a practical point of view. Dr. Oppermann is widely recognized for his numerous publications in tourism and hospitality journals, such as *Annals of Tourism Research, Journal of Travel Research, Journal of Travel & Tourism Marketing, Tourism Management*, and *Journal of Vacation Marketing*. He is Editor-in-Chief of *Pacific Tourism Review* and is currently Interim Editor for *Journal of Travel & Tourism Marketing*. He is a member of several professional and research associations, including the Council of Hotel, Restaurant and Institutional Education, the Asia Pacific Tourism Association, the International Society of Travel & Tourism Educators, and the Travel & Tourism Research Association.

Geography's Changing Role
in Tourism Marketing

Martin Oppermann

Geography is arguably the most important variable in market segmentation and tourism marketing approaches. A glance through any major textbook on marketing and/or tourism marketing quickly reveals that geographic segmentation is commonly listed as the first or second variable in the relevant chapter. However, some observers would argue that geographic segmentation has lost its pre-eminent influence and that other segmentation variables, such as life-stage and lifestyle, have gained greater importance. To what extent these other variables were and are used by the vast majority of the tourism industry remains questionable; often the academic literature suggesting yet another way of segmenting the market appears to be eclectic and not necessarily reflective of industry practice. For example, most tourism destination organizations use geographic segmentation as their primary if not only segmentation variable. Marketing budgets are usually allocated by market region and not by any other variable. In the case of New Zealand, for example, marketing budgets are established for Japan, North Asia, South East Asia, North America, etc., and not by age of travelers, family life cycle stage, adventure tourists, business traveler or alike. Most travel agencies only use geographic orientation to market to their customers with local newspapers and yellow pages being the pre-

Martin Oppermann is Senior Lecturer in Tourism Management at Waiariki Polytechnic. He is also Interim Editor of *Journal of Travel & Tourism Marketing* and Editor-in-Chief of *Pacific Tourism Review*.

Address correspondence to Centre for Tourism Studies, Waiariki Polytechnic, Private Bag 3028, Rotorua, New Zealand (e-mail: oppermam@bmt.waiariki.ac.nz).

[Haworth co-indexing entry note]: "Geography's Changing Role in Tourism Marketing." Oppermann, Martin. Co-published simultaneously in *Journal of Travel & Tourism Marketing* (The Haworth Press, Inc.) Vol. 6, No. 3/4, 1997, pp. 1-3; and: *Geography and Tourism Marketing* (ed: Martin Oppermann) The Haworth Press, Inc., 1997, pp. 1-3. Single or multiple copies of this article are available for a fee from The Haworth Document Delivery Service [1-800-342-9678, 9:00 a.m. - 5:00 p.m. (EST). E-mail address: getinfo@haworth.com].

1

dominant forms of the promotion mix. Only a few travel agencies have specialized in specific types of traveling and would accordingly use other distribution channels.

Yet, while the decline of geographic segmentation in the 1970s and 1980s cannot be disputed, it is making a major comeback in the 1990s and, I believe, will recover, if not simply retain its pre-eminent position well into the next millennium. One reason for this recovery is the issue of addressability and targetability in the age of "segments of one" (Blattberg & Deighton, 1991; Collins & Wallace, 1995; Ventresca, 1991). Market fragmentation, mass customization, and globalization are all buzzwords of the 1990s and an indication that the traditional market place no longer exists. While it is doubtful that there ever really was one mass-market, the rapid growth in the post-war era in both economic prosperity and population allowed companies to just offer a few standard products and consumers would buy anyway. Today, however, it is no longer enough to offer one standard tour package; customers want to choose between many different ones, they want to have them tailored to their wants and needs, and more importantly, the stagnant demand has turned a seller's market into a buyer's market.

However, along with increasing fragmentation of the market place comes the issue of being able to market to the individual segments effectively. While it is no problem to derive more and more, smaller and smaller segments, it becomes at the same time more and more difficult to effectively target them. Hence, addressability becomes a major issue and the introduction of Geographic Information Systems (GIS) into the marketing arena the obvious solution. The primary characteristic of GIS is that any information or data in its databank is related to a specific geographic location, for example a household. While early predecessors of today's high-powered GIS systems were used to relate, for example, demographic data to geographic area units such as states, districts or postal code areas (e.g., Baier, 1967; Kobak, 1993), they were not able to move below this level. In addition, very limited data was available on a commercial basis on individual households. Today, there is a proliferation of companies that will append information to a tourism operator's database and it is mostly a question of cost-effectiveness in relation to the intended purpose that determines the feasibility of doing so. This appending of data may be on a household level, census track or zip code level (e.g., Baker & Baker, 1993; Collins & Wallace, 1995; Drummond, 1995; Kobak, 1993; Weber, 1996). Depending on the outcome and the quality of the appending data, zip codes or households may be the more appropriate level. With the power of collecting detailed information on household level, GIS marketing programmes have made geographic segmentation once again very appealing. Databased marketing is bound to become a strong aspect of tourism marketing in the years to come (Oppermann 1996; 1997) with potential for any type and size of tourism operator.

This compendium brings together a range of contributions covering geographical issues in tourism marketing. The reader will soon notice that the contributions are very diverse, ranging from geographic segmentation of market segments or a specific analysis of subsegments within a geographical area (Lang & O'Leary; Reid & Reid) to the issue of geographic scale of the destination area and the spatial behavior and requirements of the tourists and their impact on marketing requirements (Leiper; Pearce), from "modern" promotion channels such as the Internet (Marcussen) to "traditional" ones like brochures (Lawton & Page; Zhou), and from a more theoretical contribution on the importance of the place concept in marketing (Hall) to an applied overview of the usage of GIS in tourism marketing (Bertazzon, Crouch, Draper & Waters). I trust the readers will appreciate the width of the topics covered in this compilation and will gain a greater appreciation of the influence of geography in tourism marketing.

REFERENCES

Baier, M. (1967). Zip Code–New Tool for Marketers. *Harvard Business Review* 45 (January/February): 136-140.

Baker, S., Baker, K. (1993). *Market Mapping: How to Use Revolutionary New Software to Find, Analyze and Keep Customers.* New York: McGraw-Hill.

Blattberg, R.C., Deighton, J. (1991). Interactive Marketing: Exploiting the Age of Addressability. *Sloan Management Review* 33(Fall): 5-14.

Collins, J., Wallace, J. (1995). The Use of Census Data for Target Marketing–The Way Forward for the Tourism Industry. *Journal of Vacation Marketing* 1(3): 273-280.

Drummond, W.J. (1995). Address Matching: GIS Technology for Mapping Human Activity Patterns. *Journal of the American Planning Association* 61(2): 240-251.

Kobak, T. (1993). How to Unmask Your Customer. *American Demographics* 15(7): 52-55.

Oppermann, M. (1996). The Application-Sophistication Framework of Databased Marketing in the Hospitality Industry: A Nevada Case Study. *Journal of Database Marketing* 3: 365-376.

Oppermann, M. (1997). Using Databased Marketing in the Tourism Industry–Gaining the Competitive Advantage. *Turizam* 45(1).

Ventresca, B.J. (1991). DataBase Marketing at Farm Journal, Inc. *Journal of Direct Marketing* 5(4): 44-49.

Weber, A. (1996). Enhancement–Plain or Fancy. *Target Marketing* 19(5): 42/44-45.

Traveler Geographic Origin and Market Segmentation for Small Island Nations: The Barbados Case

Laurel J. Reid
Stanley D. Reid

SUMMARY. This paper explores the effectiveness of geographic origin as a basis for segmenting visitors to small island nations that depend exclusively on international travelers as tourism markets. International visitation data drawn from the Barbados annual tourist survey, data on five geographic markets (USA, the UK, Canada, Germany, and Trinidad) are examined to determine whether country origin can be used as a segmentation criterion to effectively establish preferred visitor profiles. Visitor characteristics and profiles are found to be distinguishable by country of origin. These have implications for tourism promotion and distribution strategies for small island nations. *[Article copies available for a fee from The Haworth Document Delivery Service: 1-800-342-9678. E-mail address: getinfo@ haworth.com]*

Laurel J. Reid is Associate Professor, Brock University, Department of Recreation and Leisure Studies, St. Catharines, Ontario, Canada L2S 3A1. Stanley D. Reid is Principal, Reid Associates, #B Joe Louis Boulevard, Enterprise, Christ Church, Barbados, West Indies.

The authors acknowledge the Caribbean Tourism Organization and its Research Director, Arleigh Sobers and Technical Team: Winfield Griffith and Steven Aymes for their assistance in providing the data used in this research.

[Haworth co-indexing entry note]: "Traveler Geographic Origin and Market Segmentation for Small Island Nations: The Barbados Case." Reid, Laurel J., and Stanley D. Reid Co-published simultaneously in *Journal of Travel & Tourism Marketing* (The Haworth Press, Inc.) Vol. 6, No. 3/4, 1997, pp. 5-22; and: *Geography and Tourism Marketing* (ed: Martin Oppermann) The Haworth Press, Inc., 1997, pp. 5-22. Single or multiple copies of this article are available for a fee from The Haworth Document Delivery Service [1-800-342-9678, 9:00 a.m. - 5:00 p.m. (EST). E-mail address: getinfo@haworth.com].

5

INTRODUCTION

Understanding visitor behavior and its relevance to increasing tourism's economic benefits is critically important to all travel destinations. Such knowledge can assist decision makers to better identify visitor markets that offer opportunities for growth and formulate appropriate strategies to maximize tourism yields. Country of origin, since it typically serves as a basis for categorizing tourist markets and is universally employed as a basis for collecting and interpreting tourism data, has the potential for providing this information if it can identify preferred visitor markets.

Small island destinations have the unusual feature of operating almost exclusively in international markets. Consequently, key aspects of their tourism strategy, such as choice of transportation, travel and promotion intermediaries involve country of origin considerations. Island nations are too small to have viable domestic tourist markets and can only be accessed through international carriers. These market features suggest that a major concern for island nations should be a search for differences in tourism behaviors by origin markets to pinpoint opportunities for tourism growth.

This paper uses visitation data from an annual tourist survey to examine the link between country of origin and the behavior of tourists to Barbados, a small island destination located in the Caribbean region. The paper highlights differences in visitation patterns, travel methods, expenditures, and consumption behaviour across five different origin markets and discusses their relevance in determining preferred customer profiles. Conclusions are then drawn from the findings for strategic destination marketing of small island nations.

CONCEPTUAL FRAMEWORK

The use of geography as an effective segmentation tool in international tourism rests on the critical assumption that country of origin can distinguish preferred visitor markets—with sufficient volume and differences in market characteristics to justify using differentiated marketing strategies (Kotler, 1991; Middleton, 1994). By definition, market segments must be discrete, measurable, viable, and appropriate (Middleton, 1994). This *discrete* criterion is fulfilled when tourist origin markets have geographically separate transport, promotion, and communication links which effectively segregate the distribution system that delivers the tourist to the destination. Thus, country of origin, as a segmentation tool, defines a market that is characterized by a specific travel market structure with distinct logistics, distribution and communication channels.

The *measurability* criterion is satisfied since tourist data is collected by country of origin. This permits easy identification of market volume which is critical in determining the relative potential of a specific country market. The last criteria, *viability* and *appropriateness*, are linked since they determine the strategy required for targeting the segment. The extent to which a destination can influence demand from these markets primarily depends on its ability to implement the communication and promotional strategies appropriate for this task (Reid & Reid, 1994).

Small island nations face major constraints in this regard since they usually depend on a few travel intermediaries in the country of origin to supply visitor traffic (Go and Williams, 1993; Roop, 1994a,b). This structural feature suggests that relationships between travel distribution intermediaries and suppliers in origin countries are casual factors affecting both volume and character of tourism traffic to an island destination.

The viability and appropriateness of country of origin as a segmentation variable depends on whether these criteria identify opportunities for improving tourism performance. Destinations typically try to improve their tourism performance by: (1) increasing absolute visitation numbers; (2) encouraging visitors to stay longer; and/or (3) inducing more spending by visitors at the destination. These objectives are not mutually exclusive and underline the research question of whether targeting tourism segments defined by country of origin is a viable tourism strategy for small island destinations.

Establishing desired customer profiles by origin markets should take into account the need to identify characteristics and behaviors which have an impact on tourism expenditures (Perdue & Pitegoff, 1990). This type of focus allows the economic value of a segment to be better seen. It also has the advantage of being conceptually consistent with commonly used approaches for estimating the economic impact of tourism expenditures (Bull, 1992; Gunn, 1993; Taylor, Fletcher & Clabaugh, 1993).

Economic value is generated over an entire travel purchase cycle by spending prior to and after arriving at the destination and involves such expenditure categories as accommodation, transportation, sightseeing, activities, eating and drinking, shopping, and personal services.

Several factors affect spending patterns and levels and are relevant in determining preferred customer profiles. These include: type of trip taken (i.e., purpose, itinerary, length of stay, travel group size and composition), travel purchase characteristics (retail outlet used and type of trip, accommodation used), attractions visited and activities participated in at the destination (Bull, 1992). These variables provide data on travel decisions and characteristics that can be used to identify actionable differences in origin markets. For example, decisions involving travel mode and accommodation, the two most expensive elements of the travel product are typically combined when buying tour packages. Origin markets, however, differ in their use of travel packages and intermediaries who act as distributors (Donoghue, 1993; Skapinker, 1993).

Although patterns of information search are not proposed as a factor that influences the economic value of visitor segments, such behavior merits consideration since it can assist in determining the most effective promotion and communication channels to be used in origin markets. Destination-naive visitors engage in extensive information searches and make use of multiple information sources prior to making the travel decision (Snepenger, Meged, Snelling & Worrall, 1990). Moreover, travel intermediaries such as tour or charter operators and travel agents are frequently used as key information sources by first time travelers (Duke & Persia, 1993; Hsieh & O'Leary, 1993). These findings suggest that destinations which depend on first time visitors supplied by tours or charters have limited scope to directly influence this group's travel decisions unless this is accomplished through intermediary appeals.

Even though methods of payment used for travel products are not traditionally included in travel consumer profiles, this travel feature must also be examined in the context of geography. Credit cards are a convenient payment method for goods and services and are used by both international business and pleasure travelers (Bull, 1992; *CANA Business*, 1992; Ennew, Watkins & Wright, 1993). They provide flexibility in discretionary spending in the presence of planned travel expenditure budgets.

Widespread card ownership exists in USA, Canadian, UK, and European markets, with the latter two markets having a lower incidence of multiple card possession (Meiden, 1984). Most major credit cards are marketed independently or in co-branding or affinity relationships to promote increased spending with preferred suppliers that serve Caribbean destinations (*Insider Flyer*, 1996; Nelms, 1993). Several are linked with use of specific carriers. These include Eurocard with Lufthansa and Swiss Air, Diners Club linked with American Airlines, United Airlines and Air Canada, and American Express with affiliations extending to both US and European carriers.

The above considerations are posed as critical elements in determining preferred customer profiles based on geographic origin for small island nations. Each is analyzed below with respect to specific geographic markets visiting the Caribbean island nation of Barbados.

BACKGROUND

Barbados has direct air connections to major tourist markets provided by both scheduled international carriers and charters. It is one of the top five tourism destinations in the Caribbean, receiving more than 400,000 visitors annually drawn from North America, Europe and other Caribbean countries (DeLuca, 1993a,b). There has been a decrease in overall visitor numbers since 1989 primarily due to a decline in USA visitation (*Statistical News*, 1996).

Barbados offers a typical sun/sea/sand tourism product which includes duty-free shopping facilities, extensive marine-based activities, a limited number of land-based attractions, and a wide variety of restaurants. The Barbados Tourism Authority (BTA) is the public agency responsible for marketing the destination and primarily focuses on the USA, UK, Canada, Germany, and Trinidad which are the leading markets, accounting for nearly 80 percent of all visitors (Table 1).

The USA and UK are primary markets, collectively accounting for 54 percent of all visitors, while Canada, Germany and Trinidad are the most important secondary markets, with shares of 12 percent, 8 percent and 4 percent, respectively. Seasonal variations in visits from these markets show notable peaks such as December to March for the USA and Canada, April for UK, November to March for Germany, and July-August for Trinidad. They arise from differences in customary travel periods across these markets (McEnill, 1992) and demand stimulated by sporting and cultural events in Barbados, such as *Test Cricket* (April) and the *Crop-Over Festival* (July). These events appeal to particular origin markets, because of special interest in cricket in the UK and Caribbean and Crop-Over in Canada and the USA.

The accommodation sector consists of hotels, apartments, villas and guest houses varied in price and quality with *average* occupancy levels across the entire sector. For example, during 1993 overall occupancy was low (53.7%), peaking in February, reaching their lowest point in June. These occupancy levels vary widely by accommodation type. For the months of February and June 1993 respectively, occupancy rates were as follows: hotels: 67.2%, 29.0%; guest houses: 41.2%, 14.1%; apartment hotels: 72.3%, 59.2%; apartments: 57.5%, 36.6% (*Digest of Tourism Statistics*, 1994).

METHODS

Data are drawn from an annual tourist survey of visitors to Barbados conducted during four, three-week intervals in May 1993-April 1994 by

TABLE 1. Index of Monthly Seasonal Visitation to Barbados for Select Geographic Markets[1] (May 1993-April 1994) (May 1993 = 100).

Month	USA	(State) New York[3]	Canada	Region of Origin[1] (Province) Ontario[3]	United Kingdom	Germany	Trinidad
May 1993[2]	100	100	100	100	100	100	100
June	83	91	66	72	95	80	87
July	119	234	116	128	105	130	204
August	100	137	91	100	101	109	187
September	61	70	61	60	95	114	89
October	85	82	98	97	107	137	95
November	105	109	163	155	108	215	80
December	129	165	235	246	109	198	102
January 1994	116	104	271	280	91	176	80
February	134	124	257	279	89	173	86
March	133	122	257	276	104	191	93
April	103	113	165	164	130	135	133
• Total Visitors[4]	111,954	41,571	49,369	38,628	112,731	31,878	16,134
• Percent of Total	27.1%	10.1%	12.0%	9.4%	27.3%	7.7%	3.9%

[1]These five national markets represent 78 percent of all visitors by air (or 322,066 visitors).
[2]Actual visitors in May 1993: USA 8,665; New York 2,866; Canada 2,626; Ontario 1,975; United Kingdom 9,138; Germany 1,815; Trinidad 1,216.
[3]New York State has accounted for approximately 35-40% of the total USA market (included in USA total) and Ontario has accounted for 75-80% of the total Canadian market (included in Canada total), respectively during the last three years.
[4]Total number of visitors from all destinations was 412,746 during this period.

Source: Caribbean Tourism Organization (CTO), Bridgetown, Barbados, 1996.

the Barbados Tourism Authority (BTA) and the Caribbean Tourism Organization (CTO) at the Barbados international airport. Self-administered questionnaires were distributed to one person per travel party. Only departing passengers who were overseas residents and had stayed in Barbados for more than one night and less than one year were surveyed.

The research instrument requested information on: (1) socioeconomic and demographic variables: age, gender, region of origin; (2) travel characteristics: length of stay, purpose of visit, trip description, travel party description; (3) information sources used in travel decision; (4) prior travel experience to region and country; (5) travel expenditure, allocation and payment methods; (6) activities engaged in and attractions visited; and (7) evaluation of trip aspects. Only data from USA, UK, Canada, Germany and Trinidad respondents are used in this investigation.

RESEARCH FINDINGS AND DISCUSSION

A comparison of the visitor distribution by country of origin between the population and sample is provided in Table 2. In both instances, the country markets under investigation provide approximately 80 percent of all visitors. Germany and Trinidad are under-represented while the USA and the UK are over-represented. When considered in conjunction with the large sample size, these sampling biases indicate a robust basis for generalizing findings on visitors from these markets. A profile of Barbados visitors by geographic origin is shown in Table 3.

Purpose of Visit and Party Composition

Most stay over travelers visit Barbados exclusively for vacation purposes, irrespective of country of origin (Table 3) except for Trinidad visitors who show the highest incidence of travel for business, vacation/business and visiting friends and relatives. These findings are consistent with the country's position as an international destination for long-haul markets (three to five hours flying time) and as a major trading partner with Trinidad, its largest and geographically proximate export market.

Party composition varies by country of origin with USA and Canada markets showing the greatest similarity. Spouses/partners account for more than half the visitors from all markets, except Trinidad where only 25 percent of visitors are in this category. Families, the next largest group, account for between 21-29 percent of each visitor market except Germany where only one-tenth are in this category. Groups/friends are the third largest visitor category in the USA, Canada and UK, with single party travel accounting for less than 10 percent in these markets.

In general, these data show that Barbados as a vacation destination attracts all types of visitors, even though these may vary in relative importance and size by country of origin. These findings suggest the communication focus of the product must rest on an appeal which includes couples, families and persons traveling in groups and singles. An emphasis should be placed on promoting a wide range of activities and attractions available on the island, while reinforcing the typical sea, sand and sun components that represent core benefits sought by the market. Such a strategy is aimed at providing leisure choices unconstrained by party composition or size.

Travel Arrangements, Behavior and Itinerary

Germans principally travel on package tours and over half the UK visitors use similar arrangements. In contrast, less than half of the Ameri-

TABLE 2. Geographic Distribution of Barbados Tourist Sample versus Visitor Population.

Country of Origin	Sample (n = 15,181)	Population (N = 412,746)
• USA	33.5%	27.1%
• Canada	11.1	12.0
• United Kingdom	31.2	27.3
• Germany	4.4	7.7
• Trinidad	1.2	3.9
• Other Countries	18.6	22.0

can or Canadian visitors use this mode (Table 3). First time travelers to the destination are dominant in German, UK and USA markets. In contrast, the Canadian market is a balanced mix of first time and repeat visitors. The incidence of high package bookings and first time visitation among German and UK travel groups suggests that tour operators play an important role in the first time visit decision.

The high proportion of package travelers to the destination is of significance in view of other evidence which suggests that they behave differently to the non package visitor. For example, UK purchasers of international package tours have been found to take trips of shorter duration, travel more frequently with friends/relatives, visit more new destinations and use more information sources in trip planning when compared to non-package travelers (Hsieh, O'Leary & Morrison, 1994). These findings argue for consideration of tour package travelers in any analyses aimed at developing customer profiles for destination marketing purposes.

A significant minority of USA and Canadian visitors have previously visited the island by cruise. The cruise market provides more visitors to Barbados than air travel (*Digest of Tourism Statistics*, 1994). Since cruise travel can provide prior exposure to an island destination it, therefore, has potential as a source for generating future stay over visitors.

Trips to other Caribbean islands are taken by between 10-20 percent of visitors from all countries of origin. These side trips, which may be one-day tours or longer and are typically booked in advance as part of a trip itinerary or at the destination and are not generally available as part of a tour package. Visitors purchasing these trips are likely to stay for shorter periods at their main destination. In addition, they have first hand information on new destinations to be considered when planning future trips. These findings stress the need for continued product development and

TABLE 3. Barbados Stay-Over Visitor Profile for Select Markets (May 1993-April 1994) (n = 12,362).

Descriptor	Region of Origin				
	USA	Canada	United Kingdom	Germany	Trinidad
	(n = 5081)	(n = 1686)	(n = 4733)	(n = 674)	(n = 188)
• **Purpose of Visit**					
– Vacation	80.0%	83.0%	90.2%	96.9%	51.6%
– Business only	6.3	4.2	2.3	.7	14.9
– Vacation/Business	7.3	6.9	2.7	1.8	17.6
–Visit Friends/Relatives	2.8	3.6	1.5	.6	9.0
– Other	3.6	2.4	3.2	.0	6.9
• **Party Composition**					
– Alone	8.6	8.4	4.5	6.7	33.5
– Spouse/Partner	54.2	52.7	55.7	66.3	25.0
– Family	21.5	25.1	29.2	9.8	29.3
– Group/Friends	13.4	11.3	9.5	16.5	9.0
– Other	2.2	2.6	1.0	.7	3.2
• **Travel Arrangements**					
– Package	36.3	44.0	56.4	73.9	9.6
• **First Visit to Island**	65.5	51.2	71.6	88.4	16.5
• **Previous Visit to Island on Cruise**	13.8	17.1	7.7	2.7	11.2
• **Visited Other Caribbean Islands During Trip**	10.7	15.4	15.3	21.1	9.6
• **Accommodation Type**					
– Hotel	73.1	60.6	63.8	78.8	46.3
– Apartment/Villa	13.0	23.7	28.9	5.3	29.8
– Guest House	3.1	2.1	1.1	10.7	6.4
– Friend/Relative	7.5	9.4	3.7	4.5	14.9
– Other	3.4	4.3	2.5	.7	2.7
• **Mean Length of Stay (nights)**	7.0 nights	7.0 nights	14.0 nights	14.0 nights	4.0 nights
• **Median Daily Expenditure**	$116.00	$82.00	$77.00	$70.50	$92.50

promotion of activities and attractions as a focus for the destination marketing strategy to increase the average length of stay.

Accommodation Used

Hotels are the principal accommodation type used by visitors from all origin markets, with apartments/villas having secondary appeal to Canada,

UK, and Trinidad markets. Accommodation with friends and relatives is the third largest category of accommodation. Trinidadians show higher use of accommodation with friends/relatives than other visitors. Guest houses are least popular, with the exception of the German market which gives them second preference.

These data are relevant to increasing the relatively low occupancy levels in the accommodation sector. The results show that attracting an increased number of visitors from all origin markets would contribute to increased occupancy levels for all accommodation types, with the greatest impact on hotel occupancy. These findings suggest that packages differentiated by accommodation types can be offered to different geographic markets as a destination strategy aimed at selectively filling particular accommodation types. Apartments/villas would benefit significantly from increases in USA, Canadian, UK and Trinidad visitors while guest houses could expect their main growth from USA and German markets.

Length of Stay

There are substantive differences in length of stay at the destination across origin markets. The mean lengths of stay for the USA and Canadian markets are one week, for UK and German markets two weeks and for Trinidad visitors four days (Table 3). These values are extremely skewed for Canada and Trinidad markets (Sk > +1) (Pearson's 2nd coefficient of Skewness) which have the highest incidence of repeat visitors, a tourist category that is typically made up of long-stay visitors. In general, the length of stay is consistent with the most frequently offered packages available in the origin markets.

Visitor Spending

Mean daily expenditures are higher for US and Trinidad visitors than other country of origin markets. However, these results are highly skewed. A similar situation was found when expenditures within specific categories were examined (e.g., meals, drinks, shopping). The minimum coefficient of skewness across all expenditure types was .4, with three categories showing extreme skewness (Sk > +1), including daily spending by: (1) USA, UK and German visitors on entertainment and attractions; (2) German visitors on other meals/drinks; and (3) Trinidad visitors on shopping. The presence of extreme skewness indicates that mean daily expenditure is not an appropriate measure for indicating typical visitor spending. As a result, median values for daily expenditure while in Barbados are reported in Tables 3 and 4. Expenditures on prepaid packages and any advances paid before visiting Barbados are not included. These packages typically incorporate air travel, accommodation, and may often include some meals and ground transportation between airport and lodgings.

Median daily expenditures vary by the country of origin with the USA showing the highest daily expenditures and Germany the lowest (Table 4). Accommodation accounts for the major part of daily expenditures followed by other meals/drinks, shopping, transportation, other spending and entertainment/recreation. The varying amounts spent on accommodation by country of origin indicate that, on average, USA visitors appear to stay at more expensive accommodation than the other four geographic markets. This market represents the most lucrative one for hotels.

Overall daily spending must be interpreted within the context of length of stay since total aggregate spending per visit can come from long-stay visitors with low daily spending or short stay visitors with high daily spending. In addition, destinations may have policy preferences as to the categories of spending they want to influence. For example, Trinidad visitors who typically have the shortest length of stay (four days) would be an appropriate market for stimulating other spending expenditures.

Activity Participation

Water sports and boat trips are the most popular single category of activities that visitors pursue for all markets except Trinidad (Table 5a). Overall participation in scuba diving and fishing are low. Other activities subsumes sightseeing, golfing, attending sporting/cultural events and shopping; these enjoy participation rates varying from 29 percent to 38 percent for all markets.

Specific differences across markets are worth noting. Half the USA visitors participate in water sports; less than one-third undertake boat trips and other activities. More than one-third of Canadian visitors participate in water sports and other activities and less than one-third take boat trips. Half the UK visitors participate in water sports; nearly half take boat trips and less than one-third pursue other activities. Almost 40 percent of Germans participate in water sports while less than one-third undertake other activities. Over one-third of the Trinidad travelers pursue other activities and about one-sixth participate in water sports.

Analysis of activity by market share shows that USA and UK visitors are the principal markets for varied activity experiences offered in Barbados (Table 5b). However, the German market is an important secondary market for scuba diving and in terms of its potential, out ranks the Cana-

TABLE 4. Barbados Stay-Over Visitor Expenditures by Region of Origin ($ US) (May 1993-April 1994) (n = 12,362).

Region of Origin	Total Median DAILY Expenditure*	Median Amount Spent in Each Category					
		Accom-modation	Other Meals & Drinks	Trans-portation	Enter-tainment**	Shopping	Other
• United States (n = 5081)	$116.00	$64.0	$11.0	$5.0	$0.0	$7.0	$2.0
• Canada (n = 1686)	82.00	41.0	10.0	2.0	0.0	5.0	1.0
• United Kingdom (n = 4733)	77.00	34.0	8.0	3.0	0.0	4.0	1.0
• Germany (n = 674)	70.50	42.0	6.0	3.0	0.0	2.0	1.0
• Trinidad (n = 188)	92.50	35.0	7.0	2.5	0.0	1.0	4.0

* Median used here because the presence of extreme values (on the high side) makes the mean daily expenditure an inappropriate indicator of typical visitor spending. Total median daily expenditures are reported for all visitors, including those who came on prepaid packages. The latter group's expenditure on accommodation is, however, not included. Total mean daily expenditures reported in Table 4.
** Mean daily expenditures reported for entertainment are: USA $6.93; Canada $6.87, UK $5.53; Germany $2.85; Trinidad $7.93.

dian market which currently supplies the destination with nearly three times as many visitors.

Attractions Visited

Harrison's Cave is the major site visited by all groups, attracting four in ten Canadian, UK and German visitors, more than one-third of USA travelers and nearly one-quarter of Trinidadians (Table 6a). "Other places," which include a variety of sites that collectively form part of a typical Barbados sightseeing tour at the destination are second in popularity. The Flower Forest, Andromeda Gardens and Welchman Hall Gully are the only other individual sites with substantive visitation, with the latter site attracting 25 percent of German visitors, 16 percent of UK travelers and 10 percent or less of the USA, Canada and Trinidad markets

The key differences by country of origin are: (1) distinctive and consistently higher levels of visits to attractions by the German and UK market when compared to other groups; (2) overall lower rates of visits to attractions by the Trinidad market; and (3) the exceptionally high level of visits

TABLE 5. Specific Activities Participated in by Geographic Markets.

a) **Percent Participating by Country**

Activity	USA (n = 5081)	Canada (n = 1686)	United Kingdom (n = 4733)	Germany (n = 674)	Trinidad (n = 188)
• Scuba Diving	9.4%	6.4%	13.4%	15.3%	2.1%
• Fishing	4.7	5.0	6.1	5.2	1.1
• Water Sports	48.1	36.5	50.6	39.2	16.5
• Boat Trips	30.5	30.2	45.6	25.2	4.3
• Other Activities	37.9	35.8	29.0	28.8	36.7

b) **Overall Participation or Activity Market Share**

Activity	Total* Number Participating	Overall* Participation Rate (%)	USA	Canada	United Kingdom	Germany	Trinidad
• Water Sports	5,735	46.0%	42.5%	10.7%	41.7%	4.6%	.5%
• Boat Trips	4,394	36.0	35.2	11.6	49.1	3.9	.2
• Scuba Diving	1,326	10.7	36.1	8.2	47.8	7.8	.1
• Fishing	654	5.3	36.9	13.0	44.6	5.4	.1
• Other Activities	4,163	33.7	46.2	14.5	32.9	4.7	1.7

* Percentages based on total number of visitors participating in activities from these five origin markets.

to Welchman Hall Gully by the German travelers, when compared with other markets.

In terms of market share, the United Kingdom is clearly the dominant market for attractions (Table 6b). However, because of the peculiarly high patronage of natural attractions when compared to other visitors, German travelers assume a significant share of the market for these venues—one that is disproportionate to their total market size. These findings argue for more product development and promotion of natural attractions, given the generally high visitation levels from the primary markets and important secondary markets.

The relatively high participation levels in activities and visitation to attractions reported by visitors in Tables 5 and 6 (particularly for USA, UK and German markets) is not reflected in their daily spending on transportation and entertainment/recreation, which is typically low (Table 4). These findings suggest that Barbados has opportunities for development of saleable attractions and activities which can attract increased visitor spending.

TABLE 6. Specific Attractions Visited by Geographic Markets.

a) **Percent Visiting Attractions by Country**

Attraction	USA (n = 5081)	Canada (n = 1686)	United Kingdom (n = 4733)	Germany (n = 674)	Trinidad (n = 188)
• Welchman Hall Gully	7.8	10.0	16.1	25.2	2.7
• Harrison's Cave	34.0	41.2	44.5	42.0	26.6
• Andromeda Gardens	14.2	14.3	25.5	25.2	4.8
• Flower Forest	21.3	25.6	34.6	35.0	6.9
• Other Places	31.0	34.1	38.1	39.2	22.3

b) **Overall Visitation or Attraction Market Share**

Attraction	Total* Number Visiting	Overall* Visitation Rate (%)	USA	Canada	United Kingdom	Germany	Trinidad
• Welchman Hall Gully	1,500	12.1%	26.3%	11.3%	50.7%	11.3%	.4%
• Harrison's Cave	4,862	39.3	35.5	14.2	43.3	5.8	1.2
• Andromeda Gardens	2,343	19.0	30.9	10.2	51.6	7.2	.1
• Flower Forest	3,400	27.5	31.8	12.7	48.2	6.9	.4
• Other Places	4,260	34.5	37.0	13.5	42.3	6.1	.1

* Percentages based on total number of travelers visiting attractions from these five origin markets.

Information Sources and Their Importance

Origin markets vary in the importance they assign to information sources (Table 7). Television advertising is given a low importance rating by all visitors. Friends and relatives and other sources are rated as important or higher by USA, Canadian and Trinidad visitors. Newspaper/magazines are only considered important by Trinidad visitors while travel agents are rated as important by both UK and Canadian markets. German visitors do not rate any particular information source as important. These data are consistent with findings that first time visitors tend to use multiple information sources and travel intermediaries (Duke & Persia, 1993; Hsieh & O'Leary, 1993; Snepenger et al., 1990).

However, the overall importance rating assigned to information sources must be interpreted with caution. An information source is necessary to create awareness of a destination but may not be important in its selection. The importance rating reflects the saliency of a source to travel consumers but not its weight in making the actual destination selection. For example,

TABLE 7. Importance Rating of Information Sources Used by Barbados Stay-Over Visitors (May 1993-April 1994).

Information Source	USA (n = 5081)	Canada (n = 1686)	Median Rating by Region of Origin* UK (n = 4733)	Germany (n = 674)	Trinidad (n = 188)
• Travel Agent	3	3	2	2	2
• Newspaper/Magazine	2	1	1	2	3
• Television Ad	1	1	1	2	2
• Friend/Relative	3	3	3	2	4
• Other Sources	4	3	2	2	4

* Rating Scale: 4 = Very Important; 3 = Important; 2 = Somewhat Important; 1 = Not So Important; 0 = Not Important.

the low importance rating assigned to television advertising (Table 7) may mean that TV is important (salient) in creating destination awareness but has low importance (determinance) in the final destination selection. It is likely that television may stimulate use of other information sources which are of more help in making the final selection.

The relatively low rating assigned to television and print media by USA, Canada, UK and German visitors is an area of concern since Caribbean island nations typically spend the largest share of the promotion budget in these countries. These findings suggest that while television and print may be appropriate vehicles for promoting awareness, other information sources are of far greater significance to consumers in choosing a destination, including friends and travel agents. The results emphasize the importance of previous visitors in destination promotion, a factor which needs to be explicitly recognized in the Barbados marketing strategy.

Payment Methods

Country specific variations in card payment methods exist although cash and travelers' checks are widely used by all markets as a method of payment. Credit cards are employed as a secondary payment method by USA, Canadian, UK and German visitors (Table 8). Each country of origin shows specific brand usage with USA visitors using VISA and American Express, Canadian and UK travelers using VISA and the German market using MasterCard. These variations in credit card ownership by country of origin are significant to both increasing visitation and spending. Credit card issuers are continually in search of agreements and alliances that can keep their customers and increase their spending. Small island nations have opportunities to build partnership that are of mutual benefit. Findings

TABLE 8. Payment Methods Used by Barbados Stay-Over Visitors (May 1993-April 1994).

| Payment Method | Median Rating by Region of Origin* | | | | |
	USA (n = 5081)	Canada (n = 1686)	UK (n = 4733)	Germany (n = 674)	Trinidad (n = 188)
• Cash/Travelers Checks	3	3	3	3	3
• American Express	2	1	0	0	1
• VISA	2	2	2	1	1
• MasterCard	1	1	1	2	1
• Other Card	1	0	0	0	0

* **Rating Scale:** 3 = Widely Used; 2 = Sometimes Used; 1 = Not Used; 0 = Do Not Have.

also pinpoint where vendors of goods and services at the destination may be missing sales because specific card processing facilities are absent.

CONCLUSIONS

This study shows that country of origin provides a conceptual and practical basis for establishing preferred customer profiles and serves as a managerially efficient method of segmenting visitor markets for small island nations. It supports expanded use of geographic origin as a key variable in focusing a tourism marketing strategy for such destinations. Differences in visitation patterns by country of origin reveal markets that provide opportunities for meeting key tourism objectives.

Country of origin markets are shown to selectively contribute in: (1) increasing absolute tourist visits, (2) smoothing seasonal fluctuations in visitor arrivals and accommodations, and (3) achieving increased occupancy levels for specific accommodation types. Small island destinations can therefore effectively use country of origin based strategies in their search for a differential advantage, competitive positioning, and growth within a global industry.

REFERENCES

Barbados Visitor Survey 1993/94. (1994). Caribbean Tourism Organization, St. Michael, Barbados.

Bull, A. (1992). *The Economics of Travel and Tourism.* New York: Halstead Press.

CANA Business. (1992). Credit Cards, November: 14-26.

DeLuca, M. (1993a). International Sporting Events Give Added Boost to Tourism. *Tourism Today*, July-August, 44-48.

DeLuca, M. (1993b). Europe a Bright Spot for Caribbean Tourism. *Tourism Today*, March-April, 16-24.

Digest of Tourism Statistics 1993. (1994). Department of Statistics, Barbados: Government Printing Department.

Donoghue, J.A. (1993). Precarious European Charters. *Air Transport World*, 6 (7), 19-24.

Duke, C. and M.A. Persia. (1993). Effects of Distribution Channel Level on Tour Purchasing Attributes and Information Sources. *Journal of Travel & Tourism Marketing*, 2(2/3): 37-55.

Ennew, C., T. Watkins and M. Wright. (1993). *Cases in Marketing Financial Services*. Oxford: Butterworth-Heinemann Ltd.

Go, F. and P. Williams. (1993). Competing and Cooperating with the Changing Tourism Channel System. *Journal of Travel & Tourism Marketing*, 2(2/3): 229-248.

Gunn, C. (1988). *Tourism Planning* (3rd ed.). New York: Taylor and Francis.

Hsieh, S. and J. O'Leary. (1993). Communication Channels to Segment Pleasure Travelers. *Journal of Travel & Tourism Marketing*, 2(2/3): 57-75.

Hsieh, S., J. O'Leary and A. Morrison. (1994). A Comparison of Package and Non-Package Travelers from the United Kingdom. *Journal of International Consumer Marketing*, 6(3/4): 79-100.

Insider Flyer. (1996). Happy Birthday Frequent Flyer Miles, 37 (March 6,3), 10-12.

Kotler, P. (1991). *Marketing Management: Analysis, Planning, Implementation and Control*. Englewood Cliffs, N.J.: Prentice-Hall.

McEnill, J. (1992). Seasonality of Tourism Demand in the European Community. *EIU Travel and Tourism Analyst*, (3) 67-88.

Meiden, A. (1984). *Bank Marketing Management*. London: MacMillan Publishers.

Middleton, V. (1994). *Marketing in Travel and Tourism* (2nd ed.). Oxford: Butterworth-Heinemann Ltd.

Nelms, D.W. (1993). The Norm for World Wide Carriers. *Air Transport World*, (6), 176-180.

Perdue, R. and B. Pitegoff. (1990). Methods of Accountability Research for Destination Marketing. *Journal of Travel Research*, 28(4), Spring: 45-49.

Reid, S. and L. Reid. (1994). Tourism Marketing Management in Small Island Nations: A Tale of Micro Destinations. *Journal of International Consumer Marketing*, 6(3/4): 39-60.

Roop, E. (1994a). Shrugging Off Shoulder Periods. *Tourism Today*, July-August: 27-33.

Roop, E. (1994b). Caribbean Reaps the Rewards of Group Travel. *Tourism Today*, May-June: 30-38.

Skapinker, M. (1993). A Complete Package for the Holiday Industry. *Financial Times*, Wednesday, October 14: 31.

Snepenger, D., K. Meged, M. Snelling and K. Worrall. (1990). Information Search Strategies by Destination-Naive Tourists. *Journal of Travel Research*, 29(1), 13-16.

Statistical News. (1996). Bridgetown, Barbados: Caribbean Tourism Organization.

Taylor, D., R. Fletcher and T. Clabaugh. (1993). A Comparison of Characteristics, Region Expenditures and Economic Impact of Visitors to Historical Sites with Other Recreational Visitors, *Journal of Travel Research*, 32(1), 30-35.

Marketing European Tourism Products via Internet/WWW

Carl H. Marcussen

SUMMARY. The Internet and in particular World Wide Web (WWW) is currently one of the most significant technological developments pertaining to travel and tourism marketing. The article contains estimates of users by region in the world, by country in Western Europe in absolute figures and in percent of population. Also demographic data of the users are reviewed. Selected examples of European Web-sites are discussed. The future development on the Web goes from 'information only' to more interactive Web-presentations covering the whole spectrum from information, via inquiry service to booking and payment. Marketing and strategic implications of the development on the WWW are discussed. *[Article copies available for a fee from The Haworth Document Delivery Service: 1-800-342-9678. E-mail address: getinfo@haworth.com]*

INTRODUCTION

The Internet is in fact a network of networks. Two of the most used functions on the Internet are electronic mail and World Wide Web, also known as WWW. The Internet dates back to 1969 to the US Ministry of Defense, and developed into a working tool for Universities and research-

---

Dr. Carl H. Marcussen is Research Fellow in the field of telematics applied to tourism, Research Centre of Bornholm, Stenbrudsvej 55, 3730 Nexoe, Denmark (e-mail: marcussen@rcb.dk).

[Haworth co-indexing entry note]: "Marketing European Tourism Products via Internet/WWW." Marcussen, Carl H. Co-published simultaneously in *Journal of Travel & Tourism Marketing* (The Haworth Press, Inc.) Vol. 6, No. 3/4, 1997, pp. 23-34; and: *Geography and Tourism Marketing* (ed: Martin Oppermann) The Haworth Press, Inc., 1997, pp. 23-34. Single or multiple copies of this article are available for a fee from The Haworth Document Delivery Service [1-800-342-9678, 9:00 a.m. - 5:00 p.m. (EST). E-mail address: getinfo@haworth.com].

23

ers across the world. During the 1990s the number of users and–also commercial–information suppliers has exploded, primarily because of the establishment of World Wide Web with its user friendly Windows-like interface.

The presentations on WWW normally consist of text and as well as color photos and graphics. The graphical as well as the text-based parts of the individual presentation may be 'clickable,' i.e., by clicking on an underlined/highlighted word the user can 'jump' to other sections of the same or other presentation. It is becoming rather common to make WWW presentations as part of the promotional activities of countries, regions, organizations, and companies such as hotels.

PRESENT USE

Number of Users

Today the Internet is the world's largest computer network with 30 million users by the end of 1994 and about 40 million users by the end of 1995 (Computerwoche, 1995). The number of Internet users worldwide will probably have passed the 50 million mark by the end of 1996.

Based on statistics on the number of 'hosts' (i.e., computers connected to the Internet) in different countries and regions at the end of 1995/beginning of 1996, the overall distribution of Internet users by region is as follows: US and Canada 68 percent, Western Europe 22 percent; and the rest of the world 10 percent. The percentage for US/Canada is a maximum because a number of transnational domains (com, edu, gov, mil, org, net, and int) have been included under US/Canada.

Thus, the US and Canada have about two thirds of the world's current Internet users. For those European marketers who wish to attract North American tourists this may be an interesting target group–if these Internet users are also WWW users. After undertaking a reweighing of the data collected and reported by Nielsen (1995), Hoffman, Kalsbeek, and Novak (1996) found that 70 percent of the Internet users in the US *use World Wide Web*. This proportion is probably lower in many European countries at the moment. For example, in Denmark only 29 percent of the Internet users say they use the Internet to search in WWW (Mejlvang and Halskov, 1996) (see Figure 1).

There were about 6.3 million Internet users in Western Europe by the end of 1994, and about 8.5 million by the end of 1995. Assuming the same increase from 1995 to 96 as from 1994 to 95 (except for Finland) in absolute figures, there will be about 10.5 million Internet users in Western Europe by the end of 1996.

FIGURE 1. Estimated Number of Internet Users by Country in Western Europe in 1994, 1995, and 1996.

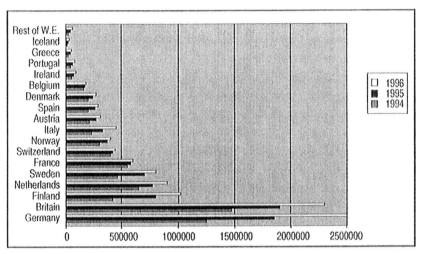

Source: Own estimate based on RIPE's statistics of number of hosts per country. Internet address: ftp://ftp.ripe.net/ripe/hostcount/History/.

Note: It is assumed that there were 6.2 users per host in 1994, 4.2 users per host in 1995, and 3.3 users per host in 1996 (year end). The number of users per country in absolute terms is assumed to increase at the same speed from 1995 to 1996 as from 1994 to 1995, except for Finland.

Germany and the UK have the largest number of Internet users in Europe *in absolute terms* which makes the Internet an interesting medium for reaching these markets.

However, Internet users only constitute 3 or 4 percent of the population in Germany and the UK, and even less in other major markets such as France and Italy (see Figure 2). In the Nordic countries as well as in Switzerland and the Netherlands the penetration of the Internet is somewhat higher. The marketing implications of the penetration of the Internet in any given market are that the lower the penetration is, the greater is the need to consider alternative media when targeting these markets. The Internet can so far hardly be used as the only medium for reaching any market in the world.

User Demographics

From a tourism marketing point of view of course it is important to know who uses the Internet. Since the USA and Canada account for about two thirds of the world's Internet users, a starting point is to look at the demographics of these. Nielsen (1995) conducted a major survey of the

US and Canadian Internet users. Hoffman et al. (1996) made a rigorous reweighing of the US part of the same data resulting in the following adjusted demographic profiles of US Internet users compared with non-users (see Figure 3).

The comparison of age distribution of Internet users with that of the total American population shows the following:

(a) Internet users are overrepresented in all the first four age groups. The overrepresentation is greatest in the age group 16 to 24 years.
(b) Men are greatly overrepresented among the Internet users, since men constitute two thirds of the users.
(c) The Internet users are better educated than the non-users. Over half the US Internet users hold a college degree or higher.

Data collected by Nielsen (1995) indicated that Internet users have considerably higher incomes per person than the American population in general, but Hoffman and Novak (1995) argued that this is at least partly due to an overrepresentation of those with high income in the Nielsen sample. Unfortunately Hoffman et al. (1996) did not take income into account in their reweighing of the Nielsen data, and therefore it is not possible to determine to what extent the Internet users (in the US) really are relatively wealthy.

The German statistical yearbook clearly suggests that the higher the income bracket, the greater is the percentage of households with computers. An exception is in the very lowest income bracket, namely students equipped with computers in spite of their low income. Undoubtedly this is the case in most countries. Since those households with high incomes generally tend to be better equipped with computers than those with low incomes, it seems fair to assume that Internet users actually have higher incomes than non-users.

Most users access the Internet from their work place (Figure 4).

A Danish survey by the market research institute Gallup reported by Mejlvang and Halskov (1996) showed that more than 6.7% of the respondents–aged 12 and over–had used Internet, which was a surprisingly high proportion, but the result may be positively biased because of a greater willingness of users than non-users to participate in the survey (Hoffman & Novak 1995; Hoffman et al. 1996). Some 70 percent of the Danish users are men, which is a slightly higher proportion than in the US. As mentioned earlier only 29 percent of the Danish Internet users say they use WWW (see Figure 5).

A comparison of the proportion of Internet users in the two first age groups shows an interesting difference between the countries: In Germany

FIGURE 2. Internet Users by the End of 1995 and 1996 as Percentage of the Population per Country in Western Europe.

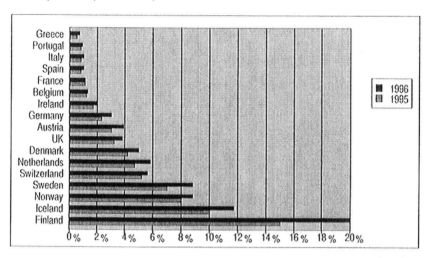

Source: Official population statistics combined with own estimates of number of users per country, cf. previous diagram.
Note: For Finland the proportion of Internet users has been revised down to 15% for 1995 and 20% for 1996 (from 19% and 23% respectively). For Iceland the proportion of users has also been reduced a little, which has been taken into account in the previous diagram. I.e., a lower number of users per host has been used for these two countries than for the others.

there are relatively few in the younger age group with low income, and relatively many in the age group 25 to 39 years with higher income. This indicates that the German Internet users have greater purchasing power than their US and Danish counterparts, ceteris paribus. This tends to increase the attractiveness of the German Internet users as a target group.

In Germany only 2 percent of the users are 17 or younger which indicates that the Internet–in Germany and probably also elsewhere–is not 'just a toy for youngsters.' In all three regions about 30 percent of the users are in the age group 40 or over. In the US 5.6 percent of the users are 55 or older, which corresponds to the situation in Denmark where 4 percent of the users are 60 or older.

In an American survey about marketing via WWW it was, among other things, stated that the most likely niche for success on the Web is travel: "Seventy-one percent of businesses with Web sites in the travel industry had some sales during the previous month, which is far higher than any other sector. Travel also had the highest mean sales per company, with the exception of real estate. In addition, 38% of those in the travel sector

FIGURE 3. Demographic Profile of Internet Users Compared with Non-users: (a) Age Group, (b) Gender, and (c) Education (USA, 1995).

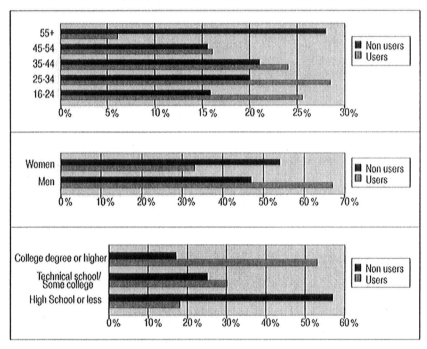

Source: Own summary based on Hoffman et al. (1996), who in turn made recalculations of Nielsen (1995).

FIGURE 4. From Where Internet Is Used in North America and Denmark.

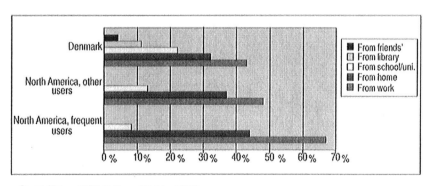

Source: Nielsen (1995); Mejlvang & Halskov (1996).

FIGURE 5. Age Distribution of Internet Users in the US, Germany and Denmark.

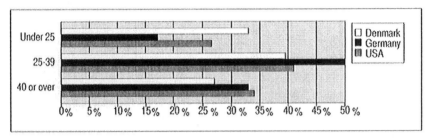

Source: US: Hoffman et al.'s (1996) reweighting of Nielsen (1995); Germany: http://www.germany.net/gast/presse/unter_3.html under http://www.germany.net/; Denmark: Mejlvang & Halskov (1996).
Note: For Denmark and the US the data provided is based on surveys. For Germany the data is in fact age distribution of the users of Germany.net rather than all Internet users. Germany.net–The German Information Highway–is Germany's largest free on-line service. The users which have registered for Germany.net may be slightly more 'serious and mature' than German Internet users in general.

stated that their sites are profitable now" (ActivMedia Inc., 1995). This 38% for travel (including tourism) is higher than the average for all industries, which was 31% in the fall of 1995, up from 22% in the spring of 1995 according to ActivMedia.

EXAMPLES OF PRESENT USE

A number of companies, organizations, cities, regions and countries have tourism-related Web-sites.

National Web Sites

Tourismus Info Internet (TII) contains links to information about flights (including the schedules of Lufthansa), rail travel, vacations in Germany, last-minute offers, hotels and lodging, touristic news, travel reports/tips, touristic information in Internet (links), and country information worldwide. It has been made possible to add a given touristic WWW presentation under any one of the above categories free of charge. For example, given destinations outside of Germany interested in attracting German tourists can add their WWW presentation under the category 'touristical information in Internet.' As another example hotels or hotel lists can add a link to their WWW presentation under 'Hotels in Internet.' The number of hits per month to TII increased from 20,000 in December 1994 to 195,000 in November 1995. During June 1996 TII measured 431,000 hits. At the

ENTER 96 conference in Innsbruck in January 1996 TII was selected as the best of about 20 competing Web-sites.

In December 1995, *British Midland*, which is Britain's second largest airline, was the first airline in Europe to introduce a reservation booking system with on-line payment via credit card on WWW called CyberSeat. Even though the Internet/WWW is mainly an information system, British Midland's introduction of their CyberSeat service shows that reservation as well as payment via WWW is possible today. However, you cannot be sure to find the cheapest flight. *The UK Guide* is developed by the University College London-Department of Computer Science. The home page is good because it contains almost 100 links to their own and others' presentations of cities and information of general touristic interest.

Holland Tourist Information from the Netherlands Board of Tourism comprises about 14,000 text-based html-files of more that 17 Mbytes in total. The categories comprise the following: Accommodation, Events, Import regulations, Leisure and entertainment, Museums, Organizations, Rental of bicycles/boats, Restaurants and party locations, and Sports/recreation. Within "Accommodation" there is a choice between several different types, for example hotels. If "hotels" are chosen, there are 12 different ways of accessing these, for example by name of city/town. There are various pieces of information about the hotel and the rooms including prices for a variety of room types and there is a quality indicator in the form of number of stars.

Global WWW-Indexes

Virtual Tourist II is one of the most common entrances to finding tourism-related information on WWW. From a world map Europe may be chosen, and on the next map any country may be chosen. It is a map-based interface to *City.Net* which in the beginning of 1996 comprised 1300 cities and 600 other destinations, which had increased to 2450 cities and 880 other destinations in the middle of 1996, i.e., only 6 months later. *City.Net* is, according to the two Americans who got the idea for the system in May 1994, the most comprehensive international guide to destinations worldwide. City.Net is updated daily and contains links to touristic Web-sites.

The *InfoHub WWW Travel Guide* contains, according to the developers, 'thousands' of links to presentations across the world within the categories destination information, activities, transport, bureaus, other travel-related subjects, and accommodation. The latter comprises hyper-links to hotels and hotel lists on the Web. Probably based on the wide range of touristic information the InfoHub WWW Travel Guide states that they are "the most comprehensive Internet travel information site." It is possible via an 'add URL form,' which is getting common in many meta Web indexes, to add a link to one's own touristic information to this guide, free of charge.

Dr. Memory includes more that 1000 tourism and travel links world-wide, some of which are European. *Hotel Anywhere* contains links to over 27,000 separate travel related web-sites, and about 1,000 new links are added per week. *Travelers' Resources* contains links to 200 touristic WWW addresses, divided into subjects and regions.

Apart from this there are some general search tools, such as *Yahoo*, *WebCrawler*, *Lycos*, *InfoSeek* and *Galaxy* which may be used to identify touristic information using a free text search, and many of them also contain the possibility of searching geographically or by subject. The subject may be 'travel' and geographically the user may start by selecting Europe, and then narrow the search to a specific country. In some of these tools, it is possible to add a link to one's 'own' home page.

International Hotel Lists Incorporating European Countries

There are a number of international hotel lists–which include European hotels (see Table 1). They vary as to the number of hotels they comprise, the type of booking facility they offer, the amount and type of information about each hotel which is included.

WorldHotel is the world's largest single source of hotel information. So far it has listed about one third of all the hotels in Western Europe. There are names, addresses, phone and fax numbers of all the hotels, but prices are not shown.

The Hotel Guide (THG) is based in Switzerland. THG on the Web is supplemented with a printed and a CD-ROM version. There are prices of all the hotels in THG–unlike a number of the other hotel lists–which makes it useful with respect to making reservations.

On 19th December, 1995, Thisco's *TravelWeb* launched a 'live' online reservations function with, among others, Best Western, Hilton, and Hyatt as participants. Online here means that a reply to a reservation request normally is received on the screen within 7 seconds. For the participating hoteliers the costs per booking received through TravelWeb is less than a tenth of the average charges by the major CRSs (Beaver, 1995).

There are also national hotel lists from many European countries.

IMPLICATIONS

The WWW is developing very quickly. Already today a significant part of the hotels in the world are included on one or more hotel lists on the

TABLE 1. International Hotel Lists

Name of list	Hotels in total listed	Hotels in W. Europe	Booking facility	Price info.
WorldHotel	200,000	64,000	e-mail	No
The Hotel Guide	50,000	21,200	Fax	Exact
Accom. Search Engine	5,276	2,800	e-mail	Range
TravelNow	12,210	2,400	e-mail	Range
All the Hotels on the Web	10,000	2,000	e-mail	No
HotelNet	1,835	1,800	e-mail	Range
Lodging Guide World Wide 84	84,000	1,500	No	No
TravelWeb	8,200	1,300	On-line	Exact

Web, although they may not know it themselves. It must be foreseen that more and more hotels and other tourism firms and organizations will choose to supplement the minimum information, namely name, address, telephone and fax number, with text and photos in order to differentiate themselves from the others.

The development on the Web goes from information to 'the whole spectrum,' namely information, brochure ordering, inquiries, booking and payment. It must be assumed that booking and payment of services within travel and tourism via the WWW will become more and more widespread in the near future. This is supported by the announcement that a common standard for payments via Internet is being developed by Visa and Master-Card (MasterCard International, 1996).

It must be assumed that the expanding use of the Internet/WWW will fuel a trend towards more direct sales between supplier and end consumer within travel and tourism. This will particularly apply to products, which the consumer perceives as commodities. The more computer literate the consumer is, the more likely is it that he or she will buy through telematics-based direct channels such as WWW. As the younger generation–which is much more computer literate that the elder generation–becomes active travelers, they are much more likely to make use of the Internet/WWW than their parents.

Tourism firms and organizations must decide *if* they will be present on the Web, and if so *when* and *how*? The general question must be raised: To what extent can the target group be reached via the medium–in this case the WWW part of Internet? The target groups may constitute certain segments of end consumers and travel agencies. Today very few travel agencies use the Internet/WWW as a source of information, but it must be assumed that information on the Web will increasingly be used for *supplementing* printed and other sources. As to the possibility of reaching certain segments of end consumers or households via Internet/WWW, the previously shown estimates of users by region, by country, and in percent of population by country may be used as a starting point. The next step would then be to take into account that only a certain proportion of the Internet users has partial or full access to WWW. Finally, demographic characteristics must be evaluated to determine to what extent there is an overlap between the target groups and the Internet users.

If a tourism firm or organization chooses to make a WWW presentation it is very important to get it registered in the relevant places so it can be found easily by those who might be interested. This could be general systems such as City.Net/Virtual Tourist II, Yahoo, Lycos, InfoSeek, Galaxy, and the more specific systems and lists of, for example, hotels or other touristic products. Those who wish to make really beautiful WWW presentations a part of their marketing effort for their tourism services might find it necessary to involve an advertising agency specializing in this field just like when producing traditional brochures.

For accommodation facilities such as hotels and others, the following question needs to be answered: Should prices be included or not? If prices are not included in the hotel list further communication will be necessary before making a sale. As a possible solution with respect to prices, it may be suggested that *list prices* are shown on the Web, which would be the price the tourist must pay by direct contact to the hotel. When a travel agency is involved as an intermediary link, the hotels can fix a certain discount factor in the annual contract negotiations depending on the expected number of rooms sold and negotiating strength. This system is well known within the business-to-business market in general.

The individual tourism firm/organization–and the firm which actually places the information on the Web–need to decide if it will only provide information (via WWW) or if it also will facilitate brochure request, inquiries, bookings, and possibly payment via WWW. Of course, it is possible to start with only providing information, but without additional sales most tourism firms and organizations would probably consider this a waste of resources. Therefore, it is important that booking, and possibly also payment, can be undertaken easily, for example via the WWW which, requires that prices and quality indicators such as stars are shown.

Travel agencies must consider to what extent the Internet/WWW–and other on-line, end-consumer oriented media–may constitute a threat for them and the agency oriented Web-sites which they use, i.e., Global and Local Distribution Systems, GDSs/LDSs. The Web can hardly be beaten, but it *can* be joined.

The possibilities of making some of the same pieces of information available both via the Internet/WWW to homes and offices on one hand and via self-service information columns and CD-ROM on the other are obvious and ought to be considered by, for example, national and/or local tourist boards.

REFERENCES

ActivMedia, Inc. (1995). Survey Stats (preview of the study Trends in the World Wide Web Marketplace), http://www.activmedia.com/charts.html

Computerwoche (1995). IDC: Unternehmen verfolgen eine zurückhaltende Internet-Politik, Sept. 22, pp. 27-28.

Hoffman, D.L., W.D. Kalsbeek & T.P. Novak (1996). Internet Use in the US: 1995 Baseline Estimates and Preliminary Market Segments, working paper, revised version, http://www2000.ogsm.vanderbilt.edu/baseline/internet.demos.july9.1996.html

Hoffman, D.L. & T.P. Novak (1995). CommerceNet/Nielsen Survey: Is It Representative? http://www2000.ogsm.vanderbilt.edu/surveys/cn.questions.html

"Host Distribution by Top-Level Domain Name," under "Internet Domain Survey, January 1996," http://www.nw.com/zone/WWW/report.html

MasterCard International (1996). Visa & MasterCard Combine Secure Specifications For Card Transactions On The Internet Into One Standard. Press release, Feb. 1, http://www.mastercard.com/Press/release-960201.htm

Mejlvang, M. & K. Halskov (1996). Internet has grown from the nerds (in Danish), Jyllands-Posten, national newspaper, April 1.

Nielsen (1995). CommerceNet/Nielsen Announce Internet Study Results. http: // www.nielsenmedia.com/news/cnet-pr.html

Nielsen (1995). CommerceNet/Nielsen Announce Internet Study Results. http: // www.nielsenmedia.com/news/cnet-pr.html

RIPE. Hostcount History directory. Internet address: ftp://ftp.ripe.net/ripe/host count/History/

Statistical Yearbook of Germany (1995). Statistisches Jahrbuch für die Bundesrepublik Deutschland.

GIS Applications in Tourism Marketing: Current Uses, an Experimental Application and Future Prospects

Stefania Bertazzon
Geoffrey Crouch
Dianne Draper
Nigel Waters

SUMMARY. The paper begins with a brief introduction to the technology of Geographic Information Systems (GIS) and a review of current literature in the field of tourism based GIS (T-GIS). This is followed by a discussion of the theoretical possibilities of using T-GIS for traditional marketing purposes and a review of the related literature. The use of T-GIS for marketing is then considered both from the demand and supply sides. The second half of the paper provides a detailed account of the use of the Internet to incorporate GIS-based models and graphics as a marketing tool for the Alberta Ski Resort industry. Further developments and prospects using this technology are also described. *[Article copies available for a fee from The Haworth Document Delivery Service: 1-800-342-9678. E-mail address: getinfo@haworth.com]*

Stefania Bertazzon, Dianne Draper and Nigel Waters are affiliated with Department of Geography and Geoffrey Crouch is affiliated with Faculty of Management at The University of Calgary, Calgary, Alberta, Canada, T2N 1N4.

[Haworth co-indexing entry note]: "GIS Applications in Tourism Marketing: Current Uses, an Experimental Application and Future Prospects." Bertazzon, Stefania et al. Co-published simultaneously in *Journal of Travel & Tourism Marketing* (The Haworth Press, Inc.) Vol. 6, No. 3/4, 1996, pp. 35-59; and: *Geography and Tourism Marketing* (ed: Martin Oppermann) The Haworth Press, Inc., 1996, pp. 35-59. Single or multiple copies of this article are available for a fee from The Haworth Document Delivery Service [1-800-342-9678, 9:00 a.m. - 5:00 p.m. (EST). E-mail address: getinfo@haworth.com].

35

INTRODUCTION

At its core, the tourism industry "sells" images of the geography of different parts of the world. If tourism marketing is to be effective in achieving the expectations of both tourism marketers and their clients, an understanding of the geography of the places that people wish to visit or to market must be a fundamental component of the marketing system. With the creation of Geographic Information Systems (GIS), the task of incorporating meaningful geographical dimensions and data into marketing efforts has become more feasible. The development of GIS and other electronic communications technology such as the World Wide Web and the Internet highlights the potential to develop much more appropriately targeted marketing tools and techniques.

In examining existing and potential uses of GIS in the context of tourism marketing, this paper briefly defines and describes GIS. The paper then turns to marketing applications of GIS in tourism where a variety of potential uses is discussed and a tailor-made example of GIS applied to tourism marketing is described. The paper concludes with comments on future prospects for GIS in tourism marketing.

GEOGRAPHIC INFORMATION SYSTEMS (GIS)

Although there are few universally agreed upon definitions of GIS (Keller and Waters 1991) most people would agree that they involve computer based systems for entering, storing, retrieving, manipulating and displaying spatial data (Maguire 1991). Overviews of the field may be found in Burrough (1986) and Maguire, Goodchild and Rhind (1991, a second edition of this seminal text is currently in preparation). Usually GIS include capabilities for carrying out spatial retrievals such as point-in-polygon analysis, spatial manipulations such as polygon overlay operations and spatial analysis such as shortest path and related network operations. (A reasonably comprehensive list of GIS functionality and software availability may be found in the *GIS World Sourcebook* (Rodcay 1996)). Wherever there are spatial data, and tourism marketing invariably involves spatial data, GIS can be used to assist with several of the marketing research steps identified by Churchill (1987) namely data collection, analysis, interpretation and report preparation.

TOURISM BASED GIS

Tourism and recreation GIS are rare. In their comprehensive review of the GIS field, Maguire, Goodchild and Rhind (1991) mention only one study. This is the paper by Duffield and Coppock (1975) describing the creation of a simple GIS, the Tourism and Recreation Information Package (TRIP), which was prepared for three Scottish agencies (Countryside Commission for Scotland, Forestry Commission and Scottish Tourist Board) in order to assist them in conducting planning and policy-making operations. In the more than twenty years since this study was completed there has been a relative dearth of GIS applications in tourism and recreation studies. During the mid-1990s this appears to be changing. For instance, Kelly (1994) carried out a study in which he created a tourist based GIS for the supply side of the equation in southern Alberta, Canada, using the MapInfo GIS package. Ryan (1994) and Sussman and Rashad (1994) have completed review articles relating to tourism and GIS.

GIS and Marketing

GIS and marketing has fared much better than GIS and tourism. Indeed, Beaumont (1991) argues that the use and popularity of GIS for marketing goods and services is the primary reason that GIS has now become central to much geographical research. A similar point emphasizing the lucrative nature of GIS for marketing is made by Openshaw (1989). GIS and market analysis usually is termed *geodemographics* and at least two journals have produced special issues on this subject (cf., *Environment and Planning A*, 1989, 21 (5) and *Journal of the Market Research Society*, 1989, 31(1)). Beaumont (1991) argues that marketing traditionally has been oriented around the four Ps of Product, Price, Place and Promotion and that geodemographics can help with a fifth P–data Processing. It is our contention that GIS can in fact be used to assist with all five Ps. We provide brief examples and demonstrate how GIS can be used to market the tourist product, advertise and set price, locate and market place, and how it can be used for promotion and to help with processing operations. We illustrate these functions with respect to the ski industry in southern Alberta, Canada, beginning with a general discussion and then turning to an application created specifically for this paper.

Marketing Product

Since 1995 GIS researchers have become more aware of the importance of the Internet both for carrying out research and for delivering software and data. Broadhead's keynote address to the GIS/LIS '95 Conference in Nashville (1995) and Dangermond's paper (1995) at the same conference illustrate this growth in awareness.

It may be argued that the Internet is a relatively elitist technology for marketing a product. Increasingly, however, the Internet is being used to sell a wide variety of products which are themselves far less elitist than the skiing industry. In addition, access to the Internet is growing at a remarkably fast and exponential rate (*The Interminablenet* 1996). We believe this technology likely will be adopted as quickly as many previous electronic technologies such as television and the telephone. While Barkow (1996) notes that in early 1996 "online households" comprise only 7 percent of households in the United States, he shows also that some electronic technologies have been adopted extremely rapidly. In the United States, for example, television grew from about a 1 percent adoption rate to over 80 percent between 1945 and 1955. Similarly, Parsons (1996) notes that home computer ownership jumped from 16.2 percent in 1990 to 28.8 percent in 1995. Cornish (1996) also suggests that "infotech" is proliferating, citing the 600 percent growth in numbers (from 2.7 to 19.3 million) of American cellular telephone subscribers between 1990 and 1994. Although in the past the Internet appeared to be a male-oriented technology with estimates that only 15 per cent of its users were female (Burstein and Kline, 1995) this is likely to change in the near future (Sinclair, 1996).

With low-cost $500 net surfing machines poised to replace or supplement computers in many homes the adopting percentage is likely to match the rate of television adoption in the 1940s and 1950s. Indeed, television and net surfing machines soon may be combined either as set-top boxes or as hybrids with game playing machines using either Apple's Pippin technology or Phillips' CD-i interactive media players (Wilson 1996). Wilson cites International Data Corporation's survey of 44,800 PC and non-PC owning households which suggested a distinct market for set-top boxes by the year 2000. However, with the distribution of GIS software via the Internet (sometimes for free as in the case of ESRI's ArcView I, GIS viewing application and the use of applets based on Java (Coriolis Group, 1995) and the Common Gateway Interface (see References for the Uniform Resource Locator)), there is a real possibility of a fundamental paradigm shift in use of household computing technology. This suggests that Internet-type marketing is likely to become one of the *de facto* standards in the near future.

The Internet provides one of the most effective ways to market ski industry products. In a later section we describe our web page for marketing the ski industry in southern Alberta. Although other web pages have been developed for marketing ski resorts in this area and other parts of Canada and the United States of America we believe that our use of GIS and related technologies incorporated into our web page is unique at the present time.

Marketing Price

GIS commonly have not been used to market price although this may well change in those industries where price is used to gain competitive advantage and where price fluctuates rapidly over space and time. In the petroleum industry, for example, marketing of downstream oil products changes rapidly in space and time. While in the past these price changes have been mapped using traditional mapping technologies (Lapaire, personal communication), at least one oil company has considered the possibility of the use of GIS technology to monitor these changes. GIS technology would allow not only the immediate production of maps of petroleum prices but also would allow the generation of "what-if" scenarios concerning future price changes and the re-optimization of delivery schedules. The new information can be distributed more rapidly to downstream retailers providing immediate competitive advantage.

Marketing Place

The most sophisticated GIS packages such as Arc/Info and TransCAD (Rodcay, 1996) include the ability to carry out location-allocation modeling. These routines allow the user to identify optimal locations for facilities such as ski resorts and other tourist destinations. In addition, by allocating tourists to these facilities the expected number of customers and their likely origins can be determined. Traditionally, these location-allocation modules have used distance calculations as the prime determinant for locating facilities and allocating customers but more sophisticated spatial decision support systems are being developed (Densham, 1991).

Marketing Promotion

In our example of the Alberta Ski Resort industry, discussed below, we argue that GIS technology could be used to coordinate the marketing of a ski package for several resorts similar to the circuit ski system used by the Dolomiti SuperSki resorts in the Dolomites of north-eastern Italy (Bertazzon, 1996). In this system, a network of lifts and slopes links each resort, allowing the customer to purchase a single ticket and to ski around the whole area. The SuperSki organization provides additional benefits including joint promotion and management and the offering of a range of tickets for different portions of the system. Such a system might be created, maintained and promoted more easily using the combination of GIS and Internet technology discussed below.

Marketing and Data Processing

Data processing has been the most commonly advocated application for GIS in marketing (Beaumont, 1991). With respect to tourism, facility owners and operators might collect data on their customers' origins and socio-economic profiles (Churchill, 1987) and use such geodemographic data for target marketing of the existing customer database to ensure their repeat visits (see Peppers and Rogers, 1993, for a discussion of this highly individualized approach to marketing). Geodemographics might be used to see what sectors of the expected, traditional market the tourist facility was not reaching, targeting these expected "no-shows" for future advertising campaigns. Finally, new, non-traditional markets could be targeted for exploitation with the use of innovative programs adapted to those not presently using the resort. For example, in our case study of ski resorts those from older age groups and those from lower socio-economic groups might be attracted by ski runs designed more specifically to their abilities and by lower priced programs, respectively.

MARKETING APPLICATIONS IN TOURISM

One way in which potential marketing applications of GIS in tourism may be viewed is to consider marketing in terms of demand for, and supply of, tourism services. Demand-oriented applications focus on the spatial task of finding, analyzing and mapping market characteristics. Supply-oriented applications, on the other hand, are concerned with the spatial tasks of locating, designing, and planning tourism development. Both types of potential applications could be used by tourism businesses or organizations involved in delivery of tourism products/services to potential travelers. In addition, GIS might find application in the travel trade (i.e., marketing intermediaries) and with tourists themselves, or as part of a hybrid system involving other types of computer-based tourism applications.

The Demand Side: Market Mapping

Tourism markets may be local, regional, national, or international. Apart from geographic bases for segmenting markets, other segmentation methods include demographic, psychographic, behavioural, product-related factors, and life-style bases. Today, many government departments and statistical bureaus collect numerous types of information about their residents and private enterprises. In the past, much of this information was held in widely different formats and systems. Currently, however, computer systems of many different departments are interlinked, greatly increasing the potential for integrating and using such data. Many government departments now charge for their information services, packaging and selling their data subject to certain privacy constraints. Market research and private companies also are engaged in gathering, packaging and selling market information. As a result, the potential for mapping markets using GIS or similar software is considerable (Baker and Baker 1993; Longley and Clarke 1995).

Tourism marketers have a wide variety of market mapping needs including information concerning the spatial distribution and location of their target markets. For example, cruise lines need to know which ports will generate most business. Airlines, too, need to know which cities will generate the greatest volumes of traffic and how population, demographic and socioeconomic trends will change these patterns over time. Hotel corporations have similar needs. As the business customer is critical to the success of many hotels, a knowledge of the industrial profile of major cities and how changes in the profile may change the attractiveness of different markets over the long term is of particular interest to hotels. Cruise lines and airlines can alter their ports readily but hotel development is a long term investment achieving the majority of its profitability well after it is built.

National Destination Marketing Organizations (often referred to as National Tourist Offices or NTOs) and Convention and Visitor Bureaus, face the task of deciding how to allocate geographically their promotional budgets, or where to locate tourism bureaus or information offices. GIS development to date has occurred principally within national borders but the availability of satellite data together with international statistics collected by various agencies including the United Nations (and its executive agency in tourism, the World Tourism Organization), the International Monetary Fund, the Organization for Economic Cooperation and Development, and the United States Central Intelligence Agency, among others, enable development of GIS which are international in scope. NTOs could use such a GIS to track changes in the potential of origin markets and thereby allocate marketing funds to different origin markets.

The Supply Side: Product and Place

Locating a suitable site for a proposed tourism development also represents a potential role for GIS in tourism marketing. Hotels and resorts, golf courses and ski hills, ecotourism projects, restaurant chains, scuba diving and river rafting operations, and sail boat rentals represent just a few of the types of tourism operations which need to determine appropriate sites for their business. Basic infrastructure information as well as location of transportation routes and modes also is important in site location. Risks due to hurricanes, bushfires, flooding, avalanches, landslides, subsidence, or earthquakes might rule out certain locations. Thus, ecological, climatic, topographic, cultural, scenic and other data will vary in significance depending on the type of development planned. GIS which combine meteorological and other natural or human-made environmental information appear to represent considerable potential for site location and development. Since it is questionable whether individual companies or organizations will be able to justify the cost of developing these systems themselves on such a broad scale, the importance of developmental partnerships is apparent.

Another potential supply side GIS application concerns route or trip planning. Spatial information is an important input to design decisions made by transportation companies regarding their routes, schedules, connections, frequencies, and capacities. Automobile associations advise travelers of the most scenic routes to take, road and traffic conditions, and worthwhile attractions or excursions along the way. Governments and travel agencies issue travel advisories warning tourists about travel risks in certain locations. Systems which take these types of spatial information and make them available to tourism marketers have definite appeal.

NTOs would find GIS-based information useful in planning and policy development for the tourism industry (Ryan 1994). For example, in many areas there is a conflict between tourism development and environmental preservation. GIS could be applied in situations where decisions must be made about appropriate forms of development on a national or regional scale. While many developmental decisions have been and continue to be made in an *ad hoc* fashion, governments and other authorities recognize the need to consider approvals for development which take into account the long term, cumulative effects of such development.

Possible Additional Uses

Other quasi-GIS applications are possible in tourism marketing. One rapidly growing development is electronic tourism marketing, most notably on the Internet (Sussmann and Rashad 1994, Canadian Tourism Commission and Canadian Tourism Research Institute 1996). Numerous destinations, airlines, hotel corporations, resorts, attractions and car rental firms, among many others, have developed Internet sites. Although many of these sites provide a passive display of information only, increasingly sites are allowing users to tailor actively the information provided to their own particular needs. For example, German or Canadian tourists wishing to visit wildlife sites in Africa might be able to enter information about the type of wildlife they wish to see, the time of year they plan to visit, and the level of service they seek. The site would then indicate the most suitable locations offering the greatest chance of seeing certain species based on their migration patterns and the time of the year. As service standards differ from one African nation to the next, the options might be further refined.

Some Internet sites allow users to make actual bookings or reservations, and some sites assist tourists in navigating subway systems such as the Paris underground. Conceivably, a tourist might use the Internet to identify golf or beach resorts which offer the highest probability of fine weather during their vacation time. Some NTOs have constructed elaborate sites on the Internet and offer a service to their industry members to enable smaller businesses to achieve a presence on the Internet. Another example of rapid growth in the electronic tourism market is the international consortium known as Services and Applications for a World Wide Market in Tourism (SAM). SAM is conducting large scale trials of communication services and applications toward a world wide electronic market place for tourism products. The possibility of using spatially-oriented information in these systems is considerable.

Other areas of computer-based information development in tourism in which geographic information may play an increasing role includes expert systems (Crouch 1991) and information kiosks. A number of prototypical expert systems have been developed for travel retailing. These systems may be used by travel agents to provide advice to customers in planning their trip. Attractions Canada plans to establish computer-based information kiosks in airports and other tourist nodes across the country. In the meetings and conventions industry, computer-based services are provided by associations such as the American Society of Association Executives and the International Association of Convention and Visitor Bureaus. Their databases enable members to access information on various conventions and convention sites including detailed information on numbers of hotel rooms, convention space and accessibility. This spatially-oriented information expedites the task of meeting planners in finding suitable convention or meeting sites.

A further computer-based development, particularly evident in airline and accommodation sectors, is the increasing use and sophistication of yield management systems. These systems seek to manage prices dynamically according to the changing sensitivity of market segments to prices over time, and thereby to maximize revenue yield. Such systems can utilize spatial information in this process, based on the geographic segment of the market involved or location of the service and indeed, airlines already do this across routes and connections.

Although these additional uses may not be classified as true GIS, they have the potential to use geographic information in increasingly sophisticated ways. With the increased integration of different computer systems and databases, hybrid GIS uses such as in the above examples, create all sorts of possibilities. As noted by Ryan (1994), as "an industry concerned with transport, environmental impacts, the use of space and places, the [tourism] industry ought to be amongst the largest users of GISs" (p. 573).

AN EXPERIMENTAL GIS APPLICATION FOR ALBERTA SKI RESORTS

In an effort to apply GIS in tourism destination marketing, this section describes the development and implementation of an experimental application using GIS to assist tourists in planning their visit to ski resorts in Alberta. A hypertext document, called Alberta Ski Resorts, was designed specifically for this paper (readers should note that this site is in the process of ongoing development).

In the Alberta Ski Resorts example, GIS has been applied to provide map displays and, in particular, to organize and convey spatial information. For users, the GIS functions at this site provide an important opportunity to move toward deeper comprehension of the spatial dimensions of the area through the calculation of traveling distance, distances between attractions and trip feasibility. Presently, this site includes direct links to other hypertext documents which add value by supplying real time information such as weather forecasts and highway conditions.

The spatial perspective that GIS provides is a relatively unique feature, rarely present in hypertext documents created by tourist destinations or marketing organizations for Internet marketing purposes. As of March 1996, for example, neither Wave Works' Western Canada Ski Guide site (http://softnc.com/waveworks/Western.html) nor Alta-Can Tours Inc. Canadian Rocky Mountain Adventures site (http://www.altacan.ab.ca/) provided spatial information. Similarly, although they offered skiing vacation packages, the American Express Travel Express site (http://www.america nexpress.com/travel/doco/vacation.html) presented no spatial information to potential clients. Additionally, although they are an independent public relations firm specializing in Internet consulting and network design, the Australian Internet Tourism Marketing Services home page (http://peg.apc.org/~travel/

itms.htm) provided no indication that spatial data display was part of their service.

Sites that include spatial data do so with varying utility of the map functions provided. For instance, Angus Reid Interactive Travel and Tourism Research Index site (http://www.angusreid.com/travindx.html) contained a link to Canadian Rocky Mountain Resorts site (http://www.worldweb.com:80/CRMR/) which included three maps. Two of these maps noted no distance or direction information in identifying the general location of the resorts. As no route numbers were indicated for "turnoffs" to the resorts, effective visitor use of the provided transportation information would be difficult. The third map contained one isolated piece of distance information but failed to note between which two points the 10 km distance measurement was relevant. Similarly, while the New Zealand Tourism Database site (http://www.cts.com/browse/jwb/index.html) permitted potential tourists to search by location, as of March 1996 the available New Zealand map contained only three active links. Destinations On-Line service site (http://dol.meer.net/) provided information on ski destinations such as Summit County, Colorado, including links to an area map and transportation information which were still under construction. In contrast, the structure of our Alberta Ski Resorts site possesses potential for more advanced GIS applications, such as geographic query and customized spatial analyses.

The Alberta Ski Resorts Hypertext Document as a Marketing Tool

Given that the GIS approach to marketing can be particularly useful in helping visitors to familiarize themselves with tourist facilities, surrounding regions and their spatial relationships, before they visit, the Alberta Ski Resorts hypertext document presents the supply of provincial ski resorts in terms of facilities and services to potential clients. Allowing tourists to gain a "feel for the place" in different and non-traditional ways could help clarify their perceptions of the region and develop a more thorough awareness of site characteristics. Not only might well-informed tourists achieve expected experiences from their vacation, but also destination managers might improve the soundness and effectiveness of their investments.

Using a GIS approach it is relatively easy to help potential visitors learn about distances and relative locations of facilities. In this respect, the use of GIS within marketing is a way of transferring geographic knowledge, which is extremely important in tourism. The inclusion of external information such as weather and road updates enhances the perception not only of geographical distance, but also of traveling time and overall accessibility of places. In light of this consideration, the Alberta Ski Resorts hypertext document offers a possibility for wider scale marketing. In a GIS approach, in fact, a whole tourist region such as the Alberta Rockies can be marketed jointly. This appears as a very promising path since various types of associations among resorts have been flourishing in recent years (cf., Wave Works' Western Canada Ski Guide).

One possibility offered by the Alberta Ski Resorts hypertext document is to plan a ski tour within the region. Prior to their actual visit, tourists could organize a tour of numerous resorts in the region, minimizing traveling time, optimizing snow and weather conditions at destinations, choosing subsequent destinations in accordance with physical conditions at other locations, optimizing their time choice by avoiding crowds and taking advantage of price specials.

Accessibility and Target Markets

The ski industry mainly targets a relatively young and reasonably affluent population, likely to have enough computer literacy to be familiar with the World Wide Web and to have increasingly easy access to a computer equipped with an Internet connection. As a marketing tool, the Alberta Ski Resorts hypertext document is designed specifically to address this market segment in an effective manner.

Our hypertext document can be accessed by any actual or potential tourist, through a personal computer connected to the Internet (in most cases via modem). An Internet browser, such as Netscape, Mosaic or Lynx also is required. Quality, speed and functionality of displayed information depend on the hardware, browser and connection used. However, the hypertext document provides extra features, such as simple text lines, which enable any user to access relevant information.

A computer is needed to access the site and for this reason the Alberta Ski Resorts hypertext document is more likely to be used as a trip planning tool, and is not designed specifically as an "on-hill orienteering tool" since skiers are unlikely to carry their own computers on the slopes. However, if terminals were available on the hill it would be possible to extend the hypertext document's capability for on-hill use. Further developments in this direction could include resort-specific information to assist skiers in their choice of runs and lifts through provision of information on open/closed runs, number of present users, wind and snow conditions. This type of aid should increase customer satisfaction and also provide a better distribution of users, thus reducing crowding and line-ups, improving the overall skiing environment, and enhancing levels of visitor satisfaction.

The Alberta Ski Resorts hypertext document also displays colors, icons, and simple maps intended to be graphically appealing and to stimulate users to further explore the hypertext document's links (Filippakopoulou and Nakos, 1996). Icons, colors, and dynamics improve the appeal and user-friendliness of the tool which is seen as an important part of the market targeting process.

A Guided Visit to the Alberta Ski Resorts Hypertext Document

The Alberta Ski Resorts hypertext document is publicly accessible. Located on the University of Calgary server, it can be reached through a net browser by typing the following address: http://acs.ucalgary.ca/~ sbertazz/maps/main.html. By typing this Uniform Resource Locator (URL) address, the user accesses our hyper-page (Figure 1). The map is "clickable" or interactive: the resort name labels on the map are hyper-links (underlined text lines) and by clicking the computer mouse on the labels, the user is lead to an attribute text file such as that for Sunshine Village (Figure 2). A list of resort names is provided below the map (Figure 1) in order to enable users who utilize limited net browsers (i.e., those with no graphics capability) to access relevant information.

As instructed at the top of the first hyper-page, a user may click on the icons on the left-hand side of the page and be brought to a "level-2" information map. Figure 3 is a level-2 map showing the ski lifts feature: both the lift symbol (for ease of interpretation) and the number of lifts at each resort is reported above or below the name label. In turn, each of the labels on the map (or the names on the list) can be clicked, leading the user to a "level-3" attribute text file which displays detailed information about lift facilities. Analogous tours can be taken by clicking on the icons for ski runs or prices. Figure 4 represents the ski area map which can be obtained by clicking on the relevant resort name in the attribute file. This map also is clickable and leads to the ski trail map (Figure 5).

By clicking on the weather or road icons, users access level-2 maps containing hyper-links to other servers which provide updated, real time information about these features. The road link leads to a map which, in turn, contains hyper-links to access more detailed information about specific subregions within Alberta. The link to the weather forecast provides the most recently available, region-wide forecasts for northern, central, and southern Alberta provided by Environment Canada, as well as detailed information for the series of weather stations in Alberta. Weather and road information is updated automatically in the specific servers. Each hyper-page provides a back-link to the lower level site, to facilitate the tour. Each page of the hypertext document provides a link to Bertazzon's electronic mail, to encourage interaction between us, as developers of the site and its users.

FIGURE 1. Welcome Page

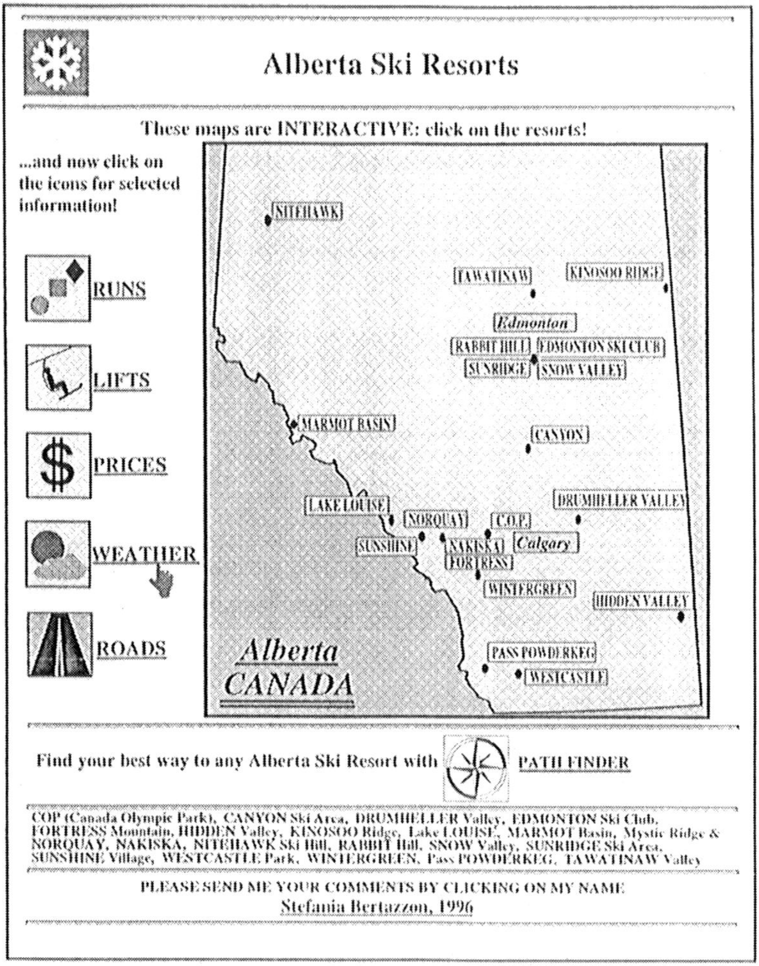

The Hypertext Document: Construction and Functioning

The hypertext document structure is similar to a home page on the World Wide Web; here, each hyper-page is composed in the HyperText Markup Language (HTML). Information is provided in a spatial fashion, mainly displayed through maps, which lead users through different features/attractions according to their interests. The database is organized by

FIGURE 2. Attribute File: Resort Highlights

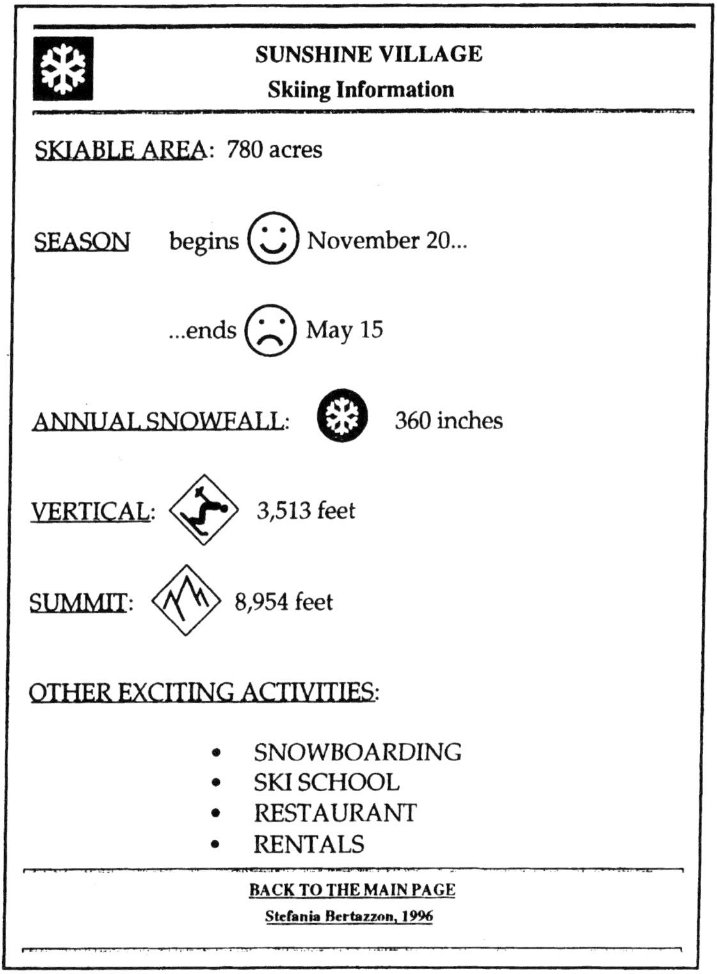

SUNSHINE VILLAGE
Skiing Information

SKIABLE AREA: 780 acres

SEASON   begins 🙂 November 20...

...ends ☹ May 15

ANNUAL SNOWFALL: ❄ 360 inches

VERTICAL: ⬦ 3,513 feet

SUMMIT: ⬦ 8,954 feet

OTHER EXCITING ACTIVITIES:

- SNOWBOARDING
- SKI SCHOOL
- RESTAURANT
- RENTALS

BACK TO THE MAIN PAGE
Stefania Bertazzon, 1996

themes and displayed in layers, each layer representing one feature. This method is a direct reflection of a GIS approach and is used to orient and lead users quickly to the specific information they are seeking. Stepwise, in a hierarchical fashion, users can obtain more detailed information by accessing subsequent sections, which are focused increasingly on specific needs. The displayed maps are a simple means to convey geographic

FIGURE 3. Feature Map: Lifts

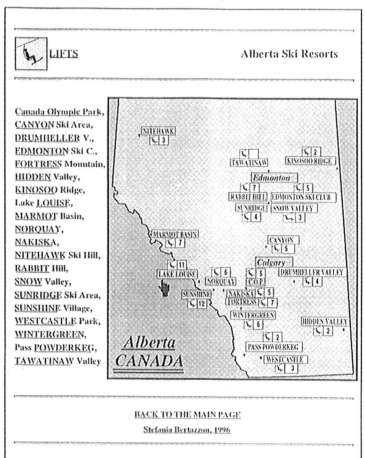

information through GIS: each geographic zone is linked to an attribute file, so that the information is accessed and organized through its spatial dimension. This clickable maps feature is supported by a system of files which specify the map zoning and establish hyper-links between map regions and attribute files.

Maps have been created by GIS software and subsequently rasterized and compressed to be incorporated into an HTML document. Other images and graphic items are imported through the same process. At

FIGURE 4. Ski Area Map

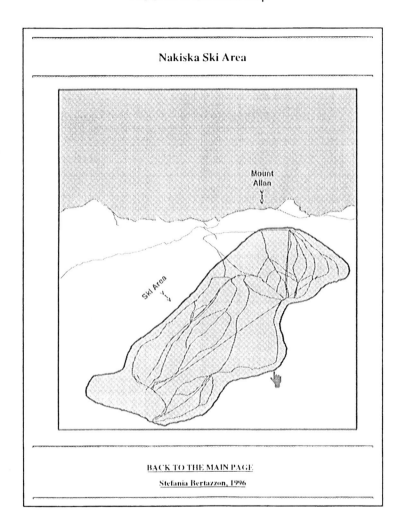

present, images have to be rasterized in order to be readable by most of the commonly used browsers. Unfortunately this causes a loss of resolution and therefore readability, and causes a significant increase in the image size, forcing the use of compression formats, such as the Joint Photographic Expert Group (JPEG) format, which are not readable by all browsers including

FIGURE 5. Trail Map

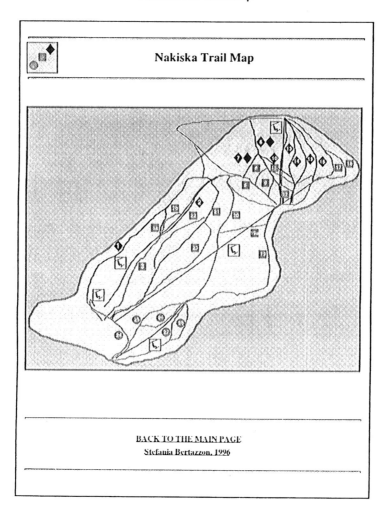

Mosaic. Refinements of the HTML are foreseen which will allow for vector images to be read directly, greatly enhancing GIS web applications.

Hyper-links connect various parts of the hypertext document to each other, usually in a bi-directional way; hyper-links also connect the hypertext document to relevant sources of information in external hypertext documents. The data needs to be updated periodically, especially immediately prior to and during the skiing season, to keep the hypertext document both current and functional. Updating includes the eventual addition of new resorts and new links to offer the widest available information and to adjust to changing needs of the market.

Further Developments

Beyond its potential as a collaborative marketing tool for the region as a whole, a GIS structure such as the Alberta Ski Resorts hypertext document may represent the organizational base for joint management of the entire region. Ski circuits or carousels, many instances of which can be found in European Alpine regions, are an excellent example. In these organizations ski resorts are physically linked to each other through a network of lifts and slopes that allow skiers to complete a ski tour of wide mountainous regions (Bertazzon, 1996). GIS would be an invaluable tool for managing and planning these organizations, and marketing would represent a highly functional interface between organizations and users.

The Alberta Ski Resorts site may be expanded to include other types of interactive maps, videos and other animations, and three dimensional representations of resorts, hills and slopes. This kind of expansion could prove particularly appropriate for on-hill use of the hypertext document, provided that terminals or personal computers were available at the base lodge or at other strategic locations. Further expansion of the Alberta Ski Resorts hypertext document could include data about roads, urban areas, geographical features and other types of tourism attractions to provide a complete guide to tourists in Alberta. Database enhancement could include summer activities offered by the included ski resorts, providing a multiple season perspective on Alberta mountain tourism. The most recent additions to the web site include database extensions that permit geographical queries (such as shortest path analysis, cf., Smith 1982, pp. 54-65), and tour planning (as in the travelling salesman model, cf., Smith 1982, pp. 205-229) and other types of customized analysis (see Bertazzon and Waters, 1996). These features are supported by on-line routines that can be added or linked to the Alberta Ski Resorts hypertext document. At the present time this has been achieved through the use of the Common Gateway Interface which is a highly flexible and effective programming tool for added true interactive GIS functionality to the web site (Bertazzon and Waters, 1996).

Future Prospects for GIS in Tourism Marketing

As electronic information technology ties the world's people together and reduces the distance barrier to international cooperation and trade, technological capabilities such as the Internet provide a crucial link in applications of GIS to tourism and tourism marketing. GIS could contribute to tourism marketing in at least three ways: enabling development of new services, improving customer services and outreach, and in market research.

This paper has emphasized the need for effective display of spatial data and has suggested that the future likely holds great potential for improvements in this area. Development of new tourist services will benefit from such improvements; for example, dramatic geographical data already may be included in digital terrain fly-bys for ski hills or for parks so that skiers and hikers can "look at" terrain before going into an area (USGS, NASA 1995). While this software is expected to be available inexpensively to private companies, its ability to be used by tourism marketers is not yet known. However, as GIS-Internet display capability is expected to grow and to be adopted by relevant users such as tourism marketers, numerous other features such as wildlife sightings or archeological information could be incorporated into interactive sites on the Internet. As a documentation resource and as a searchable information base, the GIS-Internet combination could add to tourist attractions in an area or provide guidelines to visitors regarding preservation and protection measures. However, these GIS and Internet abilities will require careful consideration of such issues as carrying capacity and environmental impacts. This suggests that there are awareness-raising, information, education and training functions possible through the use of GIS in marketing services on the Internet. Improvement in public map reading and interpretation skills could be one significant by-product of such efforts.

Growth in GIS and database transfer functions on the Internet would make it possible for marketers to undertake virtual field trips where potential clients could be taken through a multimedia tour of ski hills (or other recreational opportunities) in a region, province or country. Potential visitors might be provided with resources such as maps, pictures, sights and sounds of the ski hill itself as well as other ski hills and resorts in the region, professional personnel and services on the hill, transportation links and weather outlook options. Clearly there are marketing and business opportunities associated with determining specialized skiing (or other) interests and developing and selling specific tours or other products based on that knowledge. GIS can help generate such promotional vehicles by enabling ski hill owners, operators and marketers to answer basic questions such as where current and potential customers are located, where market gaps and opportunities may be found, how to achieve successful tourism market penetration, and where the best sites for facility expansion or site location are found (in terms of customers, market territory and competitors).

GIS may play an important supporting role in customer service and outreach programs where, because of GIS ability to contribute to strategic decision making and demand side management, marketers may be encouraged to develop highly effective micro-marketing approaches. Tourist information and product services–books, data, news user services, products and electronic ordering systems–can benefit from GIS ability to identify market niches available for "cherry-picking" (explicit exploitation). Interactive, GIS-based information kiosks can permit tourists to view travel and public transportation information, enable visitors to print ski hill, hiking or special event itineraries such as World Cup or Olympic skiing competitions, find detailed tourist attraction information, and display and print destination route maps. Customized maps should be possible, where visitors could find locations by adding landmarks and places of personal interest to address information. If cost-recovery charges are necessary for some of these services, the advent of new smart-card options might facilitate necessary fund transfers.

During the 1996 Summer Olympics, GIS assisted transportation managers in their activities through real-time mapping of road conditions and geographic analysis capabilities on over 60 miles of freeways in the Atlanta, Georgia, metropolitan area and five surrounding counties (GDS Software 1995). With data from almost 500 closed-circuit television cameras recording lane-by-lane occupancy, volume and speed, traffic managers conveyed information to motorists (many of whom were tourists) regarding accidents, alternate routes, construction and traffic delays via more than 40 overhead message signs. As part of a traveler information system which remained operational following the Olympic Games, the role of GIS in traffic management could be incorporated in current Games marketing (similar systems are already in place in Southampton, England, Cologne, Germany, and Piraeus, Greece, developed as part of the European Union's DRIVE research programme). More importantly, this event identifies a possible new link between GIS, tourism marketing and expansion of customer services in the safety field. In the context of ski hill operations, for example, marketers might identify emergency preparedness as a valuable addition to their tourist information packages. On a real-time basis, GIS can identify service and grooming vehicle routes and schedules, identify closed runs, and locate ski patrol personnel and equipment. If ski hills continue to expand and an increasingly aging population takes to the hills (Adams, 1996), such information could become an important new customer service feature.

In terms of market research for ski hill operations, GIS may contribute to improved displays of a ski hill's service territory and facilities (including property mapping details such as paved and unpaved roads, buildings, parking areas, fences, energy and water supply line locations), help in examination of competitors' locations and facilities, evaluate data about at-risk customers and generate response options, build a variety of "what-if" scenarios in order to analyze possible outcomes of potential alterations to the site, and determine economic costs of those alternative scenarios.

Clearly, GIS can contribute in similar ways to market research about other touristic operations, but in all cases, the opportunities to integrate GIS, electronic information technology and tourism marketing activities have only begun to be tapped. The globalized, cyber society that is now developing likely will experience a reduction in the influence of national and natural borders, thus enhancing the importance of GIS in production of *accurate* tourism marketing (and other) endeavours. As the Internet allows people access to great quantities of information on innumerable subjects, GIS will enable production of locally, regionally and nationally relevant data for marketing purposes.

CONCLUSION

This paper has reviewed the use of GIS technology in the tourism industry. It was shown that until quite recently the use of GIS in tourism marketing has been limited to the potential of traditional target marketing approaches using geodemographics. The second half of the paper described an innovative application in which GIS technology and the Internet are used to market the Alberta Ski Resort industry. This application involved the use of hypertext links to provide real time information on weather and road conditions within the resort region. Maps were created using GIS technology and incorporated into the web site. The use of additional GIS functionality to provide information on shortest routes and tours of the region was also explored.

The success of the site ultimately depends upon the number of tourists who visit it. Many sites provide counters to determine how many users actually access the site but we really need to know not only whether it is accessed but whether it was useful. We thus intend to build in a questionnaire at the site soliciting user feedback concerning what was effective and what was not. The continued addition of traditional GIS functionality to the site using the Common Gateway Interface is also an ongoing goal.

REFERENCES

Adams, J. (1996, February 22). Seniors no longer junior partners on mountains. *The Calgary Herald*, p. C6.

Baker, S. and Baker, K. (1993). *Market Mapping: How to Use Revolutionary New Software to Find, Analyze, and Keep Customers*. New York: McGraw-Hill.

Barkow, T. (1996). Raw Data. *Wired, 4* (4), 70.

Beaumont, J.R. (1991). GIS and Market Analysis. In Maguire, D.F., Goodchild, M.F. & Rhind, D.W. (Eds.), *Geographical Information Systems Vol. 2*. (pp. 139-151). London: Longman.

Bertazzon, S., *The Dolomiti SuperSki Circuit: A Dynamic Spatial System*, Working Papers "Nota di Lavoro" no. 96.06. Department of Economics, University of Venice. March, 1996.

Bertazzon, S. and Waters, N. M. (1996). The Use of GIS Applications on the Internet for Marketing Tourist Destinations. Proceedings of the GIS/LIS '96 Conference, Denver, Colorado, Nov. 19-21, 1996, in press.

Broadhead, R. (1995). Internet Strategies for Organizations. Keynote Address to the *GIS/LIS '95 Conference*, Nashville, Tennessee, Nov. 12-13, 1995.

Burrough, P.A. (1986). *Principles of Geographical Information Systems for Land Resources Assessment*. Oxford: Clarendon.

Burstein, D. and Kline, D. (1995). *Road Warriors: Dreams and Nightmares Along the Information Highway*. New York: Dutton.

Canadian Tourism Commission and Canadian Tourism Research Institute (1996). Online Travel Marketing Services in Canada: Report and Analysis.

Churchill, G.A., Jr. (1987). *Marketing Research: Methodological Foundations* (Fourth Edition). New York: Dryden.

Coriolis Group (1995). The Java Programming Language. Scottsdale, AZ: The Coriolis Group.

Cornish, E. (1996). The Cyber Future: 92 Ways Our Lives Will Change by the Year 2025. *The Futurist, 30*(1), 27-43.

Crouch, Geoffrey I. (1991). Expert Computer Systems in Tourism: Emerging Possibilities. *Journal of Travel Research, 29*(3), 3-10.

Dangermond, J. (1995). Spatial Database Engine Technology and How It Will Affect GIS. Presentation to the *GIS/LIS '95 Conference*, Nashville, Tennessee, Nov. 12-13, 1995.

Densham, P. (1991). Spatial Decision Support Systems. In Maguire, D.F., Goodchild, M.F. & Rhind, D.W. (Eds.), *Geographical Information Systems Vol. 1* (pp. 403-412). London: Longman.

Duffield, B. S. and Coppock, J. T. (1975). The Delineation of Recreational Landscapes: The Role of Computer-Based Information Systems. *Transactions of the Institute of British Geographers, 66*: 141-148.

Filippakopoulou, V. and Nakos, B. (in press). Is GIS Technology the Present Solution for Creating Tourist Maps? *Cartographica*.

GDS Software to Help Manage Olympic Games Traffic. (1995). *GIS World, 8*(11): 15.

Keller, P. & Waters, N.M. (1991). Mapping Software for Microcomputers. In D.R.F. Taylor (Ed.), *Geographic Information Systems: The Microcomputer and Modern Cartography* (pp. 97-128). New York: Pergamon.

Kelly, M. (1994). Partnerships for Tourism: Planning Scenarios for Municipalities Located in the Chinook Country Tourist Zone. Master's Degree Project, Faculty of Environmental Design, University of Calgary, Calgary, Alberta.

Lapaire, W. (1995). Personal Communication. Consultant to Shell Canada, Ltd., Calgary, Alberta.

Longley, P. & Clarke, G. (Eds.). (1995). *GIS for Business and Service Planning*. Cambridge: GeoInformation International.

Maguire, D. F. (1991). An Overview and Definition of GIS. In Maguire, D. F., Goodchild, M.F. & Rhind, D.W. (Eds.), *Geographical Information Systems Vol. 1* (pp. 9-20). London: Longman.

Maguire, D. F., Goodchild, M. F. & Rhind, D. W. (Eds.). *Geographical Information Systems Vols. 1 and 2*. London: Longman.

Openshaw, S. (1989). Computer Modelling in Human Geography. In Macmillan, B. (Ed.), *Remodelling Geography* (pp. 70-88). Oxford: Blackwell.

Parsons, V. (1996, January 13). Cash Driving Families on the Info Highway. *The Calgary Herald*, p. A2.

Peppers, D. and Rogers, M. (1993). *The One to One Future: Building Relationships One Customer at a Time*. New York: Doubleday.

Rodcay, G. K. (1996). *GIS World Sourcebook 1996*. Ft. Collins, Colorado: GIS World.

Ryan, C. (1994). Geographical Information Systems and Tourism Planning. In Witt, S.F. & Montinho, L. (Eds.), *Tourism Marketing and Management Handbook* (pp. 570-574). Englewood Cliffs, NJ: Prentice Hall International.

Sinclair, C. (1996). Netchick. New York: Henry Holt.

Smith, D. K. (1982). *Network Optimization Practice*. Chichester: Ellis Horwood.

Sussman, S. & Rashad, T. (1994). Geographic Information Systems in Tourism Marketing. *Progress in Tourism, Recreation and Hospitality Management, 6*, 250-258.

The Interminablenet: Why Is the Internet so Slow? And What Can Be Done About It? (1996, February 3). *The Economist, 338* (#7951), pp. 70-71.

Townshend, J. R. G. (1991). Environmental Databases and GIS. In Maguire, D. F., Goodchild, M. F. & Rhind, D. W. (Eds.), *Geographical Information Systems Vol. 2* (pp. 201-216). London: Longman.

USGS, NASA Produce Fly-by Software. (1995). *GIS World, 8*(11): 25.

Wilson, P. (1996, March 20). Set-top box could be *the* cheap entree to the Internet–or not. *The Vancouver Sun*, p. B7, B9.

INTERNET REFERENCES

Alberta Motor Association. Alberta Highway Conditions. http://www.ccinet.ab.ca/ama/home.htm

Alta-Can Tours Inc. Canadian Rocky Mountain Adventures. http://www.altacan.ab.ca/

American Express Travel Express. http://www.americanexpress.com/travel/doco/vacation.html

Angus Reid Interactive Travel & Tourism Research Index. http://www.angusreid.com/travindx.html

Australian Internet Tourism Marketing Services. http://peg.apc.org/~travel/itms.htm

Canadian Rocky Mountain Resorts. http://www.worldweb.com:80/CRMR/

Common Gateway Interface. http://hoohoo.ncsa.uiuc.edu/cgi/overview.html

Destinations On-Line. http://dol.meer.net/

Environment Canada. Public Weather Forecast. http://www.on.doe.ca/text/index.html

HyperText Markup Language Specification 3.0. http://www.w3.org/hypertext/WWW/MarkUp/htm13/Contents.html

Interactive Weather Browser. http://rs560.cl.msu.edu/weather/interactive.html

The New Zealand Tourism Database. http://www.cts.com/browse/jwb/index.html

Wave Works' Western Canada Ski Guide. http://softnc.com/waveworks/Western.html

Geography, Marketing
and the Selling of Places

C. Michael Hall

SUMMARY. Place and region have recently been rediscovered as major frameworks of analysis within the social sciences. However, both the geography of tourism and marketing have failed to adequately contextualise the concept of place within current social and cultural theory, including the concepts of production, consumption and postmodernism. This article argues that much of the place marketing literature emerges from an empiricist tradition which commodifies place as a product and fails to critically evaluate the implications of selling places on the people which constitute places. The paper concludes by arguing that contextualisation and the encouragement of argument within the disciplines is critical to their continued relevance to the public sphere. *[Article copies available for a fee from The Haworth Document Delivery Service: 1-800-342-9678. E-mail address: getinfo@haworth.com]*

The study of place and region, for long the domain of human geographers (Johnston 1991), has recently become a major element for the study

C. Michael Hall is Professor, Tourism and Services Management, Faculty of Commerce and Administration, Victoria University of Wellington, P.O. Box 600, Wellington, New Zealand.

The author wishes to acknowledge various discussions with John Jenkins, Simon Milne, Stephen Page, Rob Schaap and Kirsten Short which contributed to some of the ideas within this paper and the valuable comments of the anonymous referees.

[Haworth co-indexing entry note]: "Geography, Marketing and the Selling of Places." Hall, C. Michael. Co-published simultaneously in *Journal of Travel & Tourism Marketing* (The Haworth Press, Inc.) Vol. 6, No. 3/4, 1997, pp. 61-84; and: *Geography and Tourism Marketing* (ed: Martin Oppermann) The Haworth Press, Inc., 1997, pp. 61-84. Single or multiple copies of this article are available for a fee from The Haworth Document Delivery Service [1-800-342-9678, 9:00 a.m. - 5:00 p.m. (EST). E-mail address: getinfo@haworth.com].

61

of tourism and marketing. Indeed, throughout the social sciences there has been an increased focus on the significance of place and region. Moreover, government and industry have also focussed on the concept of place within the context of regional development and promotion.

Within the tourism and marketing literature, the concepts of 'place marketing' (e.g., Madsen 1992) also sometime described as 'selling places' (e.g., Burgess 1982; Kearns and Philo 1993), 'geographical marketing' (e.g., Ashworth and Voogd 1988) or 'reimaging strategies' (e.g., Hall 1994; Roche 1992), have come to receive significant attention over the past decade (Page 1995). As Ashworth and Voogd argue, the process of place-marketing is a new paradigm which reflects

> the way the complex functioning of cities is viewed . . . [as] .. many urban activities operate in some kind of a market . . . in which a planned action implies an explicit and simultaneous consideration of both the supply-side and the demand-side . . . [and] . . . such an approach has implications for . . . the way the cities are managed. (1988: 65)

What is the nature of this new 'paradigm'? What is its significance for the way in which we view cities and regions as a commodity to be promoted and sold (Philo & Kearns 1993), and how we regard the geography and marketing of tourism as fields of academic study with respect to places and the people within them?

This paper investigates the nature of place marketing within the context of contemporary economic and social theory. In particular it emphasises how place marketing should be considered in relation to ideas of globalisation, economic flexibility, postmodernism, heritage, identity, and changing patterns of consumption and production. The paper concludes by noting that the way place is considered highlights some of the central failings in our understanding of contemporary tourism.

THE REDISCOVERY OF PLACE: GLOBALISING PLACES

Perhaps somewhat paradoxically, the reason for the rediscovery of place as a focus of academic, government and industry interest is the globalisation of world economy and culture. According to Kotler, Haider and Rein (1993) we are living in a time of 'place wars' in which places are competing for their economic survival with other places and regions not only in their own country but throughout the world with places needing to "learn how to think more like businesses, developing products, markets, and customers" (Kotler et al. 1993: 346).

The centrality of globalisation to changing places has also been identified within other research traditions. For example, Robins (1991) argued that geographical transformations are now being brought about through the international restructuring of capitalist economies and the consequent changes to the nature and role of cities and regions as they seek to attract ever more mobile investors.

> It has created new centres and peripheries, and also new territorial hierarchies. It has produced new relational contexts and configurations . . . beyond this, there is the overarching global context. (Robins 1991: 24)

Tourism is intimately connected to the place marketing process because of the way in which it is often used as a focus for regional redevelopment, revitalisation, and promotion strategies. Tourism is seemingly almost universally regarded by government as a major mechanism for attracting investment, creating employment, and promoting regional economic growth (e.g., Hall, C. 1994; Hall, D. 1991; Williams & Shaw 1988). However, if "the promotion of a place-image becomes a matter of commodifying it through a rigorous selection from its many characteristics" (Madsen 1992: 633), then it becomes vital that we understand the context in which the new globalised place commodities are produced and consumed.

Producing Places

Many economic geographers agree that we are witnessing the onset of significant shifts in the character of contemporary capitalism (Milne, Waddington & Parry 1994). One of the most influential frameworks in the analysis of global economic change is that of 'post-fordism,' which represent a distinct break from the past economic structures associated with a dominant era of 'fordism' (Leborgne & Lipietz 1992). Fordism refers to the dominance of large vertically integrated companies producing homogeneous or standardised products for a market based primarily on price competition. 'Post-fordism,' also described within the context of 'flexible regimes of accumulation' and 'flexible specialisation' refers to the creation of a more specialized and rapidly changing market place that necessitates the use of more flexible/responsive forms of production if consumer demands are to be met (Milne 1994).

Within the tourism context, post-fordist ideas have received considerable attention in the work of Poon (1989, 1990) in the Caribbean and, to a lesser extent, in texts such as that of Shaw and Willams (1994). The focus on flexibility has considerable significance for the internal and external operations of tourism organisations. Internally, the corporate structure of a flexible tourism business revolves around the division of the labour force into core and peripheral groupings (Milne 1994; Shaw and Williams 1994). While such flexible labour forces increasingly appear to be utilised by tourism business, particularly in national economies where economic and employment deregulation has occurred (e.g., Hall 1995), there is some debate over whether contemporary tourism labour force structure is a result of economic globalisation or the nature of demand for tourism services. As Shaw and Williams (1994: 145) highlight, a flexible labour force is a long established form of internal labour-market organization in tourism services, with the temporal variation in demand resulting in the delivery of tourism services "to customers in both temporal and spatial clusters" (Shaw & Williams 1994: 145).

Externally, the concept of flexible production is tied in with the production of places as commodities to be promoted and sold to consumers. Place marketers do not see their task as simply promoting and advertising, "but also as adapting the 'product' (that is, the place) to be more desirable to the 'market'" (Holcomb 1993: 134). For Kotler et al. (1993), flexibility is inherent in the notion of place marketing, arguing that "Place marketing is a continual activity that must be adjusted to meet changing economic conditions and new opportunities" (Kotler et al. 1993: 345). Similarly, Fretter (1993), a local government employee in Britain, argued that place marketing

> calls for a demand-orientated approach rather than the supply-led approach of traditional urban planning. As such, it requires a more *flexible* approach to development plans. Above all, it requires the pro-active pursuit of the desirable rather than the reactive prevention of the undesirable. (Fretter 1993: 165)

However, although the notion of flexible economic response, whether it be by firms or places, is one of the dominant notions of the enterprise culture being promoted by governments in the Western world (e.g., see Corner & Harvey 1991), how firm are the empirical and theoretical foundations on which the apparent nexus between academic and government understanding of contemporary economic processes are based? As Milne et al. (1994) observed, our understanding of the nature of advanced capitalism has been weakened by the lack of attention paid to economic activities outside the manufacturing sphere and the narrow range of regional settings in which studies have been conducted (e.g., Amin 1989; Amin & Robins 1990; Gertler 1988, 1992; Sayer 1989).

As Thrift and Glennie observed, "paying greater attention to the historical geographies of urban life and consumption–as a variety of discourses and practices tied to different social groups, regions, cities, towns and intra-urban sites–is an essential component of rethinking the standard theorisations of modern consumption" (1993: 48). And it is a theorisation which has received only marginal attention in the tourism and marketing literature on place marketing. As Goodwin so cogently remarked, places are more than a simple coherence of production and consumption, they are

> a complex collection of individuals and communities, which in certain instances develop particular regional and local cultures, formed by social relations and practices outside of capital's narrow logic. (1993: 149)

THE PLACE MARKET

Places are now commodities to be produced and consumed. The competitive ethos of the market place became translated into a burgeoning 'place market' (Sadler 1993). The primary goal of place marketing "is to construct a new image of the place to replace either vague or negative images previously held by current or potential residents, investors and visitors" (Holcomb 1993: 133), in order to effectively compete with other places within the constraints of a global economy for a share of mobile international capital (Harvey 1987, 1989a).

> This marketing operation involved the construction or selective tailoring of particular images of place, which enmeshed with the dynamics of the global economy and legitimised particular conceptions of what were 'appropriate' state policy responses. (Sadler 1993: 175)

Place-making and promotion therefore has to be seen as deeply embedded in processes of global accumulation, in a "fragmented mosaic of uneven development" (Swyngedouw 1989: 31) in which competitive places try to secure their spot in the investment sun.

The notion of rapidly circulating international capital within the global economy is also implicit in the work of Kotler et al. (1993), probably the major place marketing text which is oriented within the mainstream empiricist marketing tradition. According to Kotler et al.

marketplace shifts and changes occur far faster than a community's capacity to react and respond. Buyers of the goods and services that a place can offer (i.e., business firms, tourist, investors, among others) have a decided advantage over place sellers (i.e. local communities, regions, and other places that seek economic growth). (1993: 18)

Kotler et al. (1993: 18) refer to the need for places to adopt a process of "strategic place marketing" for urban and regional revitalization in order to design a community "to satisfy the needs of its key constituencies." Such a process embraces four inter-related core activities:

- designing the right mix of community features and services;
- setting attractive incentives for the current and potential buyers and users of its goods and services;
- delivering a place's products and services in an efficient, accessible way; and
- promoting the place's values and image so that the potential users are fully aware of the place's distinctive advantages.

To Kotler et al. place marketing therefore means that places must be designed so as to "satisfy the needs of its target markets. It succeeds when citizens and businesses are pleased with their communities, and meet the expectations of visitors and investors" (1993: 99). Various investments can be made to a place to "improve livability, investibility, and visitability," a process made up of the four components of place:

- place as character;
- place as a fixed environment;
- place as a service provider; and
- place as entertainment and recreation (Kotler et al. 1993: 100)

However, in all of this what has become of the notion of place as people? In objectifying place as a commodity, as within the empiricist tradition of the majority of marketing, including tourism marketing, the people constituting place have been placed outside of the place marketer's frame of reference. As Hudson recognised, a

locality is *not just* a space in which to work for a wage but . . . [they are] places to which they have become deeply attached. These localities are places that have come to have socially endowed and shared meanings for people that touch on all aspects of their lives and that help shape who they are by virtue of where they are. (1988: 493-494)

In commodifying place as a product that can be revitalised, advertised and marketed places are presented not so much

> as foci of attachment and concern, but as bundles of social and economic opportunity *competing* against one another in the open (and unregulated) *market* for a share of the capital investment cake (whether this be the investment of enterprises, tourists, local consumers or whatever). (Philo & Kearns 1993: 18)

The "terrain of thinking" about local economic policies and political forms is therefore being shifted (Duncan & Goodwin 1985a, 1985b, 1988), so that a range of local institutions "now internalise the idea that the interests of a place are best served by lifting the 'dead hand' of regulation and by opening it to the sway of market forces" (Philo & Kearns 1993: 19). However, such normative arguments also lie within the academic terrain: "The public sector, being largely monopolistic in character, often lags behind the private sector in being responsive to the needs and service requirements of its citizens" (Kotler et al. 1993: 325).

It is important to note that theories are also policies (Hall & Jenkins 1995). Academic, government and industry arguments as to the role of the local state are intimately related. The last decade has witnessed the re-emergence of political structures and ideologies which are based around the notions of privatisation and deregulation, twin processes which supposedly promote the unfettered operation of so-called 'market forces' (Cloke 1992). The infrastructure of urban government is becoming increasingly privatised, along with the ideologies and discourses of regeneration and revitalisation. "Where public agencies were once seen as an essential part of the solution to . . . crisis, they are now viewed as part of the problem itself" (Goodwin 1993: 148). Thus, it is ironic that Kotler et al.'s (1993) discussion of strategic place marketing fails to address the means by which the citizenry can actually participate in the place marketing process to decide how their city should be presented to consumers, if at all. Within this context, normative assumptions about equal individual access to power and decision-making pervade much of the marketing literature (Simmons 1993). Yet, clearly, individuals to not have equal access to power and decision-making. As Hall and Jenkins (1995) argued, business interest groups dominate the tourism policy making process, while Harvey (1988) highlighted the role of growth coalitions in urban redevelopment. Similarly, Lowe commented on "the potential power of the 'regional entrepreneur' in moulding the contemporary urban landscape" (1993: 211):

A person of vision, tenacity and skill (such as a charismatic mayor, a
clever city administrator, or wealthy business leader) to put a particular stamp upon the nature and direction of urban entrepreneurialism, perhaps to shape it even, to particular political ends. (Harvey
1989a: 7)

The above observations lead us to return to a question which haunted
much urban geography and planning in the late 1960s and early 1970s
(Johnston 1991), in whose interests are cities and places being constructed,
promoted and revitalised? Or are we witnessing the creation and promotion
of places in the gaze of marketing academic, white, middle-class notions
of what constitutes civil society?

Packaging Place

Places are increasingly being packaged around a series of real or imagined cultural traditions and representations, often focussing on a particular
interpretation of the enterprise history of a place–typically without any
labour disputes! Under the enterprise economy

the ideology of locality, place and community becomes central to the
political rhetoric of urban governance which concentrates on the
idea of togetherness in defence against a hostile and threatening
world of international competition. (Harvey 1989a: 14)

The packaging of cultural images and traditions is recognised as being
significant for place marketing in the work of Kotler et al. (1993). However, whereas Kotler et al. see this as an appropriate means of forging new
images in the marketplace, other commentators argue that this may be an
inappropriate form of political socialisation whereby images of places are
manipulated in order to manufacture an apparent cultural and political
consensus designed to convince many disadvantaged and potentially dis-
affected people, "that they are important cogs in a successful community
and that all sorts of 'good things' are really being done on their behalf"
(Philo & Kearns 1993: 3). Indeed, the more intangible phenomenon of
place marketing is the process by which "cultural resources are mobilised
by urban managers in an attempt to engineer consensus amongst the residents of their localities" experience the city is basically "doing alright"
by its citizens (Kearns and Philo 1993: ix) in order to encourage them to
believe that the city is doing the right thing for its citizens.
Not only are internal marketing campaigns utilised to make citizens of a
community feel better about themselves, e.g., the 'Absolutely, Positively,

Wellington' campaign in Wellington, New Zealand, or the 'State on the Move' campaign in Victoria, Australia, but culture, in the form of heritage, history, traditions and lifestyles are sold as commodities to be consumed and utilised as mechanisms to create a unified image or history where none existed before (Philo & Kearns 1993: 3).

Issues of authenticity and inauthenticity, e.g., the creation of a 'consensus' when one does not exist, have become a major area of interest for students of cultural and heritage tourism. However, the means by which *places* are created, and the authenticity they have for tourists and the people which make up those places, particularly in western cities and regions, has not drawn much attention within the mainstream tourism literature in recent years, although it has been an issue of concern within cultural studies and social theory.

The culture of a place, however this might be understood, is intimately bound up with the history of that place and with the histories (which may *not* always be locally-rooted) of the peoples who have ended up living in that place (Philo & Kearns 1993). However, the past is often appropriated and manipulated for the presentation of a particular picture or image of the past and designed for consumption by external consumers, as well as internal consumers—the people who live in such places. The outcome has been described as 'the city as theme park' in which the architecture of the inner-city utilises historic facades from a spuriously appropriated past to generate consumption within an atmosphere of nostalgia and display. The result, according to Sorkin, "is that the preservation of the physical remnants of the historical city has superseded attention to the human ecologies that produced and inhabit them" (1992: xiv). For example, Burgess and Wood argued that as a result of the London dockland redevelopment and associated marketing places have become products offering emotional and economic benefits to their 'consumers.' Thus, the richness and diversity of the specific localities within East London have been reduced to a commodity to be packaged and sold (1989: 115).

One of the great ironies therefore, given the enterprise culture of place marketing which extols the virtues of competition and choice, is the manner in which debate over representation and redevelopment of place is denied. Throughout much of the western world, in order to ensure that urban development projects are carried out, local authorities have had planning and development powers removed by central government and have handed them to unelected institutions (Goodwin 1993). Harvey recognised that

> the new entrepreneurialism has, as its centrepiece, the notion of a 'public-private partnership' in which a traditional local boosterism is

integrated with the use of local government powers to try [to] attract external sources of funding, new direct investments, or new employment sources. (1989a: 7)

However, the partnership does not include all members of a community, those who do not have enough money, are not of the right lifestyle, or simply do not have sufficient power, are ignored. Referring to Derwentside in the United Kingdom for example, Sadler argued, place development and promotion policies

rested not so much on a basis of rational choice, but rather was a simple reflection of the narrow political and intellectual scope for alternatives. This restricted area did not come about purely or simply by chance, but had been deliberately encouraged and fostered. (1993: 190)

As Harvey (1993: 8) asked "The question immediately arises as to why people accede to the construction of their places by such a process." In many cases they do not. Communities may resist such change. However, while wins in short-term battles may save the physical fabric of inner-city communities, this will not usually win the war. The social fabric will usually change through gentrification and touristification of many areas leaving only heritage facades. Furthermore, the very 'rules of the game' by which planning and development decisions are made will often favour business over community interest groups (Hall & Jenkins 1995). Indeed, Harvey also notes that resistance has not checked the overall process of place competition. A mixture of coercion and co-optation centered around maintenance of real estate values, assumptions regarding employment and investment generation, and an assumption that growth is automatically good, has led to the creation of local growth coalitions.

Coercion arises either through interplace competition for capital investment and employment (accede to the capitalist's demands or go out of business; create a 'good business climate' or lose jobs) or more simply, through the direct political repression and oppression of dissident voices . . . (Harvey 1993: 9)

However, place packaging is not just the result of micro-political factors, it should also be placed within the context of cultural fashions and social theory. In this sense, contemporary architects, designers and other place-makers, with their penchant for the postmodern, are as responsible for the commodification of place as the real estate developer or place marketer wanting to package their product.

POSTMODERN PLACES?

Academic bookshop shelves are groaning under the escalating weight of books on postmodernism. Tourism and marketing have, so far, been little influenced by works from within a postmodern tradition (e.g., Urry 1990). However, this should hardly be surprising given their grounding within empiricist research traditions. Nevertheless, attempts at gaining an understanding of place marketing would be incomplete without exposure to some of the ideas of postmodernism, particularly postmodern architecture. Indeed, Holcomb (1993) observed that the rise of the concept of place marketing coincided with that of postmodernism as the prevailing theoretical fashion and argued that this was no mere coincidence.

> Postmodernism is a perspective, a way of seeing, a way of constructing an understanding of the world by deconstructing our experiences of it. Postmodernism is eclectic. It juxtaposes, blends, splices, copies, combines, repeats ideas, attitudes, aesthetics and forms. (Holcomb 1993: 141)

Similarly, according to Gitlin, postmodernism

> neither embraces nor criticises, but beholds the world blankly, with a knowingness that dissolves feeling and commitment into irony. It pulls the rug from under itself, displaying an acute self-consciousness about the work's constructed nature. It takes pleasure in the play of surfaces, and derides the search for depth as mere nostalgia. (1989: 52)

The postmodern architectural vision is therefore one in which difference and diversity come to dominate; one in which the austere homogeneity of the white skyscraper or block of modernist architecture "is replaced by the colourful playfulness of architects mixing and matching all manner of styles, references and materials" (Philo & Kearns 1993: 22). Indeed, the 'flexibility' of postmodern architecture can be interpreted as the cultural equivalent of the economic flexibility of postfordism.

Within postmodernist aesthetic and architectural theory it has become commonplace to favour a reintroduction of multivalent symbolic dimensions into architecture, a mixing of codes, an appropriation of local vernaculars and regional traditions. Thus Jencks (1987) suggests that architects look two ways simultaneously toward the traditional slow-changing codes and particular ethnic meanings of a neighbourhood, and the fast-changing codes of architectural fashion and professionalism. Therefore, to paraphrase Holcomb (1993), at first glance it might be assumed that place marketing, with its enthusiastic embrace of place, its appeal to the supposedly unique attractions of particular locations, and its passionate text, is anything but postmodern.

> Yet ultimately, the deconstructed discourses of the packed newly post-industrial cities replicate the same images, amenities, and potentials and contain the same silences with respect to poverty, race and blight . . . The time of places marketed is present and future. The only past that matters is the packaged past of the heritage industry. (Holcomb 1993: 141)

The selling of the 'postmodern city' therefore "entails the deliberate creation of cultural-historical packages" and "lumping together of cultural and historical elements to produce marketable pastiches" (Philo & Kearns 1993: 22)–'the city as theme park' idea noted above. Indeed, similar comments to Philo and Kearns were noted by Hewison (1987) in his critique of Britain's heritage industry; a book cited within the tourism literature, at least with respect to heritage tourism, but the fundamental thesis of which did not register on the Richter scale of tourism theory. As Philo and Kearns argued, the aim of postmodern architecture "is to manufacture an environment that will secure the acceptance and even the affection of peoples who might otherwise rebel against it" (1993: 23). Postmodern architecture is therefore not an 'architecture of the people' but still has substantial relationships to the confluence of certain values, interests, institutional arrangements and power structures (Hall & Jenkins 1995)

> with power no longer being so nakedly expressed in city form as in the days of massive skyscrapers 'pricking' the skies but being cunningly disguised amidst the homeliness of cultural, historical and (above all) local remembrances. (Philo & Kearns 1993: 23)

Within this setting, apparently public spaces, e.g., malls and festival marketplaces, are more often than not private space. In some city centres the perceived need to create a 'safe' and 'attractive' environment for consumers (of the right kind) has led to the virtual disenfranchisement from city life of young people with low spending power and of other–generally low-income–residents, whose appearance and conduct does not conform to the moral codes of well-ordered consumption enforced by shopping centre managers, in many cases with the active support of local authorities (Bianchini & Schwengel 1991). However, the homogenisation of 'public' life and space is not isolated to places of consumption. Heritage, also plays a central role within postmodernist ideas of place and representation. When cities have a crisis in terms of both urbanity and social cohesion which place marketing may seek to correct, heritage then represents "a feeble attempt to reconstruct some common identity in the face of potentially explosive social tensions and conflicts" (Bianchini & Schwengel 1991: 227).

The loss of historically rooted places, including the attempt to depoliticise and decontextualise them "so as to sell . . . places . . . to outsiders who might otherwise feel alienated or encounter encouragements to political defiance" (Philo & Kearns 1993: 24) is commonplace in tourism. Heritage centres and historical anniversaries typically serve to flatten and suppress contested views of history (Hall & McArthur 1996). However, the presentation of one-dimensional views of the past to the tourist and the community is also encountered at the destination level. In her excellent study of tourism, history and ethnicity in Monterey, Norkunas (1993) argues that the rich and complex ethnic history of Monterey is almost completely absent in the 'official' historic tours and the residences available for public viewing. In Monterey, as in many other parts of the world, heritage is presented in the form of the houses of the aristocracy or elite.

> This synopsis of the past into a digestible touristic presentation eliminates any discussion of conflict; it concentrates instead on a sense of resolution. Opposed events and ideologies are collapsed into statements about the forward movement and rightness of history. (1993: 36)

Narratives of labour, class, and ethnicity are typically replaced by romance and nostalgia. Overt conflict, whether between ethnic groups, classes or, more particularly, in terms of industrial and labour disputes are either ignored or glossed over in 'official' tourist histories. The overt conflict of the past has been reinterpreted by local elites to create a new history in which heritage takes a linear, conflict-free form. In the case of Monterey, the past is reinterpreted through the physical transformation of the canneries. Reinterpreting the past has therefore allowed the city to effectively erase from the record the industrial era and the working class and ethnic cultures it engendered. "Commentary on the industrial era remains only in the form of touristic interpretations of the literature of John Steinbeck" (Norkunas 1993: 50-51).

The theme of flattened, one-dimensional history, is a strong thread in critical discussions of heritage tourism and the postmodern city. For example, in the case of Britain's museums, Hewison argued that the contemporary presentation of heritage succeeds in presenting a curiously unified image, where change, conflict, clashes of interest, are neutralized within a single seamless and depthless surface, which merely reflects our historical anxieties . . . There seem to be no winners, and especially no losers. The open story of history has become the closed book of heritage. (1991:75)

Of significance to the manner in which heritage and urban tourism is developed Hewison went on to argue that "the time has come to argue that commerce is *not* culture . . . You cannot get a whole way of life into a Tesco's trolley or a V & A Enterprises shopping bag" (1991: 175). Such arguments are important because they run counter to the notions of commodification of place and culture as product which are intrinsic to place marketing. Furthermore, they run counter to both the macro-political narratives of postmodernism and postfordism and the (related) micro-political actions of actors within the policy making process.

The assertion of moral values, over against those commodity values which are not merely the theoretical result of the cultural logic of late capitalism, but the very practical result of the political and economic logic of the contemporary Conservative government. (Hewison 1991: 176)

As Hewison concluded, there is a need for

a version of the past that does not exclude conflict and change (the hidden agenda of Heritage being to exclude these irritants), and which admits the existence of contingency, the possibility of accident, and the reality of winners and losers. (1991: 176)

Therefore, the postmodern architecture of redevelopment—with its facadal displays, penchant for recycling imagery and theoretical rationale in semiotic theory is fully incorporated into the ideological apparatus of place marketing, and plays "a major role in mediating perceptions of urban change and persuading 'us' of the virtues and cultural beneficence of speculative investments" (Crilley 1992: 231). The postmodern skyline of the heritage waterfront is therefore more than an outcome of the pursuit of assiduous conservation policies. Instead, it is an integral part of the incorporation of cultural investment and policy into urban growth strategies, as cities and regions struggle to attract investment by amassing the correct mix of cultural infrastructure (Crilley 1993). As Harvey (1989b: 328) wrote, "aesthetics has triumphed over ethics as a prime focus of social and intellectual concern" with the consequence that inner city redevelopment resembles a "carnival mask that diverts and entertains, leaving the social problems that lie behind the mask unseen and uncared for" (Harvey 1989b: 21). Indeed, for Ghirado

> builders and developers could not in their wildest dreams have designed a strategy of such academic and intellectual status that it would successfully direct analysis toward trivial matters of surface and away from much more vexing matters of substance. (1990: 236)

Yet, if we are, as noted above, to pay greater attention to the historical geographies of urban life and consumption then why do ordinary people, going about ordinary lives, not feel themselves to be part of 'the postmodern condition'? "They do not see their everyday cultural practices as evidence of 'fragmentation' or 'depthlessness.' They do not frame contemporary popular products with notions of 'pastiche' and 'nostalgia'" (Mellor 1991: 94). Perhaps much research is asking the wrong questions. There are significant problems in trying to understand the cultural significance of the heritage industry because there is often a belief that heritage is a homogeneous phenomenon and researchers have often neglected to ask the visitor what they think.

> People should be treated as active agents interacting with real structures. People make their own cultures, albeit not in circumstances of their own choosing . . . Even in leisure, people act intentionally; although in doing so they may slice the world along a different grain to that expected by the melancholic intellectual. (Mellor 1991: 114)

Therefore, perhaps we should be asking as to whether in the communal 'visiting' to heritage sites, people are seeking the neighbourliness they feel they have lost from their real communities (Mellor 1991). If this is so, then what does this say about the success of place marketing strategies to redevelop and package places? Place-marketers are creating products. Perhaps though they have failed to revitalise or contribute to what constitutes a place, the communities and people who live there.

CONCLUSIONS

As with production and consumption, globalisation and localisation cannot be separated. Globalisation is about the achievement of a new set of global-local relations. "Globalization is like putting together a jigsaw puzzle: it is a matter of inserting a multiplicity of localities into the overall picture of a new global system" (Robins 1991: 35). Nevertheless, as Robins argues, we should not idealise the local.

> We should not invest our hopes for the future in the redemptive qualities of local economies, local cultures, local identities. It is important to see the local as a relational, and relative, concept. If once it was significant in relation to the national sphere, now its meaning is being recast in the context of globalization. (1991:35)

But 'local' in this sense does not correspond to any specific territorial configuration. 'Local' should not be mistaken for 'locality.' The 'local' should be seen as a fluid and relational space, constituted only in and through its relation to the global. For the global corporation, the local might, in fact, correspond to different regional spheres of activity depending on the product and the constituency of the market. However, place-marketers have equated place with the local. Cities are positioning themselves in an attempt to gain access to scarce international mobile capital in order to redevelop themselves, with the help of architects, as postmodern cities of pastiche and image. So that they can, again, go in search of economic and cultural capital with which to then compete against other places.

> Whether it is to attract a new car factory or the Olympic Games, they go as supplicants. And, even as supplicants, they go in competition with each other: cities and localities are now fiercely struggling against each other to attract footloose and predatory investors to their particular patch. (Robins 1991: 35-36)

Nevertheless, it is somewhat ironic that the very places which have sought to differentiate themselves have ended up looking the same, what may be described as the serial replication of homogeneity or the serial monotony of the festival marketplace, heritage precinct, art gallery, museum, casino, marina, and shopping centre (Boyer 1988; Hall 1994; Harvey 1990). The selling of cities must therefore be seen "as merely one part of a balanced approach to ensure that our urban areas are developed in a desired fashion" (Fretter 1993: 174).

The revitalisation of place requires more than just the development of product and image. The recreation of a sense of place is a process which involves the formulation of urban design strategies based on conceptual models of the city which are, in turn, founded on notions of civic life and the public realm and the idea of planning as debate and argument (Bianchini & Schwengel 1991). Unfortunately, such models have only limited visibility within the place marketing and tourism realms (Hall 1994; Hall & Jenkins 1995) as tourism and place planning is often poorly conceptualised with respect to participatory procedures, while the institutional arrangements for many of the public-private partnerships for urban redevelopment actually exclude community participation in decision-making procedures.

Policy visions, whether they be for places or for industries, typically fail to be developed in the light of oppositional or critical viewpoints. Place visions tend to be developed through the activities of industry experts rather than the broad populace. Perhaps because the vision of the wider public for a place may not be the same as some segments of business. Community involvement is undertaken through opinion polls, surveys or SWOT analyses rather than through participatory measures (Hall & Jenkins 1995). Nevertheless, as Bianchini and Schwengel (1991: 234) observed

> Cities will be re-imagined in democratic forms only by creating the conditions for the emergence of a genuinely public, political discourse about their future, which should go beyond the conformist platitudes of the 'visions' formulated by the new breed of civic boosters and municipal marketers. (1991: 234)

Tourism is intimately connected with the development of such visions. However, here, as with place marketing as a whole,

> we are presented with a set of information and evidence which . . . is overly optimistic. Nowhere is the issue of potential job loss and regional decline really addressed, nowhere are the implications of growing ownership concentration and globalized information technologies . . . analysed. (Milne 1994: 29)

As Milne, so accurately argued "the transition toward becoming competitive does not come without its costs" (1994: 30). If places are in competition in the new global economic environment there will be winners and losers and, as Williams and Shaw observed almost a decade ago

> Any evaluation of the role of tourism–and of the jobs, income and value added which it produces–must depend on particular national and local circumstances . . . There is a need, therefore, to look not just at tourism but at the opportunity costs of its development, and the alternative strategies which could be pursued by a region or a community. (Williams & Shaw 1988: 238)

In the case of place marketing, the notion of 'revitalisation' or 'regeneration' was economically based on the enterprise culture of the 1980s and aesthetically based on the foundations of postmodern architecture. Public-private partnerships were primarily property and land-based and largely failed to lay the foundations for long-term solutions to the economic and social problems of inner city areas (Bianchini & Schwengel 1991). Indeed, the 'solution' was to replace the lower socio-economic inner city populations with groups of higher socio-economic status and appropriate cultural patterns of consumption. As Parkinson's (1989: 32) review of the work of the London Docklands Development Corporation concluded:

> little attention has been paid to providing the training, jobs or low income housing to meet the needs of the original residents . . . the low income community has paid many of the economic, social and environmental prices of regeneration while deriving relatively few of the benefits.

All this is not to say that some of the people advocating place marketing do not believe in what they are doing and they do not have a humanistic sensibility for the place they are trying to regenerate. However, there

> is a certain irony that attaches to the way in which the 'New Right' discourse of individualism—the notion of individual people, enterprises, localities or whatever striving to earn their just rewards from their own resources—does not contribute in the way that might be expected to an appreciation of the *individuality* which renders one 'thing' different from any other (Philo & Kearns 1993: 20)

nor in the way that individuals within a community are able to participate in the processes of place creation. Place should therefore be seen as both a social and political construction which are, in turn, a part of spatially-grounded social processes of production and consumption. "Places are therefore not necessarily competitive: it is only a specific political packaging of the concept of place which makes them seem to be so" (Sadler 1993: 191).

To comment on the contestation of place, or lack of, as the case may be, is also to comment on the manner in which place is conceptualised. Undoubtedly, geography and marketing have secured 'place' as an important component of analysis. However, what sort of geography and marketing are we talking about? Much of the geography of tourism presents an inherently empiricist world-view which may well be able to map tourist flows, facilities and attractions on geographic information systems but contributes relatively little in terms of actually explaining the how, where, why and for whom of tourism development (e.g., Britton 1991). Similarly, in much place marketing literature, particularly that exemplified by Kotler et al. (1993), there is an empiricist tradition which fails to adequately contextualise places in terms of the global political-economic system within which they are situated. Both traditions have a fascination with techniques and tools rather than the purposes for which they are used. Much of the geography and marketing of places can therefore be characterised as instrumental in orientation, serving the purposes of those who want to package places rather than those who actually live in them. Yet it neither need, or should, be so.

Within human geography concerns over relevance have been particularly important at various times in the development of the discipline, particularly with respect to urban and social geography and resource management (Johnston 1991; Mitchell 1989). However, such concerns have only occasionally reached the surface within the geography of tourism. In the case of place marketing concerns over the nature and implications of selling places has emerged from within cultural studies rather than marketing. Such concerns highlight the often narrow academic frameworks and theoretical discourses within which much of tourism studies operate. Non-empirical studies are in the minority in the major tourism journals while 'industry orientation' is often central to tourism and marketing education. Yet such a situation is doing both fields of studies and the students within them a major disservice.

Tourism and place marketing needs to be adequately contextualised. By drawing on a wider range of theoretical discourses than is the norm in discussions of the relationship between geography, tourism and marketing, the richness and complexity of places, and some of the possibly unforeseen consequences of place marketing can be highlighted. In order to do this it becomes essential that geographers and marketers not only become aware of academic approaches outside of the normally narrow confines of their disciplines but also develop theoretical frameworks which reflect the complexity of what we are investigating and constituting in our role as 'experts.'

Postfordism, postmodernism, and the global-local nexus confronts us with the immediacy of interdependence. As Said (1989: 225) observed, the crossing of boundaries brings about a complexity of vision and also a sense of the permeability and contingency of cultures. It allows us "to see others not as ontologically given but as historically constituted" and can, thereby, "erode the exclusivist biases we so often ascribe to cultures, our own not least." However, in our postmodern world we also realise there will always be a tension between those within a discourse and those who are marginalised by it. Such conditions need to be accepted and, in fact, encouraged. As Gergen commented

> Reflexive reconsideration is required: can we now blend these richly elaborated discourses into new forms . . . that can now take us beyond text and into life? And can we do so without losing sight of context and contingency, without making fast the language, or formulating final solutions? (1991: 259)

Argument and debate about the nature of cities and for whom they are, needs to be encouraged within the public sphere in order to make places for people. Similarly, it is now vital that we encourage argument and debate and the inclusion of hitherto marginalised voices within the academic sphere, for the relevance, meaning and adequacy of our studies.

REFERENCES

Amin, A. (1989). Flexible specialisation and small firms in Italy: Myths and realities. *Antipode*, 21: 13-34.

Amin, A., & Robins, K. (1990). The re-emergence of regional economics? The mythical geography of flexible accumulation. *Environment and Planning D: Society and Space*, 8, 7-34.

Ashworth, G.J., & Voogd, H. (1988). Marketing the city: Concepts, processes and Dutch applications. *Town Planning Review*, 59(1), 65-80.

Bagguley, P. (1987). *Flexibility, Restructuring and Gender, Employment in Britain's Hotels*, Lancaster Regionalism Group, Working Paper No.24.

Bagguley, P. (1990). Gender and labour flexibility in hotel and catering. *Services Industries Journal*, 10, 105-118.

Bianchini, F., & Schwengel, H. (1991). Re-imagining the city. In J. Corner and S. Harvey (Eds.), *Enterprise and Heritage: Crosscurrents of National Culture* (pp. 212-234). London and New York: Routledge.

Boyer, C. (1988). The return of aesthetics to city planning. *Society*, 25(4), 49-56.

Britton, S.G. (1991). Tourism, capital and place: Towards a critical geography of tourism. *Environment and Planning D: Society and Space*, 9, 451-478.

Burgess, J. (1982). Selling places: Environmental images for the executive. *Regional Studies*, 16, 1-17.

Burgess, J., & Wood, P. (1989). Decoding docklands: Place advertising and decision-making strategies in the small firm. In J. Eyles & D.M. Smith (Eds.), *Qualitative Methods in Human Geography*. Oxford: Polity Press.

Cloke, P. (1992). *Policy and Planning in Thatcher's Britain*. Oxford: Pergamon.

Corner, J., & Harvey, S. (1991). *Enterprise and Heritage: Crosscurrents of National Culture*. London and New York: Routledge.

Crilley, D. (1992). The enchanting mountain: Olympia and York and the contemporary megastructure. In P. Knox (Ed.), *The Restless Urban Landscape*. Englewood Cliffs: Prentice-Hall.

Duncan, S.S., & Goodwin, M. (1985a). Local economic policies: Local regeneration or political mobilisation. *Local Government Studies*, 11(6), 75-96.

Duncan, S.S., & Goodwin, M. (1985b). The local state and local economic policy: Why the fuss? *Policy and Politics*, 13, 27-53.

Duncan, S.S., & Goodwin, M. (1988). *The Local State and Uneven Development*. Cambridge: Polity Press.

Fretter, A.D. (1993). Place marketing: A local authority perspective, pp. 163-174. In G. Kearns & C. Philo (Ed.), *Selling Places: The City as Cultural Capital, Past and Present*. Oxford: Pergamon Press.

Gergen, K.J. (1991). *The Saturated Self: Dilemmas of Identity in Contemporary Life*. United States: Basic Books.

Gertler, M. (1988). The limits to flexibility: Comments on the post-fordist vision of production and its geography. *Transactions of the Institute of British Geographers New Series*, 17, 259-278.

Gertler, M.S. (1992). Flexibility revisited: Districts, nation states, and the forces of production. *Transactions of the Institute of British Geographers New Series*, 21, 259-278.

Ghirado, D. (1990). The deceit of postmodern architecture. In G. Shapiro (Ed.), *After the Future: Postmodern Times and Places*. Albany: State University of New York Press.

Gitlin, T. (1989). Postmodernism: Roots and politics. *Dissent*, 36(1), 100-108.

Goodwin, M. (1993). The city as commodity: The contested spaces of urban development, pp. 145-162. In G. Kearns & C. Philo (Ed.), *Selling Places: The City as Cultural Capital, Past and Present*. Oxford: Pergamon Press

Hall, C.M. (1994). *Tourism and Politics: Policy, Power and Place*. London: John Wiley & Sons.

Hall, C.M. (1995). *Introduction to Tourism in Australia: Impacts, Planning and Development* (2nd ed). South Melbourne: Longman Australia.

Hall, C.M. & Jenkins, J. (1995). *Tourism and Public Policy*. London and New York: Routledge.

Hall, C.M. & McArthur, S. (Eds.) (1996). *Heritage Management in Australia and New Zealand: The Human Dimension*. Sydney: Oxford University Press.

Hall, D.R. (Ed.) (1991). *Tourism and Economic Development in Eastern Europe and the Soviet Union*. London: Belhaven Press.

Harvey, D. (1987). Flexible accumulation through urbanisation. *Antipode*, 19, 260-86.

Harvey, D. (1988). Voodoo cities. *New Statesman and Society*, 30, September: 33-35.

Harvey, D. (1989a). From managerialism to entrepreneurialism: The transformation in urban governance in late capitalism. *Geografiska Annaler*, 71B, 3-17.

Harvey, D. (1989b). *The Condition of Postmodernity: An Enquiry into the Origins of Cultural Change*. Oxford: Basil Blackwell.

Harvey, D. (1990). Between space and time: Reflection on the geographic information. *Annals Association of American Geographers*, 80, 418-434.

Harvey, D. (1993). From space to place and back again: Reflections on the condition of postmodernity, pp. 3-29. In J. Bird, B. Curtis, T. Putnam, G. Robertson & L. Tickner (Eds.), *Mapping the Futures: Local Cultures, Global Change.* London and New York: Routledge.

Hewison, R. (1987). *The Heritage Industry: Britain in a Climate of Decline.* London: Methuen.

Hewison, R. (1991). Commerce and culture, pp. 162-177. In J. Corner & S. Harvey (Eds.), *Enterprise and Heritage: Crosscurrents of National Culture.* London and New York: Routledge.

Holcomb, B. (1993). Revisioning place: De- and re-constructing the image of the industrial city, pp. 133-143. In G. Kearns & C. Philo (Eds.), *Selling Places: The City as Cultural Capital, Past and Present.* Oxford: Pergamon Press.

Hudson, R. (1988). Uneven development in capitalist societies: Changing spatial divisions of labour, forms of spatial organisation of production and service provision, and their impacts upon localities. *Transactions of the Institute of British Geographers*, 13 (New Series), 484-496.

Jencks, C. (1987). *The Language of Post-Modern Architecture* (5th ed). London: Academy Editions.

Johnston, R. (1991). *Geography and Geographers: Anglo-American Geography since 1945* (4th ed). London: Edward Arnold.

Kearns, G., & Philo, C. (1993). Preface, pp. ix-x. In G. Kearns & C. Philo (Eds.), *Selling Places: The City as Cultural Capital, Past and Present.* Oxford: Pergamon Press.

Kotler, P., Haider, D.H., & Rein, I. (1993). *Marketing Places: Attracting Investment, Industry, and Tourism to Cities, States, and Nations.* New York: The Free Press.

Leborgne, D., & Lipietz, A. (1992). Conceptual fallacies and open questions on post-fordism, pp. 332-348. In M. Storper & A.J. Scott (Eds.), *Pathways to Industrialization and Regional Development.* London: Routledge.

Lowe, M. (1993). Local hero! An examination of the role of the regional entrepreneur in the regeneration of Britain's regions, pp. 211-230. In G. Kearns & C. Philo (Eds.), *Selling Places: The City as Cultural Capital, Past and Present.* Oxford: Pergamon Press.

Madsen, H. (1992). Place-marketing in Liverpool: A review. *International Journal of Urban and Regional Research*, 16, 633-640.

Mellor, A. (1991). Enterprise and heritage in the dock, pp. 93-115. In J. Corner & S. Harvey (Eds.), *Enterprise and Heritage: Crosscurrents of National Culture.* London and New York: Routledge.

Milne, S. (1994). *The Changing Structure of the Tourism Industry: Current Trends and Their Economic Implications* (mimeograph). Montreal: Department of Geography, McGill University.

Milne, S., Waddington, R., & Perey, A. (1994). Toward more flexible organisation?: Canadian rail freight in the 1990s. *Tijdschrift voor Economische en Sociale Geografie*, 85, 153-164.

Mitchell, B. (1989). *Geography and Resource Analysis*. Harlow: Longmans.

Norkunas, M.K. (1993). *The Politics of Memory: Tourism, History, and Ethnicity in Monterey, California*. Albany: State University of New York Press.

Page, S. (1995). *Urban Tourism*. London and New York: Routledge.

Parkinson, M. (1989). The Thatcher government's urban policy 1979-89: A review. *Town Planning Review*, 4, 32.

Philo, C., & Kearns, G. (1993). Culture, history, capital: A critical introduction to the selling of places, pp. 1-32. In G. Kearns & C. Philo (Eds.), *Selling Places: The City as Cultural Capital, Past and Present*. Oxford: Pergamon Press.

Poon, A. (1989). Competitive strategies for a 'new tourism,' pp. 91-102. In C.P. Cooper (Ed.), *Progress in Tourism, Recreation and Hospitality Management*. London: Belhaven Press.

Poon, A. (1990). Flexible specialization and small size: The case of Caribbean tourism. *World Development*, 18, 109-123.

Robins, K. (1991). Tradition and translation: National culture in its global context, pp. 21-44. In J. Corner & S. Harvey (Eds.), *Enterprise and Heritage: Cross-currents of National Culture*. London and New York: Routledge.

Roche, M. (1992). Mega-events and micro-modernization: On the sociology of the new urban tourism. *British Journal of Sociology*, 43, 563-600.

Sadler, D. (1993). Place-marketing, competitive places and the construction of hegemony in Britain in the 1980s, pp. 175-192. In G. Kearns & C. Philo (Eds.), *Selling Places: The City as Cultural Capital, Past and Present*. Oxford: Pergamon Press.

Said, E. (1989). Representing the colonised: Anthropology's interlocutors. *Critical Inquiry*, 15, 225.

Sayer, A. (1989). Post-Fordism in Question. *International Journal of Urban and Regional Research*, 13, 666-695.

Shaw, G. & Williams, A.M. (1994). *Critical Issues in Tourism: A Geographical Perspective*. Oxford: Blackwell.

Simmons, D.G. (1993). Local input into destination area planning, pp. 661-668. In A.J. Veal, P. Jonson & G. Cushman (Ed.), *Leisure and Tourism: Social and Environmental Change, Papers from the World Leisure and Recreation Association Congress, Sydney, Australia, 16-19 July 1991*. Sydney: University of Technology.

Sorkin, M. (1992). Introduction: Variations on a theme park, pp. xi-xv. In M. Sorkin (Ed.), *Variations on a Theme Park: The New American City and the End of Public Space*. New York: Hill and Wang.

Swyngedouw, E. (1989). The heart of the place: The resurrection of locality in an age of hyperspace. *Geografiska Annaler*, 71B, 31-42.

Thrift, N. & Glennie, P. (1993). Historical geographies of urban life and modern consumption, pp.33-48. In G. Kearns & C. Philo (Eds.), *Selling*

Places: The City as Cultural Capital, Past and Present. Oxford: Perga-
mon Press.
Urry, J. (1990). *The Tourist Gaze: Leisure and Travel in Contemporary Societies.*
London: Sage Publications.
Williams, A.M. & Shaw, G. (Eds.) (1988). *Tourism and Economic Development:
Western European Experiences.* London: Belhaven Press.

Tourism Markets and Marketing in Sarawak, Malaysia

Douglas G. Pearce

SUMMARY. A multi-scale approach is used to analyze issues of markets and marketing with regard to the emerging destination of Sarawak in Malaysia. In particular, an analysis of market profiles and travel patterns reveals marked differences in the demand for tourism in Sarawak and in peninsular Malaysia and suggests different strategies might be needed for marketing the state. Issues of state marketing within a federal system are then explored. *[Article copies available for a fee from The Haworth Document Delivery Service: 1-800-342-9678. E-mail address: getinfo@haworth.com]*

Most tourism marketing studies focus on a single spatial scale, be it international, national, regional or local. Market research is undertaken for individual countries, regional marketing studies are carried out and issues of promoting local destinations or resorts are examined but the linkages between these different levels of analysis usually receive little consideration. In this respect marketing has been treated little differently from other fields of tourism research where the emphasis has again been on single scale problems or phenomena.

Douglas G. Pearce is Associate Professor, Department of Geography at the University of Canterbury, PB 4800, Christchurch, New Zealand.

This paper draws on research undertaken by the author as a member of the Tourism Resource Consultants-Lincoln International Consortium engaged in the preparation of the Second Sarawak Tourism Masterplan for the State Government of Sarawak. The views expressed are those of the author.

[Haworth co-indexing entry note]: "Tourism Markets and Marketing in Sarawak, Malaysia." Pearce, Douglas G. Co-published simultaneously in *Journal of Travel & Tourism Marketing* (The Haworth Press, Inc.) Vol. 6, No. 3/4, 1997, pp. 85-102; and: *Geography and Tourism Marketing* (ed: Martin Oppermann) The Haworth Press, Inc., 1997, pp. 85-102. Single or multiple copies of this article are available for a fee from The Haworth Document Delivery Service [1-800-342-9678, 9:00 a.m. - 5:00 p.m. (EST). E-mail address: getinfo@haworth.com].

Nevertheless some attention has been directed to multi-level research in tourism and to synthesizing phenomena at different scales. The notion of a spatial hierarchy is central to a number of models which underpin the geography of tourism, including those of Miossec (1976), Britton (1982) and Lundgren (1982). Pearce (1987, 1990) has analysed different scales of tourist travel patterns, showing how flows at one scale are linked to those at another, with resultant implications for the impacts which tourism may generate. Mathieson (1985), too, argues that greater attention should be given to "the scale of impact for the spheres of influence of tourist development vary and their consequences may be viewed differently depending upon whether they are assessed from a local, regional, national or international perspective." Pearce's (1992) application of interorganizational analysis to tourist organizations also highlighted the importance of inter-scale linkages, with the activities of higher and lower order organizations being a critical external factor impacting on any organization's operational environment.

Marketing was one of the key functions of the tourist organizations examined by Pearce. While domain consensus regarding marketing activities occurred in some countries at given periods, often marked inter-scale tension existed in others. In Great Britain, overseas tourism promotion was limited by the 1969 Development of Tourism Act to the national body, the British Tourist Authority (BTA). During the late 1970s and early 1980s this situation was strongly contested by the Scottish Tourist Board (STB) which sought the right to promote Scotland abroad. Passage of special legislation in 1984, argued on the grounds of Scotland's special case and the need to combine domestic and overseas marketing, eventually gave the STB the authority to undertake such promotion but the corresponding resources allocated to do so were rather modest. As a result, the official marketing of Scotland abroad continues to depend heavily on the BTA. Subsequently, marketing differences occurred between the STB and the Highlands and Islands Development Board and the smaller scale Area Tourist Boards. As the Regional Tourist Boards in Ireland matured over a similar period and developed aspirations to market their regions internationally, relations between them and the national body, Bord Failte, became strained. Within Hawaii, a tier of island organizations has emerged because operators on the Neighbour Islands were not wholly satisfied with the marketing directions of the Hawaii Visitors Bureau and sought to develop stronger images and niches for their own islands.

Different arguments have been put forward by the higher and lower order organizations regarding their marketing functions and programmes. National Tourist Organizations (NTOs) are generally content to leave domestic marketing to the regions and make a case for a strong central co-ordinated marketing effort to create the biggest impact with usually limited resources in competitive international markets. NTOs normally see their role as being to develop a strong national image and to promote the country as a whole, arguing that multiple campaigns by a host of regional and local organizations will confuse the market and lead to duplication of effort. Moreover, central government's prime reason in funding NTOs is generally to boost the balance of payments with the result that the marketing thrust is on the growth in total arrivals rather than issues of regional dispersion.

Regional and local organizations, on the other hand, are less concerned with overall growth and generating foreign exchange, than with increasing visitor numbers and revenue in their own regions and resorts. Growth for them is often perceived to be directly related to marketing and promotion. National strategies are rarely seen as giving sufficient prominence to specific regions or forms of tourism associated with particular areas. Consequently, regional and local organizations develop a desire to become more directly involved in marketing their own destinations abroad. This is especially so where there are marked regional differences in market preferences and products, in which case the regional concern is marketing to their given strengths or spending more money in the markets most disposed to visiting them. But even where regions offer similar attractions and appeal to the same segments, a desire may exist to extend the national programme with regional organizations feeling some additional activity would give them an edge over their competitors.

The purpose of this paper is to examine these issues further with reference to a South East Asian example, Sarawak, a state of Malaysia. After briefly reviewing the context of the study area, attention is directed firstly at the size and structure of Sarawak's markets compared to those of the country as a whole in order to determine any specific characteristics that might set the state apart. The marketing implications of these characteristics are then examined in terms of state/federal relationships and conclusions are drawn.

Tourism in Sarawak and Malaysia

Malaysia is a federation of thirteen states formed in 1963 (Figure 1). Eleven of these are located in West or Peninsular Malaysia; two, Sabah and Sarawak, occupy the northern and northwestern parts of the island of Borneo. These two non-contiguous areas are separated by 650 km of the South China Sea. Sarawak (37.7%) has almost the same surface area as the peninsula (40%), but only 10% of Malaysia's 17.7 million inhabitants, compared with 83% in Peninsular Malaysia and 7% in Sabah. Kuala Lumpur, the capital and largest city, is located on the peninsula.

While each state has its own constitution and government, much of the power and responsibility is vested in the Federal Government. Central economic direction has been provided by a series of five year plans. It was not until the latter part of the Fourth Malaysia Plan (1981-1985) that the government attached much significance to tourism, recognizing in particular the sector's potential for generating foreign exchange. Priority under the Fifth Malaysia Plan (1986-1990) was to be given to the enhancement of existing destinations, particularly Kuala Lumpur and the established island destination of Penang. Secondary destinations on the peninsula were also targeted for development, along with the islands of Langkawi and Tioman. However, in order to complement Kuala Lumpur and Penang, Kuching and Kota Kinabalu, the state capitals of Sarawak and Sabah, were also to be designated as primary destinations. A federal Ministry of Culture, Arts and Tourism was established in 1987, under which was placed the Tourist Development Corporation (now the Malaysia Tourism Promotion Board (MTPB)) which had been set up in 1972. The number of international arrivals in Malaysia increased from 2.5 million in 1981 to 7.5 million in 1990. While no tracking studies are available to monitor the effect of marketing and development activities, some of this substantial increase, especially in the latter part of the period, might be attributed to the new importance accorded to the sector, for example organization of Visit Malaysia Year in 1990.

Sarawak receives little specific mention in the 1991-1995 plan. However, the state might be expected to play a central role in the development of Malaysian tourism given the plan's emphasis on natural and cultural attractions and the diversification of tourism product. In contrast to the urban and coastal attractions of the peninsula, international visits to Sarawak have developed around the state's cultural and physical diversity. In particular, visits to Iban longhouses have developed over the last twenty years into a distinctive attraction, complemented by a fine state museum and, more recently, the Sarawak Cultural Village. Coastal tourism is also being developed at Damai Beach and the state's rainforests and other natural features, notably the Niah and Mulu Caves, are beginning to attract visitors. Miri, in the north, is also drawing a growing number of short-stay, cross-border visitors from Brunei.

Although a significant amount of new hotel building has gone on in recent years, access has improved and national parks have been opened up, tourism in Sarawak is still at a youthful stage of development and most operations remain modest in scale. The sector has, however, been ac-

FIGURE 1

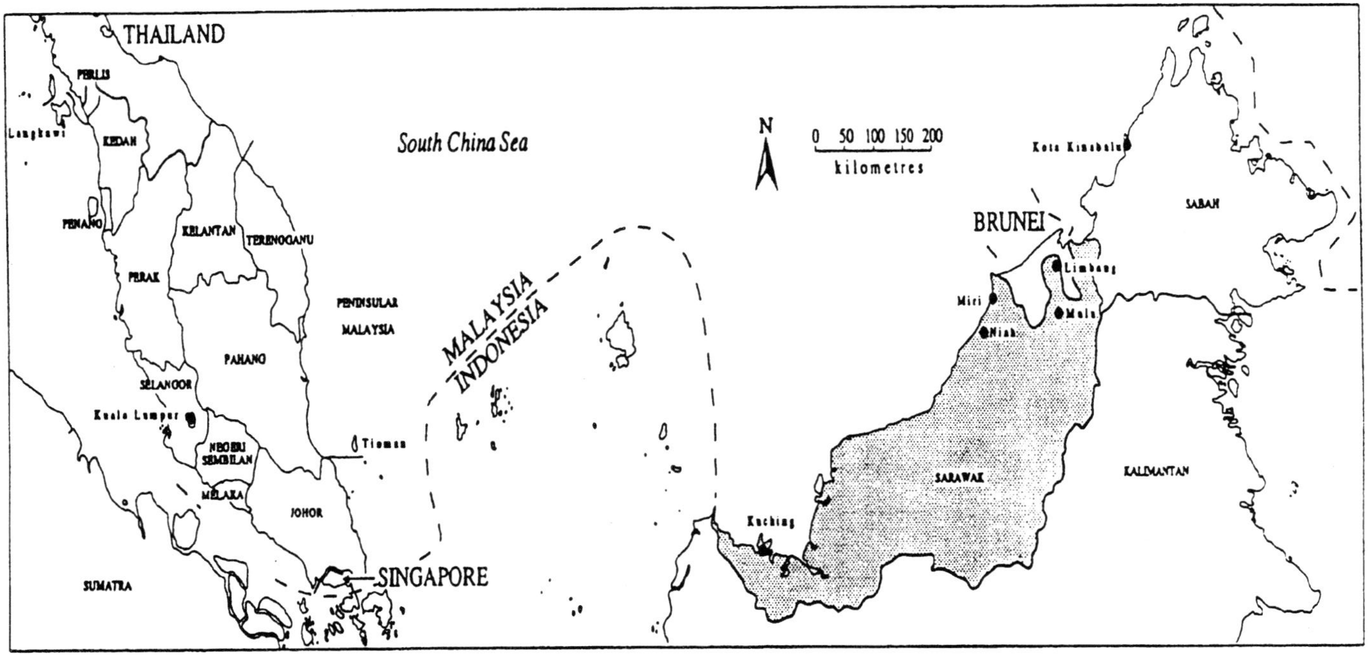
THAILAND
PERLIS
Langkawi
KEDAH
PENANG
KELANTAN
TERENGGANU
PERAK
PAHANG
SELANGOR
Kuala Lumpur
NEGERI SEMBILAN
MELAKA
JOHOR
SUMATRA
SINGAPORE
PENINSULAR MALAYSIA
Tioman
South China Sea
MALAYSIA
INDONESIA
N
0 50 100 150 200
kilometres
BRUNEI
Miri
Niah
Limbang
Mulu
Kota Kinabalu
SABAH
SARAWAK
Kuching
KALIMANTAN

corded growing importance by the state government, especially in terms of diversifying the economy. In 1992 it commissioned, with the federal Ministry of Culture, Arts and Tourism, the Second Sarawak Tourism Masterplan to guide the orderly development of tourism in the future. Preparation of the masterplan provided a timely review of the state's markets and associated marketing activities.

Markets

The conceptual framework for the preparation of the masterplan stressed a multi-scale approach which set Sarawak explicitly in the national context and that of the wider ASEAN region (Pearce, 1995). In terms of the market analysis this meant not considering Sarawak in isolation but rather in relation to the rest of the country, particularly Peninsular Malaysia, with regard to market share and composition. Attention was also directed to the ways in which the state was linked into the national and regional systems through an analysis of tourist travel patterns.

Tourism in Malaysia is at present heavily concentrated on the peninsula (Table 1). Peninsular Malaysia recorded 91.6% of all hotel guest arrivals in 1990 (94.4% of foreign guest arrivals). One third of all hotel guest arrivals were registered in Kuala Lumpur and Penang. International tourism was more concentrated (43.5% in Kuala Lumpur and Penang) than domestic tourism (25.8%). Other significant destinations for both international and domestic guests were Johor, Melaka, the hill resorts (Genting and Cameron Highlands) and Perak, particularly for Malaysians. Emerging destinations which experienced rapid rates of growth and increased market share in the period 1988-90 were the island resorts (Langkawi, Tioman . . .). East Malaysia recorded only a modest share of visitor arrivals: 8.4% of all hotel guest arrivals, 5.6% of foreign hotel guest arrivals. Sabah's share was greater than that of Sarawak.

Whatever measure is used (Tables 1 and 2), it is clear that Sarawak has only a small share of the total Malaysian tourism market:

- 2.3% of total foreign hotel guests in 1990, i.e., 97,972, compared with 4,170,914 for all Malaysia.
- 5% of all domestic hotel guests in 1990 and 3.8% of total hotel guests in Malaysia that year.
- 1.7% of Peninsular Malaysia's arrivals by air in 1990, i.e., 56,520 for Sarawak compared with 3,192,505 for Peninsular Malaysia.
- 5.8% of all foreign arrivals in 1990, i.e., 434,379 out of a total of 7,476,772 and 8.4% of Peninsular Malaysia's foreign arrivals for 1991, i.e., 509,597 compared with 5,543,376. In both cases it should

be noted that many of the arrivals are excursionists–about half of Sarawak's recorded arrivals are cross-border visitors who do not stay overnight.
- 5.1% of total tourist expenditure in 1989 (5.7% of international expenditure, 3.6% of domestic tourism expenditure).

The imbalance in Sarawak's share of Malaysia's tourism is particularly noticeable when it is recalled that Sarawak and Peninsular Malaysia are almost the same size. Even in terms of its smaller proportion of the country's population, Sarawak's tourism is underdeveloped.

The composition of Sarawak's international tourism markets differs significantly from that of Peninsular Malaysia's leading markets (Table 2). When all foreign arrivals are compared, it can be seen that Sarawak draws heavily on the cross-border traffic from Brunei and Indonesia while Peninsular Malaysia depends on neighbouring Singapore and Thailand. Important secondary markets for Sarawak are the United Kingdom and Other Europe whereas Peninsular Malaysia also draws on Japan and Taiwan.

In terms of arrivals by air only, Sarawak relies heavily on one market, Singapore, whereas the peninsula exhibits a more balanced demand. Brunei and long-haul markets (UK, Other Europe, Australia/NZ) are important secondary markets for Sarawak. Peninsular Malaysia draws on its neighbours (Thailand, Singapore) and intra-regional markets (Japan and Taiwan).

Sarawak's recent pattern of growth in visitor arrivals differs significantly from that of Peninsular Malaysia (Table 3). Growth in Visit Malaysia Year 1990, when a major programme of promotional activities was undertaken, was less than on the peninsula but continued in 1991 in contrast to the decline there. In 1991, Sarawak experienced declines only in the Singaporean, European and Canadian markets whereas decreases were widespread in the markets of the peninsula. These different rates of growth may reflect differences in market composition, a lack of regional uniformity in the effects of Visit Malaysia Year and the Gulf Crisis of 1991, together with differences in product development.

Differences would also appear to exist in the motivations of tourists visiting Sarawak and Peninsular Malaysia. Results from an exit survey of holiday visitors leaving the state through Kuching Airport in November 1992 indicate Sarawak's cultural diversity, its lifestyles and friendly people were the major elements visitors enjoyed, followed by scenery, outdoor activities/beaches and, to a lesser extent, food and shopping (Table 4). While this general pattern holds across the five markets, differences do occur. The Europeans appreciate in particular the cultural diversity and scenery and are particularly prominent amongst longhouse visitors.

TABLE 1. Distribution of Hotel Guest Arrivals in Malaysia 1990

Locality	All hotel guests			Foreign hotel guests			Domestic hotel guests		
		%	% change 88/90		%	% change 88/90		%	% change 88/90
Kuala Lumpur	1,666,800	17.76	21.48	1,041,449	24.97	47.93	625,351	11.99	– 6.39
Penang	1,494,330	15.92	116.51	773,362	18.54	88.66	720,968	13.83	157.23
– Beach area	447,540	4.77	59.04	295,245	7.08	32.66	152,295	2.92	158.84
– City area	1,046,790	11.15	156.06	478,117	11.46	155.18	568,673	10.91	156.81
Selangor	357,146	3.81	69.84	219,378	5.26	113.01	137,768	2.64	28.40
Kedah	151,161	1.61	26.37	7,561	0.18	25.16	143,600	2.75	26.44
Perus	26,290	0.28	10.19	1,642	0.04	152.62	24,648	0.47	6.20
Perak	713,974	7.61	45.96	225,139	5.40	278.96	488,835	9.38	13.75
Negeri Sembilan	113,035	1.20	66.93	20,020	0.48	103.80	93,015	1.78	60.76
Melaka	540,427	5.76	48.48	277,249	6.65	56.97	263,178	5.05	40.47
Johor	1,143,131	12.18	47.08	383,335	9.19	78.05	759,796	14.57	35.21
Pahang (excl resorts)	349,379	3.72	6.84	108,320	2.60	– 14.28	241,059	4.62	20.52
Terengganu	275,968	2.94	71.28	79,371	1.90	41.28	196,597	3.77	87.34
Kelantan	211,347	2.25	86.50	54,949	1.32	136.85	156,398	3.00	73.54
Hill Resorts	887,239	9.45	26.10	464,129	11.13	32.58	423,110	8.11	19.68
Island Resorts	536,869	5.72	277.34	255,936	6.14	322.41	280,933	5.39	243.91
Port Dickson	130,838	1.39	47.33	24,162	0.58	58.09	106,676	2.05	45.10
Peninsular Malaysia	8,597,934	91.61	52.17	3,936,002	94.37	69.86	4,661,932	89.41	39.87
Sabah	426,702	4.55	64.77	136,940	3.28	40.26	289,762	5.56	79.60
Sarawak	360,495	3.84	69.29	97,972	2.35	107.02	262,523	5.03	58.50
Malaysia	9,385,131	100.00	53.30	4,170,914	100.00	69.40	5,214,217	100.00	42.46

Source: TDC Annual Tourism Statistic Report, 1990.

TABLE 2. Composition of Visitor Arrivals in Sarawak and Peninsular Malaysia

	Sarawak	%	Peninsular Malaysia	%
All foreign	Brunei	43.60	Singapore	64.10
arrivals	Indonesia	20.60	Thailand	7.20
	Singapore	6.80	Japan	6.90
	UK	4.50	Other Europe	3.50
	Other Europe	4.46	Taiwan	2.60
	Aust/NZ	2.10	UK	2.60
Arrivals	Singapore	38.30	Thailand	16.00
by air	Other Europe	11.00	Japan	15.70
	Brunei	8.30	Singapore	12.00
	Aust/NZ	7.00	Taiwan	6.10
	UK	6.90	UK/Ireland	6.00
	Japan	3.50	Aust/NZ	5.50

Sources: Visitor Arrival Statistics, Sarawak, PATA Annual Statistical Report, TDC Annual Tourism Statistical Report 1990, Malaysian Tourism Statistics Update 1991.

TABLE 3. Evolution of Arrivals in Sarawak and Peninsular Malaysia

	Sarawak Arrivals		Peninsular Malaysia Arrivals		Malaysia Arrivals	
	No.	% change	No.	% change	No.	% change
1988	247,675	–	n.a.	–	3,623,636	7.90
1989	325,114	31.30	4,553,392	–	4,846,320	33.70
1990	434,379	33.60	7,079,107	55.40	7,476,772	54.30
1991	509,597	17.30	5,543,376	– 21.40	6,182,973†	– 17.30

† estimate based on totals for Sarawak, Peninsular Malaysia and Sabah (130,000).

Sources: Immigration Statistics, Sarawak, TDC Annual Tourism Statistical Report 1990.

Other Asians, in contrast, exhibit a more diverse pattern of enjoyment, attaching less importance to the cultural element while appreciating other aspects of Sarawak such as its food, shopping and the urban features of Kuching. Similar patterns, the urban feature excepted, are found amongst the Malaysian and Singaporean respondents.

Directly comparable information is not available for Peninsular Malaysia but the spatial pattern of demand there suggests a pronounced bias

TABLE 4. Things Visitors Enjoyed Most in Sarawak, 1992

Country of residence

	Malaysia (216) %	Singapore (216) %	Other Asia (205) %	Other Western (180) %	Europe (207) %
Cultural diversity/ lifestyles	23	19	13	24	33
People	16	15	18	23	16
Scenery	12	18	11	19	24
Outdoor activities, beaches	12	12	11	9	11
Food	8	12	10	6	5
Shopping	6	5	8	2	
Museum	6	4	3	5	2
Calm, relaxing	5	6	2	1	1
City clean and well organised		1	9	2	2
Weather not too hot	2	1	3	3	1

Source: Kuching Airport Exit Survey.

towards urban attractions and beach resorts as well as to more specialized destinations such as the hill resorts for their refreshing climate, entertainment and gambling (Table 1).

Analysis of tourist travel patterns can provide further insights into the roles of regional destinations, particularly their place in a broader tourist circuit, thereby contributing to a better understanding of the nature of the demand and how such destinations might be marketed.

The majority of foreign visitors to Malaysia appear not to travel very widely within the country. Results of a 1990 exit survey at Malaysia's two main gateways, Kuala Lumpur and Penang airports, revealed that pleasure visitors on average overnighted in only two locations (Oppermann, 1992). The flows which do exist from one locality to another are concentrated along the west coast of the peninsula, with the largest flows occurring between the capital and Penang. Very few of the respondents had spent any time in Sarawak. While these patterns are clearly influenced by the locations at which the survey was undertaken, they are consistent with Sarawak's small share of the national total.

Conversely, a significant share of visitors to Sarawak spend time elsewhere in the country. Results from the Kuching Airport Exit Survey reveal major differences in the travel patterns of short-and long-haul visitors to Sarawak (Table 5). As might be expected, the majority of Malaysian and Singaporean visitors are making Sarawak the sole focus of their visit. Where overnight stays are made elsewhere, they tend to be mainly in other parts of Malaysia (including Sabah) and Singapore. In contrast, virtually all long-haul visitors from Europe and Other Western (primarily North America and Australasia) markets combine a visit to Sarawak with visits elsewhere. Just over and just under half of these markets respectively visit Malaysia and Singapore, with a significant proportion (28% and 16%) visiting both. Other countries may also be visited, notably Indonesia and Thailand. On average, European and Other Westerners visit two countries in addition to Sarawak. Other Asians constitute an intermediate group, visiting on average one other country (most likely Singapore), with about a third making Sarawak their sole destination. Certain "Other Asia" segments would be considerably under represented in the Kuching exit survey, notably visitors from Brunei who concentrate on Miri and Limbang but who at present do not appear to go much further afield and who appear to spend all their trip in Sarawak.

Further details of the relative weight of Sarawak in the overall trip can be obtained by calculation of the Trip Index (Pearce and Elliott, 1983) using the formula:

$$\text{Trip Index} = \frac{Dn \times 100}{Tn}$$

Where Dn = the nights spent at the destination, in this case Sarawak

Tn = the total nights spent on the trip

Trip Index values of 100 indicate that all nights have been spent in Sarawak. Lesser values represent the percentage of all nights spent in Sarawak, for example a Trip Index of 50 shows half the trip was spent there. Thus while confirming that the majority of Singaporeans and Malaysians made Sarawak the sole focus of their trip, the Trip Index values in Table 6 show three quarters of Europeans and Other Westerners and one third of Other Asians were spending half or less of their trip in the state.

These two different patterns of travel, at one end the Singaporean "short break," at the other, long-haul "circuit travel," are also reflected in the comparatively short visits which most tourists make to Sarawak. About half of all Singaporean, Other Asian and Other Western respondents spent four nights or less in Sarawak and upwards of two thirds of all visitors were there for seven nights or less. Singaporeans had the shortest

TABLE 5. International Travel Patterns of Visitors to Sarawak, 1992

Country of residence

	Malaysia (216) %	Singapore (216) %	Other Asia (205) %	Other Western (180) %	Europe (207) %
No other countries visited	70	80	31	6	7
Malaysia only	11	11	12	12	10
Malaysia plus (excl. Singapore)	2	1	5	19	14
Singapore only	9	1	26	15	13
Singapore plus (excl. Malaysia)	2	–	7	17	18
Malaysia and Singapore	–	–	5	9	14
Malaysia, Singapore plus others	1	–	6	7	14
Other countries excl. Malaysia and Singapore	3	7	7	14	10
All combinations incl. Malaysia	16	12	28	47	52
All combinations incl. Singapore	12	1	38	48	59
All combinations incl. both Malaysia and Singapore	1	–	11	16	28
Mean number of countries visited	0.33	0.23	1.03	2.24	2.09

Source: Kuching Airport Exit Survey.

lengths of stay and fewer Malaysians were there for very short trips. The slightly higher mean average lengths of stays for Other Asian and Other Westerners appears to be boosted by a small number who spent more than two weeks in Sarawak, possibly visiting friends and relatives.

For virtually all long-haul European and Other Western visitors, Sarawak constitutes but one part of a trip to the ASEAN region. To a large extent this reflects the conditions of access, a trip to Sarawak from these markets necessitating a transfer if not an overnight stop at some other point, usually Singapore or Kuala Lumpur. The Trip Index values also indicate, however, that many of these places are not visited just in transit but visitors are actively combining a visit to Sarawak with stays elsewhere in the region to justify the distances covered and costs incurred. Indeed in many cases a visit to Sarawak constitutes a minor part of the overall trip, at least in terms of time spent.

Marketing Implications

Differences in the size and structure of Sarawak's markets vis-à-vis those of Peninsular Malaysia produce a range of issues for marketing tourism to the state. The limited growth of tourism in Sarawak to date cannot be attributed solely to marketing matters. Access and product development have also been and remain major constraints, but they must be addressed with some urgency if tourism is to make a greater contribution not only to the development of the state but to the national economy.

In many respects a special case can be made for Sarawak. Geography and history have endowed Sarawak with a different range of potential products than Peninsular Malaysia which is reflected in the composition of the state's nascent tourist traffic. When differences in product and markets occur within countries, key questions which arise are what is the national image which is being promoted, what are the markets being emphasized, and how do both of these correspond to the interests of the focal region, in this case, Sarawak?

These questions become especially crucial when a marked imbalance in resources available to the federal and state bodies occurs. In 1990, for example, the TDC's budget was 86 million ringgit, of which 56.6 million ringgit was allocated for marketing and a further 3.6 million ringgit for conventions promotion. With such resources the TDC has been able to operate a dozen overseas offices and take a lead role in marketing the country abroad. In contrast, the Tourism Division of Sarawak's Ministry of Environment and Tourism has had an annual budget of just over two million ringgit in recent years. Consequently, Sarawak has been largely dependent on federal marketing activities, as well as those of the private sector. The extent to which the federal programme creates a platform on which states can build, and below them individual products can be sold by the private sector, depends in large part on the commonality of central campaigns and state strategies.

As noted in Table 2, the main markets of Peninsular Malaysia currently do not parallel those of Sarawak, particularly in terms of the relative importance of the intra-Asia markets which have been a major focus of TDC attention. Nor has the big city/beach thrust of recent years corresponded fully with what Sarawak has to offer. On the other hand, there was a marked commonality of interest in the 1991 "Malaysia Naturally" campaign and with the TDC's 1992 product positioning strategy, namely: "To project Malaysia as a value for money destination offering unique natural products of acceptable international standards oriented towards family travel."

For Sarawak a real issue of identity and image arises. Currently Malaysia, in comparison to its neighbours of Thailand, Singapore and Indonesia, does not enjoy a very strong or clearly positioned image, particularly in the long-haul markets. In terms of name recognition, Sarawak might be better served in these markets, especially Europe, by stronger identification not with Malaysia but with Borneo, as Sabah, "Borneo's Paradise," has done. Such a strategy, however, does not complement federal objectives of national integration on the one hand nor of promoting a Malaysia image on the other. Sarawak has recently sought to develop its image by undertaking independent promotions abroad, for example taking a separate booth at trade fairs such as the 1992 World Travel Mart in London.

Related issues also arise out of the circuit nature of much travel to Sarawak. As Tables 5 and 6 illustrated, for most long-haul tourists a visit to Sarawak is combined with visits to other destinations, most commonly Singapore, other parts of Malaysia or some combination of both. There are obvious advantages in cooperative marketing and packaging visits to Sarawak through Singapore, given its dominance as a regional hub, the volume of passengers arriving at Singapore International Airport and the number of medium-and long-haul flights it serves. Such a strategy, however, does not correspond to the federal policy of building up Kuala Lumpur as an international gateway attempting to compete not only with Singapore but also with Bangkok.

One consequence of this policy has been a reluctance to open up access to Sarawak to carriers other than the national airline, Malaysia Airlines (MAS). Sarawak in 1992 had thrice-daily services from Singapore by

TABLE 6. Trip Index of Visitors to Sarawak by Country of Residence, 1992

Country of residence

Trip index %	Malaysia (216) %	Singapore (216) %	Other Asia (205) %	Other Western (180) %	Europe (207) %
1-10	–	–	7	9	12
11-20	4	4	7	21	19
21-30	3	2	7	20	18
31-40	2	2	13	11	11
41-50	5	4	12	13	16
51-60	5	4	7	4	4
61-70	5	2	7	5	6
71-80	3	–	3	6	4.0
81-90	3	–	4	3	2.0
91-99	–	–	3	2	2
100 (all nights spent in Sarawak)	70	80	31	6	7

Source: Kuching Airport Exit Survey.

MAS but only two services a week from Singapore International Airlines. Granting international air service agreements, it should be recalled, is a federal prerogative. The national carrier has been active in developing tourism to Sarawak, for example through its Golden Holidays packages and by facilitating the visits of agents and publicists and assisting participation in overseas trade shows. However, there can be little doubt that opening up Sarawak's skies to other carriers out of Singapore would not only improve access but also bring increased exposure to the state through the other airlines' marketing activities and range of sales outlets.

As for linkages with other Malaysian destinations, Sarawak might do well to emphasize the complementary nature of visits to the state and how they might generate new visits to other parts of the country. In other words, greater promotion of Sarawak would be good not only for the state but also for Malaysia. More international visitors to Sarawak would generate additional foreign exchange earnings, and boost federal tax revenues. Joint packaging of Sarawak and Sabah also has potentially strong advantages; visitors to the Mulu Caves, for instance, may also be attracted by a trip to Mount Kinabalu. The First Sarawak Tourism Masterplan (Thompson Berwick Pratt, 1981), initiated by the TDC, advocated a development concept based on the joint promotion of Sarawak and Sabah and the marketing of Kuching and Kota Kinabalu as a visitor destination package. Cooperative marketing at an official level subsequently foundered as a result of political differences between Sabah and the Federal Government (resolved in 1994). A number of tour operators already offer Sarawak-Sabah trips, usually as part of a Borneo package.

In contrast, "Sarawak Only" campaigns might be targeted at both the Singapore and domestic markets. Visitors to Sarawak from both these short-haul markets at present frequently make the state the sole focus of their trip, in the first case as a "short-break" to get away from Singapore, in the second, often as a trip to visit friends and relations. The Singapore short-break market is a keenly contested one, with resorts in West Malaysia, Southern Thailand and in Indonesia offering very competitively priced packages. Cost, an underdeveloped image and competition from more accessible resorts are major handicaps to overcome in attracting domestic tourists from the peninsula. The federal policy of promoting national integration saw the establishment of the Feri Malaysia passenger ferry service between West and East Malaysia under the Fifth Malaysia Plan (1986-1990) but this was not successful and was subsequently withdrawn.

Sarawak adopted a more aggressive approach to tapping these two short-haul markets, opening Sarawak Tourism Centres in Singapore in 1990 and in Kuala Lumpur a year later. In addition to disseminating information and having an important public relations role, particularly organising familiarisation trips, the STCs concentrated on developing heavily-discounted packages and marketing these through special consortia of Singapore and Kuala Lumpur based agents. After a promising beginning in 1990 when more than 6,000 tourists arrived from Singapore on Hornbill Escapades, the number of packages sold in following years declined significantly while similar packages out of Kuala Lumpur proved even less popular. As the result of a management review recommended by the masterplan, both the STCs were subsequently closed and replaced by 0800 telephone services.

In addition to the activities of the official destination associations and the airlines, marketing is also carried out by the private sector. Given the generally small scale of Sarawak tourist enterprises and the low level of overseas investment, the amount of marketing undertaken directly by the sector outside of the state is limited. The larger state- or federally-owned hotels are operated under international hotel franchises, notably Holiday Inn and Hilton, and benefit from inclusion in the promotional activities of these chains. A number of tour operators participate in trade fairs abroad but often draw a significant share of their business from wholesalers based elsewhere, for example in Singapore or Europe. Many of the private enterprises, especially the smaller ones, would also appear to draw much of their business from informal word of mouth sources, particularly in terms of the Sarawak's small internal market and the cross-border traffic from other parts of Borneo.

CONCLUSIONS

Given the size of Sarawak's tourist traffic and its share of national demand, scope exists for improving the marketing and development of tourism in the state. While closer coordination and cooperation between the state and federal organizations is needed, the differences in product and market composition outlined here suggest Sarawak's tourism marketing function also requires considerable strengthening. Following the recommendations of the second tourism masterplan, the establishment of the Sarawak Tourism Board, a new marketing body separate from the ministry, was announced in late 1993. Such a body should be better able to build on the national programme and complement it by selectively targeting those segments for which Sarawak has most appeal, particularly in culture and nature based tourism. These special interest markets require different strategies than the campaigns to attract the mass tourists of the peninsula and developing them is appropriate to the regional organization most directly involved. In targeting these segments consideration will have to be given to cooperative ventures with other destinations, both within Malaysia and elsewhere in the region, particularly Singapore. As tourism within Sarawak grows, attention will also have to be directed downwards to ensure that the efforts and interests of destinations beyond the Kuching area are fully and effectively mobilized and coordinated to avoid any local/state dislocation and to maximize statewide activities. With the expansion of tourism the state tourist organization will progressively fulfill a pivotal intermediate function, reaching both upwards and outwards as well as down to the individual localities within the state.

More generally, it is argued, the preceding sections have demonstrated the utility of moving beyond a single spatial scale of analysis, that just of the state, to consider not only markets but also marketing at several levels. Setting Sarawak's markets and marketing activities in the national and at times broader regional context has provided greater understanding of opportunities and constraints and ways in which these might be addressed more effectively. Such considerations apply not just to Sarawak and to Malaysia for they are relevant to the planning and marketing of most destinations.

As Tables 1 to 6 have shown, more general application of this approach will require analysis of a wider range of marketing data than is often used. In particular, standard national arrival data need to be complemented by comparable sub-national figures as well as by other more specific profile and motivational information. This will almost inevitably mean undertaking special purpose surveys. Analytical techniques which directly measure linkages between the focal destination and other areas, such as use of the Trip Index, will also be required.

In addition, more attention needs to be directed at other issues such as the hierarchical structure of relevant destination marketing organizations, their goals and policies and the factors, for example political, influencing them. In other words, greater consideration needs to be given not only to the markets but also to the marketing agents. The notion of positioning might thus well be extended to include not only how well the focal destination, especially at a sub-national level, is situated with regard to particular markets but also to how effectively it is placed in the overall administrative and decision-making process relating to marketing and other associated issues such as economic planning and civil aviation policies. A comprehensive multi-scale approach to marketing therefore requires not only taking into account phenomena at different levels, from the local to the international, but also widening the scope of the analysis to take account of broader contextual and implementation factors.

REFERENCES

Britton, S.G. (1982). The political economy of tourism in the Third World. *Annals of Tourism Research*, 9(3): 331-351.

Lundgren, J.O.J. (1982). The tourist frontier of Nouveau Quebec: Functions and regional linkages. *Tourist Review*, 37(2): 10-16.

Mathieson, A.R. (1985). Social impacts of tourism: A state of the art. In *Issues in Tourism Research in The South Pacific* (pp. 15-19). Aix-en-Provence: Centre des Hautes Etudes Touristiques.

Miossec, J.M. (1976). *Eléments Pour Une Théorie de l'Espace Touristique*, Cahiers du Tourisme, C-36. Aix-en Provence: Centre des Hautes Etudes Touristiques.

Oppermann, M. (1992). Intranational tourist flows in Malaysia. *Annals of Tourism Research*, 19(3): 482-500.

Pearce, D.G. (1987). *Tourism Today: A Geographical Analysis*. New York: Wiley. Harlow: Longman.

Pearce, D.G. (1990). Tourist travel patterns in the South Pacific: Analysis and implications. In C.C. Kissling (Ed.), *Destination South Pacific: Perspectives on island tourism* (pp. 31-49). Aix-en-Provence: Centre des Hautes Etudes Touristiques.

Pearce, D.G. (1992). *Tourist Organizations*. New York: Wiley. Harlow: Longman.

Pearce, D.G. (1995). Planning for tourism in the nineties; an integrated, dynamic, multi-scale approach. In R.W. Butler and D.G. Pearce (Eds), *Change in Tourism: People, places, processes* (pp. 229-244). London: Routledge.

Pearce, D.G. and Elliott, J.M.C. (1983). The Trip Index. *Journal of Travel Research*, 22(1): 6-9.

Thompson Berwick Pratt (1981). *Sarawak Tourism Masterplan Technical Report*. Kuala Lumpur: Tourist Development Corporation.

Big Success, Big Mistake, at Big Banana: Marketing Strategies in Road-Side Attractions and Theme Parks

Neil Leiper

SUMMARY. As a road-side attraction for 24 years after its construction in 1965, the Big Banana succeeded in three respects, by providing the basis of a profitable business for the proprietor and staff, a satisfying experience for many travellers, and a promotional symbol for its locality. In 1989, perceiving a growing tourist market, new owners built a horticultural theme park. Within months the business failed, and went into liquidation. Examining the case suggests that road-side attractions and theme parks relate to different elements in systems of tourism geography and, therefore, to different kinds of markets. These differences were not clearly recognised in the feasibility report prepared in 1988. Moreover, they tend to be overlooked by perceptions of tourism that focus on destinations and products there, a focus that marketing practice has tended to follow. Pathological research of the sort represented in this review of business at the Big Banana, pinpointing problems in a business venture, might help entrepreneurs, investors and tourism marketing analysts avoid similar mistakes in the future. *[Article copies available for a fee from The Haworth Document Delivery Service: 1-800-342-9678. E-mail address: getinfo@haworth.com]*

Dr. Neil Leiper is Associate Professor, School of Tourism and Hospitality Management, Southern Cross University, Lismore 2480, Australia (e-mail: nleiper @scu.edu.au).

[Haworth co-indexing entry note]: "Big Success, Big Mistake, at Big Banana: Marketing Strategies in Road-Side Attractions and Theme Parks." Leiper, Neil. Co-published simultaneously in *Journal of Travel & Tourism Marketing* (The Haworth Press, Inc.) Vol. 6, No. 3/4, 1997, pp. 103-121; and: *Geography and Tourism Marketing* (ed: Martin Oppermann) The Haworth Press, Inc., 1997, pp. 103-121. Single or multiple copies of this article are available for a fee from The Haworth Document Delivery Service [1-800-342-9678, 9:00 a.m. - 5:00 p.m. (EST). E-mail address: getinfo@haworth.com].

INTRODUCTION

The subject of this case history is the Big Banana, located just north of Coffs Harbour, a provincial city on Australia's east coast. During the past thirty years, at different times two kinds of business have been conducted at the site, under the same name. The first, commenced in 1965, can be described as a simple road-side attraction. It was a successful business. The second, launched in 1989, was an extension of the first. It can be described as a horticultural theme park. The development was a mistake, and led to a $30 million loss.

The central theme discussed below is an analysis of why the first venture succeeded and the second failed. The analysis is based primarily on a theory of whole tourism system geography and its marketing implications (Leiper 1981, 1990, 1995). The first venture, the road-side attraction, depended mainly on markets in tourist transit routes. The second, the horticultural theme park, lost most of that original market and was reliant instead on other markets, in a tourist destination region. Those destination-based markets were too small to support the large investment. A supplementary theme is a review of business strategies and, a key issue in this case, a feasibility report prepared in 1988 by a firm of consultants specialising in tourism marketing and management, a report which was used to justify investments in the theme park.

Research for the present study included interviews with persons knowledgeable about the case (from the perspectives of investors, managers of tourist businesses, bankers, tourist association officials, academics and other local residents) and a search of newspaper archives. The writer's observations at the site, on intermittent occasions since 1967, have also informed this study.

The first topic below is the origin of the Big Banana. The second is the successful road-side attraction, reviewed using two sets of theories: one concerning tourist attractions and the other about business strategies. The third topic is the proposal in 1988 to construct a horticultural theme park. This leads into a fourth topic, a review of why that venture failed, and a fifth, a review of the feasibility report which predicted great success. Then two conclusions are drawn. Certain issues are discussed relating to a model of tourism geography and its marketing implications. A final topic considers the benefits of pathological approaches in business studies.

BIG THINGS ON THE ROAD: BIG BANANA'S ORIGINS

Thirty years ago "Big" things began appearing along Australian provincial highways. The first, at Nambour in Queensland, was a pineapple just large enough for a person to step inside and peek through a hole. It was a small copy of a Big Pineapple in Hawaii. Later a truly big one replaced Nambour's initial attempt, which was carted away with a label which is simultaneously true and doubly false—"The Original Big Pineapple" and now sits in a gas station on the Pacific Highway at Ballina, dwarfed by what looms in the sky nearby . . . the Big Prawn. "Big Things" represent rural themes; Australia's highways now have a Big Ram, Big Cow, Big Oyster, Big Bull, Big Trout, and so on. Each symbolises a feature of its provincial locality, an allegedly endemic personality with a blatant promotional message. This was the origin of the Big Banana.

In 1963 an American scientist, John Landi, travelled to Australia to study bananas and settled in Coffs Harbour. He subsequently purchased land for a plantation and set up a stall on the highway to sell produce. Devising an opportunity for innovative promotion, Landi suggested that the regional Banana Growers' Federation pay half the cost of constructing a larger-than-life banana to be located adjacent to his stall. Seen by travellers on one of the busiest highways in rural Australia, its promotional effects would be synergistic, inducing them to eat more bananas and to perceive Coffs Harbour as a distinctive place associated with this tropical fruit.

The idea stimulated the first of many stories and letters about this particular banana in *The Advocate*, Coffs Harbour's main newspaper. For many locals, the idea was problematical. Many did not like it and, worse, regarded it as detrimental to the district's interests (see letters and articles in *The Advocate* during 1964-5). The district was being proudly promoted to residents, tourists, prospective immigrants and others less fortunate as "Pacific Beautizone." According to the sensibility of Coffs Harbour's civic leaders, a giant artificial banana was not a thing of beauty. As several were reported as saying, it was something they imagined "might be seen in Hawaii or Queensland." Despite the controversy, the thing was built in 1965 at a cost of 1,200 pounds ($A 2,400 dollars, approximately $A 20,000 in 1996 value).

In 1972 the controversy evaporated. Presumably, locals upset in 1965 became accustomed. More immediately, a decision in Sydney, four hundred miles south, helped change sentiments in Coffs Harbour. One of Australia's leading department stores decided on bananas as the theme for summer promotions. This caused a re-think in Coffs Harbour. If Grace Brothers imagined that bananas would promote sales in Sydney, then Pacific Beautizone's civic leaders could believe that an over-sized model of the fruit would boost tourism and development in Coffs Harbour. "Pacific Beautizone" was suddenly out-moded. To replace it, the Coffs Harbour Tourism Association devised and launched campaigns promoting the Banana Coast and Banana Republic. These gave Landi's symbol status as a semi-official symbol linked with tourism development. The Big Banana has retained that status to the present time.

A SUCCESSFUL ROAD-SIDE ATTRACTION

In the period from 1965 to 1988, the Big Banana can be analysed as a popular tourist attraction. In this context, certain concepts from models by Gunn (1972) and MacCannell (1976) will be used, along with a composite model assembled by Leiper (1995) which combined selected features from the earlier two and added extra details.

The designation of a name ("Big Banana") represented MacCannell's first phase of sight sacralisation, the naming phase. A large sign proclaimed the name, its information functioning as an example of MacCannell's on-sight marker, which is termed "contiguous marker" in Leiper's model–designed for general applications including and beyond sightseeing attractions. The banana, about six metres in length, was constructed to lie on its side. It was what Gunn termed the attraction's nucleus. Set on a dais, it attained, from the start, MacCannell's second phase of sight sacralisation–framing and elevation. Framing was also achieved by a small area of lawn around the nucleus, providing what Gunn calls an inviolate belt.

Throughout the day, people came in off the highway to look at the Big Banana from close up, to touch it, walk through it and make comments. These *in situ* touristic experiences–personal interaction with the nucleus of an attraction and with its marker elements (information about the nucleus) are experiences which Gunn, Leiper and others have indicated to be the central theme in tourists' behaviour, in tourism.

Countless tourists have photographed the Big Banana. Afterwards, such photographs can fulfil the eighth of ten functional roles of markers identified by Leiper. This role is information acting as a souvenir of a visit or a vacation, helping people remember their experiences.

Gunn prescribed that facilities and commercial services should be placed apart from a nucleus, separated by what he termed an inviolate belt. This principle was evident at the Big Banana. There was no commercial or service activity in or immediately alongside the nucleus. However a short distance away was a store selling drinks, souvenirs, snacks, postcards, clothes, honey, bananas. There was also a parking bay for cars and tour coaches. An important facility was the spacious public toilet, welcome relief for travellers who had been on the road for hours.

Commercially, the business depended on sales in the shop. Everything else was free. This can be interpreted as another facet of the inviolate zone, and an effective feature in a successful business strategy. (This was in an era before the "user pays" principle became popular, encouraging foolish managers to put a price on everything used by consumers.)

In its original formulation, the Big Banana was a profitable business, no doubt envied by proprietors of many other road-side attractions. It became the best-known "Big Thing" on Australian provincial highways. Travellers found that a brief stop could satisfy a range of needs. These bundled satisfactions represented the core of a successful business strategy. The principle that marketing is concerned with satisfying consumers' needs is a central theme in the marketing concept prescribed for more than thirty years (Kotler, 1967: 17-27).

Certain factors in the satisfaction derived from the Big Banana have been noted above. Another source of satisfaction can create mild excitement–pleasant or disturbing, explicit or subconscious, depending on the individual–stemming from the fact that a larger-than-life banana has sexual connotations. Marketing theory has long recognised sexual factors in consumer behaviour, especially latent and repressed desires explicable in terms of Freudian psychoanalysis (Kotler, 1967: 105-108). Published records of the Big Banana controversy in 1964-5 repressed any hint of sexual connotations but three decades later, the media have fewer inhibitions of this sort. Among examples that could be cited, perhaps the most candid comes from the current edition of a popular (vulgar in both senses) guide book for independent tourists, where the Big Banana is described as "A huge erection . . . modelled on a friend of ours–Duncan, take a bow" ("Day 6: Surfers to Bellingen" in *The Oz Experience: Australia Adventure Guide, Summer 95-96* , 4th ed., no pagination).

Another satisfaction is also notable. Many travellers on the Pacific Highway, using private vehicles and coaches, stop at Coffs Harbour not merely because it is a convenient place to rest, use a toilet, buy a snack, fill the tank. Also, "Coffs" is a stage marker on the busiest long-haul route in Australia, seven hours driving time north from Sydney, four hours south from the Gold Coast. After 1965 the Big Banana became a popular site for these "pit stops."

THE RISE AND FALL OF THE BIG BANANA

In 1988 the Big Banana, its shop and the plantation on the hill behind were acquired by a company which had a thriving business growing and marketing vegetables and fruit. The acquisition was a step in the company's plan for a theme park around horticultural displays, with supplementary rides, restaurants and shops.

A subsidiary company, Horticultural World Pty Ltd, was established to operate the Big Banana. A manager was employed, allowing Directors of the parent company to continue their existing interests. The manager hired two consultants. Total Project Control Pty Ltd was engaged for site development, while a firm specialising in tourism, Horwath and Horwath Services Pty Ltd, was hired to conduct feasibility studies to ensure that the investment was likely to be profitable, and to help get bank financing.

Two levels of strategies can be identified, as follows. The top level is corporate strategy, as described by Andrews (1991), Bowman and Ash (1996) and others. It exists when a company owns, or contemplates, more than one kind of business and it involves decisions about the mix. The entrepreneurs who created Horticultural World saw potential for diversifying into a new kind of business, new kinds of markets, new industries. Beyond growing and marketing, they envisioned a business based on horticultural displays, in the form of a theme park. This is one of the four kinds of strategic diversification identified by Galbraith (1991).

A theme park with a horticultural theme could interest Australian and international tourists; in turn, tourists' experiences could induce more consumption, back home, of horticultural produce. Asians were a key target since Horticultural World's parent company was marketing Australian fruit and vegetables in Asia and Asian tourists were coming to Australia in increasing numbers. The corporate strategy was clearly synergistic.

A second level of strategy are business strategies. Rumelt (1991), Kotler et al. (1996) and others have discussed this level. It involves a marketing mix aimed at particular types or groups of consumers. In other words "the focus of strategy at the business level will be how a strategic business unit (SBU) competes in a particular industry or marketplace with particular products, marketing . . . and so on" (Bowman and Asch, 1996: 119). A leading text on marketing contains the observation that core questions about business strategy "are simple sounding (but are) among the most difficult a company will have to answer . . . Successful companies continuously raise these questions . . . What is our business? What should our business be?" (Kotler et al., 1996: 28).

Proposals for the theme park at Big Banana represented strategies for an SBU. If many tourists were visiting a road-side attraction and spending $5 on average in a shop, why not add features and services on a large site behind the shop, additions which would induce visitors to spend more and also attract greater numbers than were coming in to use the toilet, buy a Coke and photograph a banana? A distinctive theme park was envisaged, a small version of Disneyland with an environmental theme endemically suiting its regional location.

Optimism was encouraged by signs that tourism was in boom phase, with increases recorded in the numbers of visitors to Australia, especially from the USA, Japan and New Zealand. In 1988, Brisbane Expo had recorded several million visits. The Marketing Manager from Brisbane Expo was recruited for the corresponding position at Big Banana. Other encouraging signs were Japanese investors inspecting properties to buy in Coffs Harbour while their Australian agents willingly described to locals the fortunate prospects in the near future when many Japanese tourists would be visiting.

Not all signs pointed to optimism about a Japanese tourist boom in provincial regions. A study widely-distributed by Qantas (Leiper, 1985) forecasted that more Japanese tourists would visit Australia, but showed how and why, in the foreseeable future, they would be heavily concentrated in certain urban destinations: Sydney, Melbourne, Cairns, Gold Coast. Most other places such as Coffs Harbour would see relatively few.

The report by Horwath and Horwath (1988) ignored cautionary warnings of that sort and instead, presented a very optimistic scenario. It forecasted that the park would capture, from its first year, high penetration rates of several target markets: transient tourists passing along the Highway; domestic (i.e., Australian) tourists staying in Coffs Harbour; day trippers from surrounding districts; international visitors in Coffs Harbour; residents of Coffs Harbour and district. The highest projection was for international visitors, where the report predicted a market penetration rate of 60% for the theme park. The lowest forecast penetration rate was for residents of Coffs Harbour and district, at 15% in 1989 and 10% in later years.

The estimated penetration rates were applied to optimistic predictions, from researchers in various organisations, about future growth in tourist arrivals in Coffs Harbour. For example, the report predicted 120,700 international tourists and 439,600 domestic tourists in 1990/1. The report forecasted that the total visitors to the Big Banana in 1993/4 would number 1,108,600. This came from segmentation analysis, shown in Table 1.

The report projected a cash flow from operations, before debt, costs and income tax, of $5,872,000 in 1989-90 rising to $7,375,000 in 1993-4 (Horwath and Horwath, 1988, p. VIII-6). The main revenue source in the report is admission fees, projected to earn $6,655,000 in 1989-90, when 924,300 visitor arrivals were expected, paying $7.20 (mean average) per head. Smaller sums of revenue were projected to come from lease payments from food and beverage outlets, retail outlets, and farmers' market,

TABLE 1. Horwath and Horwath's Forecasts (in 1988) for Visits and Market Share at the Big Banana in 1993-4.

Market Segment	Number of Visits ('000)	Share of Total Visits %
Coffs residents	9	1
Area residents	10	1
Domestic tourists	499	45
International tourists	94	9
Transient tourists	496	45
Total	1,108	100

Source: adapted from table (p V-19) Horwath and Horwath (1988).

and "a minimum figure of $275,000 per annum" from corporate sponsorship. The report noted that "negotiations are proceeding with various companies for naming and sponsorship rights within the theme park" (p. VIII-3).

After reviewing these positive projections, the banking industry provided funds to top-up investment by the parent company, and the theme park was built. The precise cost is unknown: various sources say $22 million was invested, of which more than half came from the parent company and almost half from three Australian banks. The largest bank investment (about $5 million) came from AGC, a subsidiary of Westpac Banking Corporation.

A train on a concrete rail was the most expensive capital item. The rail meandered up the hill and back, through a plantation, alongside lakes where a monster lurked underwater—rearing up its grotesque iron head and spraying water as the train passed, and on to a number of stations. At one, a hydroponics vegetable farm was built. At another were displays of ecological notions and futuristic technology. Another station allows spectacular sightseeing over the sea and inside are tables for a hundred diners, and a dozen open kitchens to serve a range of European and Asian cuisines.

The first months of trading after June 1989 were hugely successful. Several thousand visitors came. Suddenly the growth stopped and the trend went into reverse. Within five months of opening, by late 1989, the business was insolvent. During this period the directors recognised a crisis so one of them, Mr. Bob Johnson, stepped in as Managing Director on the site.

Johnson implemented strategies for dealing with crises, of the sort described by Starbuck (1991) and strategies for attempting to "turn-around" failing ventures (Hofer, 1991). For example Johnson said (personal communication, 1994) he found that the manager of the site had engaged four times as many employees as were needed to operate at full capacity. Instead of 60, only 15 were needed, besides sub-contractors in the restaurants. Johnson said he reduced costs by cutting overheads and increased sales by low-cost promotional tactics. Within months, by early 1990, the business was earning more income, at lower costs, sufficient to cover operating expenses but not nearly enough to pay the interest owing each month to the bankers, nor give a profit to the investors.

In mid 1990, after one year's operations, the company folded, when the bankers arranged through the courts to place an official receiver in charge. While trading in receivership, the Big Banana was offered for sale and sold to the highest bidder.

A successful bid in 1991 by Mr. Kevin Rubie was a fraction of the $22 millions invested three years earlier. He paid less than $2 million for the assets, and said it was "the best deal of my life" (personal communication, 1995). Under his management the operation has been scaled down and the strategy changed. There is no entry fee. The restaurants are closed and the train operates only on busy days. A small bus, cheaper to operate, conveys people (for a fare) up the hill to the views, plantation, hydroponics farm and display of eco-technology. Alternatively, they can walk up for free.

Since 1992 a principal focus of business strategy at the site is the shop, as it had been before 1989. It is the main source of income. With a relatively small amount of capital invested, the Big Banana now needs far fewer visitors to break even. It can be economically sustainable on a small scale. In effect, it has reverted to a road-side attraction with the remnants of a theme park.

REVIEWING THE 1988 PROPOSAL

The feasibility of developments like the theme park depends on many factors. Six critical ones can be suggested: (a) the quality of strategic decisions; (b) the quality of top managers; (c) the amount, cost and mix of capital; (d) market potential; (e) estimated market penetration rates; (f) projected cash flows. If any of these six is seriously deficient, or if they do not match up, the venture is likely to fail. Other issues such as middle level management, staffing and promotional strategies are not usually critical, because they can be fixed fairly quickly if deficient.

Assessing the 1988 proposal requires separating corporate strategy from business strategy. The former was clever and plausible, for reasons described earlier. The latter, relating to the site at Coffs Harbour, was deficient in all the crucial issues noted above, which meant it should have been seen as highly risky. If the business strategy were to fail, the corporate strategy would go down with it.

The business strategy did not build on past success, nor did it take care to keep existing customers: it ventured into a new industry and depended on a different kind of consumer. The park was grossly over-capitalised. The market potential for a theme park in Coffs Harbour was not nearly so large as the developers imagined and the consultants estimated. Most severe was the deficiency in market penetration rates, between what was forecast and what was achieved. Cash flows, rather than generating millions of dollars from the first year, were large and negative outflows.

The feasibility study prepared by Horwath and Horwath Services in 1988 was accepted as valid by the investors and bankers, possibly blinded by its professional tone, its detailed data and its conclusions which reinforced the general mood at the time of unfettered optimism regarding tourism development.

Business strategies proposed for the theme park might have seemed reasonable to persons transfixed by mass propaganda, in the Australian media and in local business circles, about the scale and growth of tourism. However, a close and objective study of the markets for the new business should have revealed the fact that they were small in relation to the amount of capital required, as will be shown below. Moreover, the new strategies largely killed off custom from the established markets, passing trade, another point explained below.

All this meant that the probability of positive cash flows was virtually zero. The theme park should have been seen as doomed from the outset. That it went ahead suggests that senior officials in certain Australian banks might lack competence in judging the feasibility of business proposals. The sums involved meant that the decisions were not made at local branch level, but in head offices of AGC and two other banks. Other persons were also parties to the mistake, but the bankers were the key decision makers for the proposal to become an investment.

That the proposal went ahead also indicates that entrepreneurs can launch grandiose and impractical visions if they are skillful in selling the visions–and themselves–to bankers and tourism boosters. None of this is news or unusual, as Sykes' (1994) case histories have shown. Nor is Horwath and Horwath the only firm of management consultants professing expertise in tourism to be a party in failures of this sort; feasibility reports endorsing tourism investments which failed dramatically have been prepared by many such firms. The development would not have proceeded without Horwath and Horwath Services' (1988) report, because the investors and bankers accepted its optimistic findings and it was the basis for the banks' decision to help with capital finance. The report's key contents are summarised above. In the next section, alternative analyses are set out.

REVIEWING KEY NUMBERS UNDER TWO STRATEGIES

Having questioned the theme park's business strategy, the discussion can now analyse its feasibility. This will be considered alongside the feasibility of the road-side attraction. Data have been assembled from independent estimates, without specific information from anybody associated with the Big Banana.

To service capital of $22 million in the late 1980s a net return of at least $3 million annually was needed, assuming cost of capital was around 12%. (It was probably higher.) This represents $8,219 per day. There was also a need to cover operating costs and earn a profit.

How much money would an average visitor spend in this sort of theme park? Assume $30, a mean in a range of $10 to $50. Besides entrance fees, this includes food, drink, film, souvenirs. For simplicity, the restaurants are assumed to be part of the company operating the park; in this case they were under lease.

For every $30 revenue, the businesses incur direct costs of, say, $15 to pay for supplies. This would leave $15 to contribute to overhead expenses (such as wages, rates, office costs, advertising, etc.), interest and service charges on the $22 million investment and, ideally, a remaining contribution to a profit. Assume that overheads were $3,000 per day.

The first 200 visitors every day would, in effect, cover the overheads (200 × $15 = $3,000). If another 548 arrived, the daily cost of the $22 million of capital investment would also be covered (548 × $15 = $8,219). Thus, 748 visitors (200 + 548) were needed daily on average (more precisely 273,000 were needed per year) to break even. If an average of 749 or more was achieved, the business became profitable. The probability of averaging 749 was remote. This is explained below.

The next question is the size of market segments. From this, judgements can be made about penetration rates and then estimates of visitor numbers. These can be matched with income, expenses and capital costs, to see if the venture is feasible.

Analysing markets for road-side attractions and theme parks is not a matter of assessing the total market–all persons who might visit–but the size and likely penetration rates in key segments. Segmenting a market can be done in many ways. Traditional methods, by demographic variables (age, gender, etc.) are misleading in many modern tourist markets. Psychographic segmentation (dissecting by behavioural variables) might be more appropriate.

An approach for this case identifies three categories of persons, distinguished by behaviour relating to road-side attractions and theme parks. They are (a) permanent residents of the region; (b) tourists travelling along the highway; and (c) tourists staying for leisurely visits in the region. They are discussed below.

Permanent residents in the locality of a theme park often provide a significant percentage of customers. The brief boom when Big Banana opened as a theme park was caused by residents of the region. Curious about a new and unusual local feature, many locals came to see. Most never returned. Repeat visits by local residents are what sustains Disneyland (Real, 1977) and are also important in many other theme parks.

Why few locals revisited the Big Banana is not salient to this analysis because even if many did, the population is too small to generate much demand. Theme parks on Queensland's Gold Coast (e.g., Dreamworld, Sea World, Movie-World) draw on a resident market numbering 2 million in the day-tripping range. Disneyland has 30 million. The Big Banana has fewer than 100,000. Thus the Big Banana had to be more dependent on tourists, compared to the norm for theme parks. This represented a risk not seen in the 1988 feasibility study.

A second segment comprises tourists and others passing by, in transit, passing through Coffs Harbour by private vehicle, line coach or tour coach, perhaps stopping overnight but not visiting for longer than two nights. Many of these persons are on trips for holidays or to visit friends and relatives, regarding the region as transit route, not a tourist destination, and this is reflected in their behaviour related to sites they might visit. This market segment, termed "transiting tourists," is huge.

Coffs Harbour is the largest stopover point for tourists in New South Wales outside Sydney. Estimates can be drawn from sources such as Domestic Tourism Monitors and International Visitor Surveys for the period 1986 to 1989, reported in *Tourism Trends in New South Wales* (Bureau of Tourism Research, no date, circa 1990). Another source is four surveys of visitors in 1992 and 1993 reported in the *Coffs Harbour Tourism Association Newsletter* in November 1993. The four surveys found that between 52% and 61% of visitors staying at least one night regarded the region as a transit point.

From those sources, the number of journeys past the Big Banana by transiting tourists (including overnighters) can be estimated at between 1,500,000 and 2,000,000 per year, about 300 per hour in daylight hours, in the late 1980s. This estimate counts movements in both directions, north and south, and assumes that most travel by day. Because of Brisbane Expo and other bicentennial events, 1988 was a boom year, up 20% or so. Volumes decreased in 1989, back to normal.

A small proportion of persons in this transit segment visited the Big Banana in its original form, before 1989. But the segment is so huge that a small proportion is a large number. A penetration rate of 5% represents 87,500 visitors per annum (see Table 2).

Whatever the quantities of transiting tourists who visited the Big Banana when it was a road-side attraction before 1989, far fewer visited the theme park throughout the period 1989-1991. The decrease is explicable. Transiting tourists tend to avoid sites that occupy an hour or more, which is what a theme park requires. They prefer short stops, since their typical priority is getting to destinations. Money is another factor. The theme park's entrance fee obviously deterred many motorists who would have stopped before 1989, the multitude who want a "pit-stop" on the highway, not a fee-based experience. As shown in Table 2, the theme park's penetration rate for this segment can be estimated at 1%, giving 17,500 visits annually.

The third segment of the market was identified as tourists staying for leisurely visits in the region. Many of these persons, on holidays of various sorts in Coffs Harbour and nearby districts, have the necessary conditions to become visitors to a theme park: free time, motivation, and money intended to be spent on pleasurable (or time-consuming) experiences.

This "tourist visitor" segment is very small compared with the transit tourist segment. Its size in the late 1980s is estimated at about 300,000 tourists per annum, using sources noted above. But the penetration rate achieved by a theme park could be much higher among tourist visitors than among transit tourists. A 10% penetration rate might be feasible.

It is unlikely to be greater than 10% in a theme park such as this one. The Big Banana was and is the nucleus in a secondary attraction, not a primary attraction, for many tourists. Very few persons travel to Coffs Harbour for the specific purpose of visiting the Big Banana. The main market had to be visitors already in the region. Surveys by the local tourism association, noted above, found in several months that between 10% and 16% of visitors said they "might be attracted" to the Big Banana. Assume 10% did go there. This gives a total of 30,000 per annum, or 82 visitors per day on average.

TABLE 2. Big Banana: Estimates of Market Segments, Penetration Rates and Profitability for Two Business Options

Estimated Item	Roadside Attraction	Theme Park
(a) Local residents	90,000	90,000
penetration rate	2%	5%
market potential	2,000	5,000
(b) Transit tourists	1,750,000	1,750,000
penetration rate	5%	1%
market potential	87,500	17,500
(c) Tourist visitors	300,000	300,000
penetration rate	10%	10%
market potential	30,000	30,000
Total visitors	119,500	47,500
Break-even visitors	89,000	273,000
Capital Invested	$2 million	$22 million
Total visitors as % of break-even visitors	134%	17%
Profitability forecast	Profits probable	Huge losses certain

Estimates for three segments can now be assembled. Table 2 compares estimates of market size, penetration rates, visitor numbers, income and break-even data for the two kinds of business: road-side attraction versus theme park.

The profitability and low risk of the Big Banana as a road-side attraction is evident. Total visitors are 119,500 which is 34% above break even, a comfortable margin. In contrast, the theme park is revealed as a very bad idea. Revenue per visitor is higher but visitor numbers are way below those under the road-side attraction option. The lost market share is in the huge transit segment. To break even it would have to lift penetration six-fold. That is impossible.

Anyone with experience in following statistical and qualitative analyses of markets should have found problems in Horwath and Horwath's report, in at least two areas. One defect is the over-estimation of penetration rates. The second problem area is more basic. The report describes a proposal for people to freely enter a foyer where videos would preview the theme park. These people would then decide whether or not to pay to enter through turnstiles. Later in their report when calculations are set out, Horwath and Horwath implicitly assume that everyone entering the foyer will proceed through the turnstiles. All the market estimates and revenue projections in the report are based on projected numbers of visitors in the foyer. This was either a naive error of judgement or a gross oversight when editing the draft report, because certainly a proportion of visitors in the foyer, probably a sizeable proportion, would decide against paying an entry fee and spending an hour or two in the theme park. A second estimate of penetration rates, representing that proportion, should have been inserted in the consultants' report.

A MARKETING ISSUE IN THE GEOGRAPHY OF TOURISM

Every tourist's itinerary contains at least three places, in three elementary roles. These places become geographical elements in whole tourism systems. They are (a) a traveller generating region, where each trip begins and usually ends; (b) at least one tourist destination region which are places that tourists choose to visit, a decision made in advance or in transit–when a decision is made to remain for a day or more; and (c) one or more transit routes where travelling (as against visiting) is the main activity. That geographical concept, suggested by Mariot (cited by Matley, 1976), has been developed and applied by Leiper (1981) in a model of whole tourism systems, which combines three geographical elements with industrial and human elements, all in the nature of open systems interacting with complex environments.

A tourism business strategy can be deceptively dependent on markets in one geographical element in whole tourism systems. Strategically, roadside attractions are positioned at a point on transit routes. Strategically, changing a road-side attraction into a theme park represents a re-positioning, towards the destination element in whole tourism systems, where tourists behave differently and where the local resident population becomes an important market segment. This re-positioning issue was not adequately understood by those responsible for the investment decisions at Big Banana in 1988.

In transit routes, tourists' behaviour tends to be distinctive in some degree. Mainly concerned with travelling along the route, in order to get to a destination, tourists in this geographical element are not inclined to spend time in leisurely activities beyond necessary rest and minimal entertainment. Moreover, mass tourism seems dominated by desires to experience destinations, with the result that many tourists are incapable of pausing to enjoy travelling along transit routes. A striking observation on this behaviour follows:

> By making the object of the journey the destination rather than the journey itself, we rob ourselves of an important element in living. I truly believe that to really live is to be engrossed in the moment. Waiting for the future kills experience, wastes life–as if our purpose is merely waiting to die. (Macartney-Snape, 1992: 130)

Do marketing messages from tourism industries tend to reinforce the behaviour which Macartney-Snape despises? Possibly. Occasionally advertisements invoke the travel-for-travel's-sake philosophy (cf., Robert Louis Stephenson's "I travel not to go anywhere, but to go"). However the contents (graphic and copy) usually promote a specific destination, or sequence of destinations, or type of destination.

Statistical reports issued by tourism organisations reinforce this focus, and so encourage researchers to ignore the fact that a lot of tourism occurs in transit routes. From sources ranging from United Nations' agencies to Australian States' Government agencies, official statistics imply that tourists' itineraries comprise places of origin and destinations. Officially, transit routes are non-existent.

CONCLUSIONS

From 1965 to 1988 (and after 1991) the business strategy at the Big Banana positioned the enterprise on a transit route in whole tourism systems. Large numbers pass by, so a low market penetration rate is sufficient to attract large numbers spending small amounts of money. It requires a low-risk skimming strategy in a large market.

From 1989 to 1991, as theme park, the principal markets had to be tourists visiting the region for longer periods than a transit stop. This strategy positioned the Big Banana in a tourist destination region. Given the small resident population and the small tourist visitor stock, it is a much smaller market, requiring a higher penetration rate, which is difficult to achieve. This required a market dipping strategy. The probability of failing to attract sufficient consumers was higher than before. Also, the amount of capital was much higher, so a greater financial risk compounded the effect of a greater marketing risk.

Losses of $22 million were incurred by equity investors and by banks who loaned finance. Public opinion in Coffs Harbour is that local businesses and workers also lost money, perhaps $8 million. Thus the total loss was $30 million. Losses like these are paid for, indirectly, by everyone in society: wage earners, consumers, businesses, investors, tax payers, borrowers. That is why large business losses should be matters of public interest and why failing investments should be studied. Regional economies cannot avoid losses on some investments. However, by studying past failures, by pathological research, the incidence or severity of future ones might be reduced. This view follows Sykes (1994) who, after discussing dramatic cases of corporate collapse, argued that a lot could be learned from past business failures and claimed that such lessons were ignored by most business leaders and politicians.

A final comment relates to education. Typical case studies used in business education are about successes, after facing problems or challenges. A prominent professor of management has recommended that bias: "I have concentrated on success stories because I am sure we can learn more from successes than from failures" (Hilmer, 1985: vi).

Hilmer is mistaken. Anyone interested in business can learn from a range of cases, including successes and failures. Success inspires others to succeed, and provides clues for imitation. Failures point to high risks and pitfalls, providing clues for what to avoid. Since both seem beneficial, perhaps an equal balance is best? Arguably not. More can be learned from failures, from a pathological approach.

Modern science supports that opinion. Medical research and education relies largely on pathology–dissecting corpses to discover the causes of death and disease, rather than studying healthy persons and their organs to find out why they are alive and healthy. That tradition, established for a century, is explained by the science of cybernetics (Wiener, 1950) in a way that is well-summarised by Morgan (1986: 84-88 and 356-358).

The ability to engage in self-regulating (i.e., learned) behaviour "depends on processes of information exchange involving negative feedback" (Morgan, 1986: 85). By that interpretation, learning involves avoiding noxiant states. Even seemingly simple tasks, like picking up a pencil, involve double-loop learning systems. A hand seems to reach for a pencil, but in fact, as Morgan shows in a clever diagram, an eye-brain-hand-system works, not by a positive reach, but by negative feedback. Likewise, we might imagine that we learn "how to" manage something. However, as Morgan explains, the truth is that we also learn "how not to," by avoiding anything that seems to take us away from our goal. The Big Banana case contains several lessons of "how not to," lessons of negative feedback, for students of marketing management, especially those interested in tourism industries.

REFERENCES

Andrews, K.R. (1991). The Concept of Corporate Strategy (pp. 44-51). In H. Mintzberg and J.B. Quinn (Eds), *The Strategy Process.* Englewood Cliffs: Prentice-Hall.

Bowman, C. and D. Asch (1996). *Managing Strategy.* London: Macmillan.

Bureau of Tourism Research (1990). *Tourism Trends in New South Wales.* Canberra: BTR.

Galbraith J. (1991). Strategy and Organizational Planning (pp. 315-323). In H. Mintzberg and J.B. Quinn (Eds), *The Strategy Process.* Englewood Cliffs: Prentice-Hall.

Gunn, C. (1972). *Vacationscape: Designing Tourist Regions.* Austin: University of Texas.

Hilmer, F.G. (1985). *When the Work Runs Out: The Future for Australians at Work.* Sydney: Harper & Row.

Hofer, C.W. (1991). Designing Turnaround Strategies (pp. 793-799). In H. Mintzberg and J.B. Quinn (Eds), *The Strategy Process.* Englewood Cliffs: Prentice-Hall.

Horwath and Horwath Services Pty (1988). Market Study With Financial Projections for Proposed Big Banana & Horticultural World. Unpublished report for Horticultural World Pty Ltd. Brisbane: Horwath and Horwath Services Pty.

Kotler, P. (1967). *Marketing Management Analysis, Planning and Control.* Englewood Cliffs: Prentice-Hall International.

Kotler, P., Peter Chandler, Linden Brown and Stewart Adam (1996). *Marketing in Australia and New Zealand,* 3rd ed. Sydney: Prentice-Hall.

Leiper, N. (1981). Towards a Cohesive Curriculum in Tourism: The Case for a Distinct Discipline. *Annals of Tourism Research* 8: 69-84.

The Japanese Travel Market and Its Potential for Australian Tourist Destinations (1985). Sydney: Qantas Airways.

Tourism Systems: An Interdisciplinary Perspective (1990). Palmerston North: Massey University, Department of Management Systems.

Tourism Management (1995). Melbourne: RMIT Press.

Macartney-Snape, Tim (1992). *Everest From Sea to Summit.* Sydney: Australian Geographical Society.

MacCannell, Dean (1976). *The Tourist: A New Theory of the Leisure Class.* New York: Schoken.

Matley, Ian (1976). *The Geography of International Tourism.* Washington, DC: The Commission on Geography.

Mintzberg, H. and J.B. Quinn (Eds.). (1991). *The Strategy Process.* Englewood Cliffs: Prentice-Hall

Morgan, G. (1986). *Images of Organization.* Newbury Park: Sage.

The Oz Experience: Australia Adventure Guide, Summer 95-96, 4th ed. Sydney: Oz Experience Ltd.

Real, M. (1977). *Mass-Mediated Culture.* Englewood Cliffs: Prentice-Hall.

Rumelt, R. (1991). The Evaluation of Business Strategy (pp. 52-59). In H. Mintzberg and J.B. Quinn (Eds.), *The Strategy Process.* Englewood Cliffs: Prentice Hall.

Starbuck, W.H., A. Greve and B.L.T. Hedberg (1991). Responding to Crises (pp. 785-792). In H. Mintzberg and J.B. Quinn (Eds.). *The Strategy Process.* Englewood Cliffs: Prentice Hall.

Sykes, T. (1994). *The Bold Riders: Behind Australia's Corporate Collapses.* Sydney: Allen and Unwin.

Weiner, N. (1950). *The Human Use of Human Beings: Cybernetics and Society.* London: Eyre and Spottiswold.

Analysing the Promotion, Product and Visitor Expectations of Urban Tourism: Auckland, New Zealand as a Case Study

Glenda R. Lawton
Stephen J. Page

SUMMARY. Urban tourism is generally not recognized as a concept. There appears to be a lack of understanding by many tourism operators that tourists visit urban destinations primarily because they are multifunctional and offer a wide variety of activities. This study reports the findings of an analysis of 160 tourism brochures by 120 different Auckland-based operators and a survey of 170 tourists. The results indicate that there appears to be a mismatch between supply and demand with tourists undertaking urban activities while the industry is primarily offering outdoor and adventure type activities. The challenge for the future is

---

Glenda R. Lawton is Tutor and doctoral candidate in Tourism Management, and Dr. Stephen J. Page is Senior Lecturer in Tourism Management, Department of Management Systems, Massey University-Albany, Private Bag 102 904, North Shore Mail Centre, Auckland, New Zealand.

The authors aknowledge the support and assistance of Mr. B. Roberts, Tourism Auckland.

This paper is derived from research undertaken by Glenda Lawton for her Honours thesis entitled "Tourist promotional literature in Auckland" in 1995 in the Department of Management Systems, Massey University-Albany. In 1996, the thesis was awarded a Tourism Auckland Research Prize for its contribution to research and knowledge with a practical application for the Auckland Tourism industry.

[Haworth co-indexing entry note]: "Analysing the Promotion, Product and Visitor Expectations of Urban Tourism: Auckland, New Zealand as a Case Study." Lawton, Glenda R., and Stephen J. Page. Co-published simultaneously in *Journal of Travel & Tourism Marketing* (The Haworth Press, Inc.) Vol. 6, No. 3/4, 1997, pp. 123-142; and: *Geography and Tourism Marketing* (ed: Martin Oppermann) The Haworth Press, Inc., 1997, pp. 123-142. Single or multiple copies of this article are available for a fee from The Haworth Document Delivery Service [1-800-342-9678, 9:00 a.m. - 5:00 p.m. (EST). E-mail address: getinfo@haworth.com].

123

to reformulate and promote an image which is consistent with the supply attributes. *[Article copies available for a fee from The Haworth Document Delivery Service: 1-800-342-9678. E-mail address: getinfo@ haworth.com]*

INTRODUCTION

There has been a growing interest during the 1980s and 1990s in place-marketing and promotion (Gold and Ward, 1993; Kotler, Haider and Rein, 1993) based on the formulation of appropriate place-images to sell cities as urban tourism destinations. Yet this interest is not new, since the promotion and advertising of cities as leisure environments for tourists can be dated to at least the nineteenth century (Brown, 1985). Place-marketing is now recognised as a vital process in facilitating the development of urban tourism (Ashworth and Voogd, 1990) since it assists in recognising how "many urban activities operate in some kind of market . . . in which a planned action implies an explicit and simultaneous consideration of both the supply-side and the demand-side" (Ashworth and Voogd, 1990: 65) of tourism and the way in which cities are managed as visitor destinations (Page, 1995). In other words, place-marketing requires the public and private sector to consider the market context and competitive position of cities as tourism destinations supply of attractions, facilities and activities available in the destination.

Place-marketing is important as a concept in tourism management because it acknowledges that tourists select particular place products (i.e., destinations) in their holiday decision-making process often on the basis of limited knowledge of the destination and available options (Kent, 1990). As Goodall (1990: 260) observed, the holiday may be as much the place as the place is the holiday for the tourist. In contrast, the various businesses and organisations associated with tourism focus on specific aspects of the place product (e.g., an attraction or facility). The organisation charged with marketing the city will tend to adopt a composite view of the city and its place product in selling the destination to potential visitors yet they may do so without a real understanding of the diversity of the services and products being sold by the tourism industry within the locality. This can lead to a more generalised image of the urban tourism destination and influence the way in which it is constructed and sold to visitors by agencies responsible for marketing and promotion.

To date, no major academic research has evaluated whether specific forms of place-marketing for destinations at a city-region level are appropriate in relation to the supply of attractions, facilities and activities available in the destination. In other words, research needs to consider whether the images which tourism operators promote are at variance with the city-wide image of the destination. One explanation for the paucity of research is that urban tourism is a buoyant and growing sector for domestic and international tourism markets and as a result many cities have tried to keep pace with this growth and sought further expansion without adopting a critical view of the effectiveness of such marketing. In fact most public sector agencies usually assume that place-marketing automatically contributes to the growth in visitor arrivals. However, this paper argues that in some urban tourism destinations there may be a major mismatch between the place-product being promoted to visitors and the place-image used to entice visitors to destinations.

Auckland is New Zealand's major international gateway and leading destination and offers a wide range of urban tourism and recreational activities (Pearce, 1992). A key feature of Auckland is the Waitemata Harbour and as a destination the city has consistently been marketed and branded as the *"City of Sails"* by Tourism Auckland, (the regional tourism organisation), Air New Zealand, and the New Zealand Tourism Board even though the harbour is difficult to access by tourists. Using Auckland as an example, this paper examines the way in which the place-image is now at variance with both the supply of tourist services and products and the actual expectations and attitudes of urban visitors. The paper commences with a discussion of the concept of place-marketing and its role in urban tourism as a basis for a critical review of the situation in Auckland. The paper also examines how the promotion of urban based tourism activities by means of operators' brochures may shape and influence urban tourists' activities. It also considers the effect of place-marketing in developing an awareness of the destination which may facilitate or constrain the activity patterns of international visitors. In particular, the paper argues that inappropriately focused place and activity based marketing may constrain the geographical activity patterns and spatial distribution and dispersion of visitors throughout urban destinations.

Place-Marketing and Urban Tourism

The term place-marketing (Madsen, 1992), selling places (Burgess, 1982) or geographical marketing (Ashworth and Voogd, 1990) in an urban context is based on the principle that the city is a place product which can be marketed and promoted to potential customers. Ashworth and Voogd argued that "the complexity of places, makes it impossible for either buyer or seller to be aware of, let alone give active consideration to, all but a fraction of the place attributes and their possible uses" (1990: 2). In promoting a city a critical component of the marketing strategy is positioning or creating an appropriate "place identity" or image (Dredge and Moore, 1992; Echtner and Ritchie, 1993; Judd, 1995). Studies suggest that destinations with strong positive images do influence tourist behaviour and are more likely to be chosen in the travel decision process (Hunt, 1975; Goodrich, 1978; Pearce, 1982; Woodside and Lysonski, 1989). Buck (1993, cited in Laws, 1995: 112), commented that "tourism is an industry based on imagery, its overriding concern is to construct . . . an imagery that entices the outsider to place himself or herself into that symbol-defined space" implying that place imagery and the role of tourism attractions within this process is an important determinant of visitor perception and activity.

Projected images are ultimately derived from the structure of the tourism supply, while received images are related to the consumers' predisposed constructs. Images are "projected through a set of cultural codes" (Ashworth and Voogd, 1990: 79) which are transmitted through a variety of channels thus leading to distortion and interference. Images are formed by impressions chosen from a flood of information (Reynolds, 1965) and help simplify information storage retrieval. Imagery is a process of conceptually representing information (MacInnis and Price, 1987) with the outcome of this process being an image (Cossens, 1994). Research indicates that consumers often suffer from "information overload" and are therefore selective in the information they access (Jacoby, 1984). Most potential visitors will be making decisions based on little experience and, therefore, mental imagery can act as a model in the absence of the original stimulus (Morris and Hampson, 1983). A tourist destination is widely regarded as an intangible product and because of the strong ties with self, the strong impact of travel on emotions and the complex nature of the decision, it is likely that images held of a destination will be influential in the travel decision (Cossens, 1994). Dichter (1985) defined a destination-image as "not only individual traits or qualities but also the total impression an entity makes on the minds of others" (Dichter, 1985: 79). Image is a set of beliefs, ideas and impressions that a person holds of an object (Kotler, 1991). In fact Echtner and Ritchie (1993) suggested that a destination image should be envisioned as consisting of two main components; those that are attribute based and those that are holistic. Each of these components of a destination image contains functional, or more tangible, and psychological or more abstract, characteristics. Therefore, images of destinations can also range from those based on "common" functional and psychological traits to those based on more distinctive or even unique features, events, feelings or auras. In addition, Milman and Pizam (1995) suggested that destination image consists of three components:

- the product (quality and variety of attractions, price, uniqueness and categories of users);
- the behaviour and attitude of the employees who come into direct contact with the tourists;
- the environment, such as weather, scenery, landscape and physical layout of the destination, the quality and types of accommodations, and restaurants.

Cities that find it easy to project a tourist image are characterised by memorable cityscapes or icons such as the Eiffel Tower in Paris, the Sydney Opera House or the Statue of Liberty in New York, to name a few. Successful destinations will have a distinct character built upon unusual or unique features whereas those that lack image cannot easily be promoted (Dredge and Moore, 1994; Judd, 1995). A destination image should be as original as possible, truthful and capable of being implemented at a cost appropriate to its attractiveness (Lawson and Baud-Bovy, 1977). Research indicates that the effectiveness of a destination image is also dependent upon the ease of its recognition (Ashworth and Goodall, 1988).

It should be noted however, that the promoted images are often not consistent with most residents' perceptions of their own country (Laws, 1995). In most cases, governments are responsible for shaping the place image of their country, but they may also be simultaneously creating and projecting other competing images for different purposes. A number of other agencies including local governments and sections of the tourism industry also create destination images and this can lead to conflict between the images promoted by different agencies (Ashworth and Goodall, 1988). Laws (1995) also noted that the way a destination is portrayed can structure tourists' activities after arriving in a destination. One way the tourism industry seeks to portray an image is through the use of brochures and there have been few attempts in urban tourism to compare the nature of place-marketing at a city-wide level with the specific marketing activities of tourism operators through their brochures and publicity material. For this reason it is important to consider the role of brochures in tourism promotion in order to understand how they may influence tourists' decision making and their desire to visit urban tourist attractions and to undertake activities.

The Use of Brochures in Tourism Marketing and Promotion

One of the most important ways a destination and its attractions are portrayed is through the dissemination and use of brochures. Previous available research into the use of brochures in the tourism decision-making process focused on tour operators brochures which advertise package tours. In contrast, there has been a complete neglect of the role of brochures advertising individual attractions or activities and their ability to provide a consistent image in relation to that promoted at a city-wide level.

Consumers of tourism products and services are dependent upon the information found in brochures and other sales media to assist in their travel decision-making (Wick and Schuett, 1991). Once motivated to travel, potential tourists need to gather sufficient information on various aspects of their planned trip. Mansfeld (1992) noted that the search process consists of two parts: an internal search which relies on past experiences and information, and an external search which uses new information. It is in the latter context in which brochures are important in destination areas.

Gitelson and Crompton (1983) also recognised that the external search is important for the following reasons:

- because a trip is a high risk purchase and involves the use of discretionary dollars during an individual's free time;
- the consumer is unable to actually observe the potential purchase;
- holiday-makers tend to visit new and relatively unfamiliar destinations.

During the information-gathering phase, the consumer first gathers enough information to ascertain that any attractive destinations offered or chosen are within the constraint limits. Secondly, the consumer uses the information "to evaluate each alternative on a 'place utility' rather than on a constraint basis" (Mansfeld, 1992: 406). Mansfeld (1992) found that tourist information emanates mainly from two sources. First, formal sources such as travel agents, brochures, travelogues, travel books and maps; secondly, informal sources such as the recommendations and impressions of other people and long term personal knowledge acquired during previous travels.

For producers, the most important objective of the brochure is providing general information followed by the promotion of specific attractions. Marketing strategies tend to be largely undifferentiated. Distribution channels are either direct (i.e., using computer mailing lists) to reach specific target markets or indirect (i.e., through visitors' bureaux, local libraries, travel agents and coach tour operators). Purchased direct mailing lists are rarely used (Wicks and Schuett, 1991). Consumer choice is influenced by the way an agency displays brochures (Wicks and Schuett, 1991). Clients spend 40 percent more time scanning the racks for potentially suitable material than they do reading the brochures (Gilbert and Houghton, 1991). This indicates that the initial visual component of the brochure is extremely important. Factors affecting brochure "pickup" include the use of travel agents' stickers, brand name recognition, and the perceived validity of images, i.e., if consumers thought the cover looked "cheap and shoddy" they felt the advertised holiday was likely to be inferior.

For many potential visitors, the brochure actually represents the destination or product they are purchasing. Brochures are relatively permanent and may be passed on or kept as a long-term reminder. Nearly 20 percent of those who used brochures kept them for six to twelve months (Wicks and Schuett, 1991). Customers compare brochures and the best brochure is most likely to receive the business (Coltman, 1989). Stabler (1988) found that once visitors had reached their destination, over 80 percent did not make use of any local brochure or guide. However, Gitelson and Kerstetter (1994) indicated that tourist information from friends and relatives at the destination is very important in the tourist decision-making process. Nearly one-third (29%) of friends or relatives actually decided the length of time non-locals should stay and 39 percent decided what non-locals would do when tourists stayed with them. These findings suggest that the role of locally supplied travel information is relatively minor although no other research has been undertaken to question the validity of this.

Methodology

Two separate surveys were conducted in order to compare the supply and demand sides of the tourism industry in Auckland and to identify whether the image being promoted was consistent with both the product available and visitor expectations. The first survey was conducted to analyse the supply side of Auckland's tourism industry and focused on promotional brochures advertising tourism activities or attractions within the Auckland region. This was undertaken to identify the geographical spread of attractions and activities and to identify strategic issues concerning the tourism distribution channel. The geographical sampling frame used was Auckland with the focus being on both the spatial distribution of sites from which visitors would seek information and the various points of contact from which tourism brochures are disseminated within Auckland such as transport, accommodation and Visitor Information Centres. One hundred and sixty brochures promoting different tourist activities, attractions or services and published by 120 different operators were collected from eight locations. All brochures in stock were collected at each location in order to be representative of the entire range of attractions and activities. Obviously the results of this method depend on how well stocked the racks are, but discussions with the Visitor Information Centres indicated the attractions or activities which resulted were representative of the Auckland tourism industry. This was preferable to a random sample of a large number of sites due to the existing knowledge of the key locations from which tourists select brochure literature as indicated by the Visitor Information Centres. The initial purpose was to ascertain the total number of brochures available, the type of activities or attractions promoted by each brochure, the locations at which each brochure is available, and the number of brochures available at each location. In addition, the location of each activity or attraction within the wider Auckland region were derived and the image presented by the cover of each brochure was also identified.

Each brochure selected was analysed to determine the activity or attraction being promoted. In the absence of previous research, the basis of classification was derived from the New Zealand Tourism Board (1993) *Visitor Information Survey* and therefore includes a wide range of categories. Some brochures featured more than one activity and therefore the total number of activities or attractions exceeds the total number of brochures collected. A brochure was categorised as promoting an activity or attraction if it contained two or more sentences specifically featuring that activity or attraction.

The small pilot study of 170 tourists (limited by budget constraints) was undertaken to analyse tourism demand in Auckland. A questionnaire was administered on a random basis to overseas tourists outside the two visitor information centres located on Queen Street, Auckland's central thoroughfare. This was undertaken in order to identify tourist demographics, how visitors perceive Auckland as a destination, the activities they undertake and their use of tourism brochures at a destination.

Results of Tourist Brochure Analysis

As Table 1 suggests, the three main activities promoted by these brochures were outdoor activities, guided tours and adventure activities. This is somewhat different to the prevailing image of Auckland as a destination promoted as the *"City of Sails"* with a paucity of activities aside from the principal tourist attractions of the War Memorial Museum and Kelly Tarlton's Underwater World. What is even more surprising is the number of eco-activities incorporating a bush walk and adventure activities.

Within the 163 brochures, the main geographical area promoted in Auckland was the Waitemata Harbour which is consistent with the traditional place-image of the *"City of Sails."* While this reflects the dominance of one major tourist operator–Fullers Ltd, a ferry operator–only 3% of all tourist activities promoted in brochures involve any form of sailing. In contrast, Downtown Auckland is the second most important area promoted in brochures followed by Auckland City and then the remaining

TABLE 1

Type of activity/attraction being promoted in Auckland by brochure		
	Number of brochures	**% of total**
Outdoor activities	72	44%
Guided tours	51	31%
Adventure activities	40	25%
Restaurants	32	20%
Shopping	27	17%
Beach based activities	25	15%
Historical attractions	18	11%
Theme park/zoo	17	10%
Transport	16	10%
Maori culture	14	9%
Museums/art galleries/observatory	13	8%
Sporting/cultural activities	9	6%
Nightlife activities	9	6%
Geothermal/hot pools	6	4%

areas of North Shore City, Waitakere City and Rodney District. Thus, the marketing of Auckland as the *"City of Sails,"* fails to recognise the spatially dispersed nature of the Auckland region across five cities and the fact that only 34 percent of promoted tourist activities are located in the Downtown or harbour area which has been conventionally identified as the city's central tourist district (Getz, 1993). As Table 2 indicates, the natural environment such as beaches or the New Zealand bush is by far the most important image used on the front cover of the brochures which appears at odds with the conventional stereotyped image of Auckland as New Zealand's main gateway city and a traditional urban destination.

Survey of International Tourism Demand in Auckland: Urban Tourism Expectations and the Role of Promotional Literature

A pilot study of 170 international tourists was undertaken in Downtown Auckland in November 1995 to examine their perception of Auckland as a destination, their use of activity brochures, and the extent to which the material was memorable and influenced their decision to undertake an activity or visit an attraction in Auckland. This survey was based in Downtown Auckland and was therefore seen as an important comparative research tool (Pearce, 1993) in view of the weaknesses in existing New Zealand Tourist Board (NZTB) data being based on an exit survey of major gateways that did not contain any questions on the use of brochures

TABLE 2

Image on covers of promotional brochures collected in Auckland		
	Number	**%**
Natural environment	71	43%
Adventure	21	13%
Bus tours	14	9%
Cityscape	13	8%
Theme parks/museums	13	8%
Transport	11	7%
Restaurants	11	7%
Shopping	7	5%
Total	163	100%

in visitors' activity patterns. The results of this pilot study differ from NZTB results and may be explained by the fact that visitors to Downtown Auckland are in fact a separate segment within New Zealand's wider visitor mix and have not previously been specifically identified. Another factor that may have influenced these results is that visitors were interviewed outside the two visitor centres at either end of Queen Street, Auckland's central retail thoroughfare and business tourists, package tourists and those visiting friends and relatives may be less likely to use the visitor centres and thus are less likely to be identified within this study. The major source markets are evident but the resulting visitor mix and profile of visitors is quite different from those identified in NZTB and Tourism Auckland surveys (Table 3) with nearly one third (32%) of those surveyed coming from Great Britain, 17 percent from Other Europe, 13 percent from North America and 12 percent coming from Germany. The age profile of visitors was spread between the 25-30 age group (31%), the 20-25 age group (35%) and the 31-40 age group (19%). Among the respondents, 32 percent described themselves as professional or managerial workers, 25 percent as students and 17 percent as skilled with these findings being consistent with the widely acknowledged proposition that tourists tend to be drawn from the better educated social groups. This was also reflected in the income status of respondents with 17 percent who earned NZ$20-30,000, 18 percent NZ$30-40,000 and 18 percent NZ$40-50,000 with only 6 percent earning NZ$50-60,000 although 16 percent earned in excess of NZ$60,000 per annum. Some 49% stayed in backpackers hostels (compared to 9 percent in the NZTB survey) while 21 percent stayed with friends and relatives and 10 percent stayed in a quality hotel.

Following the socio-demographic profile of respondents, a range of

TABLE 3

Nationality of international visitors interviewed in Auckland		
	This survey	**NZTB survey**
Great Britain	32%	9%
Other Europe	17%	5%
North America	13%	15%
Germany	12%	5%
Australia	9%	32%
Japan	8%	12%
Other	7%	11%
Other Asia	3%	7%
Taiwan	0%	3%
Total	100%	100%

questions were asked concerning visitor impressions, perceptions and expectations of urban tourism in Auckland in relation to the marketing of tourism, their use of brochures, and the extent to which visitor information leaflets had increased their knowledge of the range of attractions, facilities and activities available. Visitors were asked to identify those activities or attractions they felt were located or available in Auckland (Table 4) and the primary activities or attractions identified were shopping (84.7%), the Auckland Museum (83%), bar/nightclubs (83%), the Art Gallery (80%) and live theatre/concert (77%). The role of leisure shopping as a major activity for urban tourists is well established (Jansen-Verbeke, 1994) and it is important to note that all of these attractions or activities can be found in most major cities. The attractions and activities unique to Auckland that scored well were the Maritime Museum (69%), Mt Eden/One Tree Hill (66%) and Kelly Tarlton's Underwater World (60%). Sailing (65%) and scenic boat cruises (65%), while not unique to Auckland, indicate that over half of the tourists are aware that the city is located on a harbour although only 54 percent knew that Auckland had beaches suitable for swimming and 21 percent were aware that the Hauraki Gulf Islands were located in Auckland. Approximately 60 percent of the respondents expected to find a Maori cultural performance in Auckland which probably indicates an awareness of Maori culture as a recognisable part of the total New Zealand tourist experience. Geothermal activities are another well-publicised feature of the New Zealand tourist experience yet there is little awareness (16%) that geothermal hot pools are located in the Auckland region. Overall there was a low awareness that the Auckland region offers a number of activities and attractions based in the natural environment. It is also interesting to note that although NZTB data indicates that the most popular activity undertaken by tourists in New Zealand are short bush walks, only one third of those interviewed (31%) knew that short bush walks could be taken in the Auckland region. These findings suggest that although Auckland has a large number of tourist activities located in a natural environment, tourists neither know about them nor expect to find such activities in an urban destination.

Respondents were also asked to identify which activities or attractions they *had visited* during their stay in Auckland. As Table 5 shows, the most popular activities or attractions undertaken by tourists in Auckland were shopping, visiting Parnell Village, a shopping attraction, frequenting bars and nightclubs and the Auckland War Memorial Museum. The Maritime Museum and Kelly Tarlton's Underwater World could both be considered unique to Auckland yet only 22 percent and 16 percent respectively of all those interviewed had visited these sites.

Tourists were also asked what activities or attractions they *planned* to visit and, as Table 5 also shows, the most popular were shopping, attending a Maori cultural performance and visiting a bar/nightclub. The only activities unique to Auckland that rated significantly were Kelly Tarlton's Underwater World (20%) and Mt Eden/One Tree Hill (19%). Overall these results would indicate that tourists arrive in Auckland with little real idea of what they plan to do and reiterate the notion that tourists visit cities primarily for the urban-based activities and attractions such as shopping, bars/nightclubs and art galleries. Although the Waitemata Harbour is the most highly promoted geographical area of Auckland, only 15 percent of respondents planned to take a scenic cruise, 12 percent planned to go sailing and 6 percent planned to go fishing, which indicates that high levels of promotion do not necessarily translate into high levels of visitor usage. Yet, to what extent were tourists' intended activities shaped by their use of brochures?

Use of Brochures by Visitors

Among the respondents, 82 percent had collected brochures during their stay in Auckland. Some 30 percent of visitors collected three to five brochures, while 29 percent and 24 percent collected six to ten and more than ten brochures respectively. Only 16 percent of visitors collected one to two brochures. Respondents were asked how often they took brochures or read brochures promoting activities or attractions they did not intend to visit. Table 6 shows that tourists read brochures more often than they take them with only 24 percent who *always* or *nearly always* take them compared to 41 percent who *always* or *nearly always* read them. These

TABLE 4

Activities and attractions in Auckland identified by tourists		
	Number	**%**
Shopping	144	85%
Museum	142	84%
Bar/nightclub	142	84%
Art gallery	136	80%
Live theatre or concert	131	77%
Maritime Museum	118	69%
Mt Eden/One Tree Hill	113	66%
Scenic boat cruise	111	65%
Sailing	111	65%
Maori cultural performance	102	60%
Kelly Tarlton's Underwater World	102	60%
Wildlife park/zoo	102	60%
Historic site	95	56%
Beach activity, e.g., swimming, sunbathing	91	54%
Parnell Village	89	52%
Golf	89	52%
Fishing	86	51%
Wine tasting	78	46%
Scenic flights	69	41%
Walk in bush or countryside—less than half day	53	31%
Wildlife in natural settings (e.g., gannet colony)	46	27%
Rafting/kayaking	45	26%
Walk in bush or countryside 1/2 to 1 day	41	24%
Hauraki Gulf Islands	35	21%
Farm show	95	56%
Geothermal (hot pools)	27	16%
Rock climbing/mountain biking	24	14%
Other	11	6%

findings appear to contradict previous research (Gilbert and Houghton, 1991) which found that clients in a travel agent's office spend 40 percent more time scanning racks for suitable material than they do actually reading them. The discrepancy between the results of these two surveys may be linked to the difference between the cost and time factors associated with the tourism product being purchased (i.e., a package tour compared with visiting a single attraction) with time constraints being more pressing when tourists are actually on their holiday. When asked what they do with brochures after they have taken them, 45 percent of respondents stated that they *keep the brochures in case they can use them later*, while 18 percent *take them back to their home country*, 14 percent *throw them away as soon as they have read them*, and 12 percent *take them to their next destination*

TABLE 5

Activities and attractions in Auckland	Already visited by tourists		Tourists plan to visit	
	Number	%	Number	%
Shopping	87	51%	47	28%
Other	56	33%	15	9%
Parnell Village	48	28%	24	14%
Bar/nightclub	46	27%	38	22%
Museum	43	25%	12	7%
Maritime Museum	38	22%	22	13%
Art Gallery	28	16%	31	18%
Kelly Tarlton's Underwater World	27	16%	34	20%
Wildlife in natural settings (e.g., gannet colony)	27	16%	20	12%
Maori cultural performance	20	12%	41	24%
Walk in bush or countryside (less than one day)	13	8%	17	10%
Live theatre or concert	12	7%	21	12%
Beach activity (e.g., swimming, sunbathing)	12	7%	22	13%
Wildlife park/zoo	11	6%	22	13%
Scenic boat cruise	11	6%	26	15%
Geothermal (hot pools)	9	5%	28	16%
Historic site	8	5%	25	15%
Wine tasting	8	5%	16	9%
Walk in bush or countryside (1/2 to 1 day)	8	5%	16	9%
Golf	5	3%	7	4%
Fishing	5	3%	10	6%
Sailing	5	3%	20	12%
Mt Eden/One Tree Hill	5	3%	32	19%
Farm show	4	2%	18	11%
Hauraki Gulf Islands	4	2%	8	5%
Rock climbing/mountain biking	4	2%	11	6%
Scenic flight	2	1%	5	3%
Rafting/kayaking	2	1%	16	9%

and discard them there. Only 3 percent *give them to someone else* and less than 1% of the respondents *throw brochures away without reading them.* These results also confirmed other research which shows that brochures are relatively permanent (Wicks and Schuett, 1991), yet indicates that tourists tell each other about activities and attractions but do not pass on brochures when doing so.

Respondents were asked to rank different factors that influenced their decision-making process during their holiday and were instructed to rate the most important influence with one, the second most important with two and so on. The results were weighted and then added with the factor receiving the highest total being the factor most likely to influence the

TABLE 6

Brochures taken and read by International tourists				
	Brochures Taken		Brochures Read	
	Number	%	Number	%
Always	19	12%	24	15%
Nearly always	19	12%	41	26%
Sometimes	64	40%	55	34%
Rarely	32	20%	21	13%
Very rarely	19	12%	15	9%
Total	162	100%	160	100%

decision-making process on holiday. As Table 7 shows, the recommendation of friends and relatives is the most important factor influencing what tourists do while on holiday and secondly, the recommendation of other tourists met while travelling. When respondents were asked whether they had ever visited an activity or attraction *only* on the basis of reading a brochure about it, 66 percent of respondents answered that they had. These results appear to confirm other results from a study of people requesting tourism brochures by mail (Wicks and Schuett, 1991) which showed that 84 percent of those who received the brochures then visited the site. This indicates that brochures do have an important place in the tourism distribution channel when local knowledge or information from other travellers is not accessible. Respondents were also asked whether brochures collected in Auckland had influenced what they had done during their time in the city and 72 percent replied that the brochures had. However, respondents were not asked how or why the brochures had influenced their activities and further research is needed to understand the role of destination based brochures in the tourism decision-making process.

When asked what they would do if they read a brochure advertising a really appealing activity or attraction about which they previously knew nothing, some 87 percent of respondents indicated they would try to ask other tourists or friends about it before visiting, 71 percent would ask staff at their hostel or hotel whereas only 43 percent of the respondents would visit without asking another person for further information. These findings again emphasise the high importance tourists place on personal recommendations.

TABLE 7

Factors likely to influence activities undertaken by tourists while on holiday							
	1	2	3	4	5	6	7	Total
Recommendation by friends and relatives	66	24	8	7	4	4	1	695
Recommendations in travel guidebooks	22	21	21	10	9	17	6	492
Recommendation by staff at accommodation	1	14	24	26	17	16	5	403
Recommendation by Visitor Information Centre staff	6	12	11	25	30	13	11	396
Recommendation by travel agent in home country	6	12	11	25	30	13	11	396
Advertising brochures	4	11	10	11	26	23	20	332

CONCLUSIONS

Urban tourism is not generally recognised as a concept (Page, 1995) and this is demonstrated in the way Auckland's tourism industry has developed and is currently being promoted. There appears to be a lack of understanding by many tourism operators that tourists visit urban destinations primarily because they are multi-functional and offer urban based activities such as shopping, visiting bars and nightclubs, museums, and art galleries. Tourists arrive in a destination with expectations based on their previous tourist experience (Ahmed, 1991; Hunt, 1975; Milman and Pizam, 1995) or their experience in other similar destinations (Chon, 1990; Milman and Pizam, 1995) and many tourists visiting Auckland would not expect to find outdoor and adventure activities within the boundaries of New Zealand's largest city. There appears to be a mismatch between demand and supply of the tourist product in Auckland, with tourists undertaking urban attractions and activities while the industry is primarily offering outdoor and adventure type activities. There also appears to be an oversupply of outdoor and adventure activities with a high degree of substitutability between them and therefore a major rationalisation is likely to occur before the industry becomes sustainable. Analysis of the spatial features of tourism in Auckland highlights a further mismatch with the majority of activities and attractions located on the periphery of the Auckland region while tourists mainly undertake activities and visit attractions located within the centre of the city thus giving rise to a central tourist district. This pilot study indicates that only a small number of Visiting Friends and Relatives (VFR) tourists use the resources of the city and therefore an important tourist function of Downtown Auckland may be as a centre of tourist information, a function that may be of less importance to VFR tourists.

The Waitemata Harbour appears to be highly important on the supply side, yet few tourists actually undertake harbour-based activities. This could indicate that it may be inappropriate to use the *"City of Sails"* brand for marketing Auckland to overseas tourists. Unlike the Eiffel Tower or the Sydney Opera House, the Waitemata Harbour is difficult to access or view and few tourists therefore undertake activities located on the Harbour. Auckland appears to have no single recognised activity or attraction that most tourists plan to view or visit and that can be used to set the city apart as a destination (see Table 5) which is in contrast with many major urban destinations where tourists arrive with a knowledge of the "must do" attractions and activities located there. It is perhaps not surprising that in the absence of a major focus for Auckland, the Waitemata Harbour is viewed by tourism marketers as a unifying theme, given the city's domestic association with sailing. But few tourism operators appear to endorse this theme in their own marketing efforts.

Tourist brochures are kept by tourists for a reasonable length of time and nearly all tourists (81.6%) collected brochures while in Auckland which was unexpected as Stabler (1988) had indicated that tourists make little use of brochures at a destination. These findings could be attributed to the type of tourist interviewed: predominantly free independent travellers with high levels of education. Although brochures were rated low overall in relation to those factors influencing tourist activities while on holiday, nearly three quarters of tourists (71%) indicated that brochures *had* influenced what activities they undertook while in Auckland. This could imply that few of those interviewed had access to other sources of influence such as family, friends or other travellers during their stay in Auckland. It also suggests that within Auckland, brochures are an effective way for tourism operators to advertise, particularly to the Free Independent Traveller (FIT) tourists.

The low number of VFR tourists interviewed could indicate that they do not visit Downtown Auckland to any great extent and the usual direct marketing channels such as the Visitor Information Centres are therefore less useful for reaching this segment. In order to reach the large VFR segment in Auckland, the tourism industry may need to identify or develop other promotional channels which include the local residents. The role of the tourism distribution channel within Auckland also appears to be poorly understood by many of the smaller tourism operators, many of whom appear to have no awareness that to attract a large percentage of potential visitors, promotion is necessary at more than one central city outlet.

Because of the multifaceted nature of Auckland as a destination, it is vital that a suitable image highlighting the city's urban and cultural characteristics be identified and promoted. Although it appears that tourists primarily seek urban activities when visiting an urban destination, there is potential for Auckland to increase demand for adventure or outdoor-based tourism and thus develop that segment of the industry alongside that of urban tourism. This would assist in the geographical dispersion of visitors from central Auckland to the urban fringe. Therefore this research has indicated that Auckland, like many other urban tourism destinations, has sought to expand its international visitor market but place-marketing appropriate to the 1970s is no longer acceptable in view of the expansion and growing complexity of the urban tourist (Page, 1995). A simple *"City of Sails"* image conveys the wrong impression to visitors in terms of the potential range of activities, the likely visitor experience available and the geographical extent of their actual and potential activity patterns within the city. While this may be appropriate for Tourism Auckland given that a large proportion of its operational budget is derived from Auckland City Council with its focus on the Waitemata Harbour and the prospects for the America's Cup in the year 2000. The challenge for the 21st century is to reformulate and promote an image which is consistent with the supply attributes of the destination to provide a focused and meaningful experience for the visitor.

REFERENCES

Ahmed, Z.U. (1991). The influence of the components of a State's tourist image on product positioning strategy. *Tourism Management*, 12: 331-340.

Ashworth, G., and Goodall, B. (1988). Tourism images: Marketing considerations (pp. 213-238). In B. Goodall and G. Ashworth (eds.), *Marketing in the Tourism Industry*. London: Routledge.

Ashworth, G.J., and Voogd, H. (1990). *Selling the City*. London: Belhaven Press.

Brown. B.J.H. (1985). Personal perception and community speculation: A British resort in the nineteenth century. *Annals of Tourism Research*, 12: 353-369.

Buck, J. (1993). *Paradise Remade, The Politics of Culture and History in Hawai'i*. Philadelphia: Temple University Press.

Burgess, J.A. (1982). Selling places: Environmental images for executives. *Regional Studies*, 16(1): 1-17.

Chon, K.S. (1990). The role of destination image in tourism: A review and discussion. *The Tourist Review*, 45(2): 2-9.

Coltman, M.M. (1989). *Tourism Marketing*. New York: Van Nostrand Reinhold.

Cossens, J. (1994). Destination Image: Another Fat Marketing Word? (pp. 579-600). In J. Cheyne and C. Ryan (eds.), *Tourism Down-Under: A Tourism Research Conference*, Massey University.

Dichter, E. (1985). What's in an image? *Journal of Consumer Marketing*, 2(1): 75-81.

Dredge, D., and Moore, S. (1992). A methodology for the integration of tourism in town planning. *Journal of Tourism Studies*, 3(1): 8-21.

Echtner, C.M., and Ritchie, J.R.B. (1993). The measurement of destination Image: An empirical assessment. *Journal of Travel Research*, 31(4): 3-12.

Gilbert, D., and Houghton, P. (1991). An exploratory investigation of formal design and use of U.K. tour operators brochures. *Journal of Travel Research*, 30(2): 21-25.

Gitelson, R.J., and Crompton, J.L. (1983). The planning horizons and sources of information used by pleasure vacationers. *Journal of Travel Research*, 22(3): 2-7.

Gitelson, R.J., and Kersteller, D. (1994). The influence of friends and relatives in travel decision-making. *Journal of Travel & Tourism Marketing*, 3(3): 56-68.

Gold, J., and Ward, S. (eds.) (1993). *Place Promotion: The Use of Publicity and Public Relations to Sell Cities*. Chichester: Wiley.

Goodall, J. (1990). The dynamics of tourism place marketing (pp. 259-279). In G.J. Ashworth and B. Goodall (Eds.), *Marketing Tourism Places*. London: Routledge.

Goodrich, J.N. (1978). The relationships between preferences for and perceptions of vacation destinations: Application of a choice model. *Journal of Travel Research*, 16(1): 8-13.

Hunt, J.D. (1975). Image as a factor in tourism development. *Journal of Travel Research*, 13(3): 1-7.

Jansen-Verbeke, M. (1994). The synergy between shopping and tourism: The Japanese experience (pp. 347-362). In W. Theobald (Ed.), *Global Tourism: The Next Decade*. Oxford: Butterworth-Heinemann.

Jacoby, J. (1984). Perspectives on information overload. *Journal of Consumer Research*, 10: 432-435.

Judd, D.R. (1995). Promoting tourism in US cities. *Tourism Management*, 16: 175-187.

Kent, P. (1990). People, places and priorities: Opportunity sets and consumers' holiday choice (pp. 42-62). In G.J. Ashworth and B. Goodall (eds.), *Marketing Tourism Places*. London: Routledge.

Kotler, P. (1991). *Marketing Management: Analysis, Planning, Implementation and Control*. Englewood Cliffs: Prentice Hall.

Kotler, P., Haider, D.H., and Rein, I. (1993). *Marketing Places: Attracting Investment, Industry and Tourism to Cities, States and Nations*. New York: Free Press.

Laws, E. (1995). *Tourism Destination Management. Issues, Analysis and Policies*. London: Routledge.

Lawson, F., and Baud-Bovy, M. (1977). *Tourism and Recreational Development*. London: Architectural Press.

MacInnis, D.J., and Price, L.L. (1987). The role of imagery in information processing: Review and extensions. *Journal of Consumer Research*, 13: 473-491.

Madsen, H. (1992). Place-marketing in Liverpool: A review. *International Journal of Urban and Regional Research*, 16: 633-640.

Mansfeld, Y. (1992). From motivation to actual travel. *Annals of Tourism Research*, 19: 399-419.

Milman, A., and Pizam, A. (1995). The role of awareness and familiarity with a destination: The Central Florida case. *Journal of Travel Research*, 33(3): 21-27.

Morris, P.E., and Hampson, P.J. (1983). *Imagery and Consciousness*. London: Academic Press.

New Zealand Tourism Board (1993). *New Zealand International Visitors Survey 1992/93*. Wellington: New Zealand Tourism Board.

Page, S.J. (1995). *Urban Tourism*. London: Routledge.

Pearce, D.G. (1993). Introduction (pp. 1-8). In D.G. Pearce and R.W. Butler (eds.), *Tourism Research: Critiques and Challenges*. London: Routledge.

Pearce, D.G. (1992). *Tourist Organisations*. London: Longman.

Pearce, P.L. (1982). Perceived changes in holiday destination. *Annals of Tourism Research*, 9: 145-164.

Reynolds, W.H. (1965). The role of the consumer in image building. *California Management Review*, 24(1): 69-76.

Stabler, M.J. (1988). The image of destination regions: Theoretical and empirical aspects (pp. 131-161). In Goodall, B. and G. Ashworth (Eds.), *Marketing in the Tourism Industry: The Promotion of Destination Regions*. London: Croom Helm.

Wicks, B.E., and Schuett, M.A. (1991). Examining the role of tourism promotion through the use of brochures. *Tourism Management*, 12: 301-312.

Woodside, A.G., and Lysonski, S. (1989). A general model of traveller destination choice. *Journal of Travel Research*, 17(4): 8-14.

Destination Marketing:
Measuring the Effectiveness of Brochures

Zongqing Zhou

SUMMARY. This article reports the findings of an exploratory study defining effectiveness for assessing impacts of brochures. Using data collected from 2,400 information-inquirers of a destination, five major variables are identified to be important for measuring effectiveness: readership, on-site consultation of brochure, influence on decision-making, influence on spending, prior experience of the destination. Implications and recommendations are discussed for developing quality brochures and marketing strategies. *[Article copies available for a fee from The Haworth Document Delivery Service: 1-800-342-9678. E-mail address: getinfo@haworth.com]*

INTRODUCTION

The importance of tourism in national and regional development has caused increasing competition in efforts to attract and lure tourists. According to the U.S. Travel Data Center (1995), every state in the United States maintains an agency or division to promote inbound travel. The budget for these offices ranges from $860 thousand in Delaware to over

Dr. Zongqing Zhou is Assistant Professor, Institute of Travel, Hotel and Restaurant Administration, Niagara University, Niagara University, NY 14109.

The author wishes to thank Dr. Donald Holecek and Dr. Dan Spotts of Michigan Travel and Tourism Center, Michigan State University for their support and assistance with the research project for this paper.

[Haworth co-indexing entry note]: "Destination Marketing: Measuring the Effectiveness of Brochures." Zhou, Zongqing. Co-published simultaneously in *Journal of Travel & Tourism Marketing* (The Haworth Press, Inc.) Vol. 6, No. 3/4, 1997, pp. 143-158; and: *Geography and Tourism Marketing* (ed: Martin Oppermann) The Haworth Press, Inc., 1997, pp. 143-158. Single or multiple copies of this article are available for a fee from The Haworth Document Delivery Service [1-800-342-9678, 9:00 a.m. - 5:00 p.m. (EST). E-mail address: getinfo@haworth.com].

$22 million in Texas. Across the states, an average amount of $2 million was allocated to state promotional efforts. The bulk of this money is allocated to advertising efforts, with one of the primary objectives being the generation of requests for information packages (e.g., brochures) that have been prepared by the state.

Brochures are a unique medium of communication and marketing, not only in terms of their content, format, and design, but also in terms of their varied means of distribution. There are many means for distributing brochures, such as mailing them to people who request them, handing them out on site or displaying them in the lobbies of hotels, in convention centers, in rest areas, in travel agency offices, and in tourist information centers. Consequently, studies related to the effectiveness of brochures vary greatly in terms of focus and emphasis. In this paper, only the effectiveness of brochures requested by and mailed to potential tourists will be examined.

There are two major issues concerning studies of the effectiveness of brochures. The first involves the question of defining the word effectiveness; that is, what are the criteria used in measuring the effectiveness of brochures. The second is concerned with the relationship between effectiveness of brochures and the characteristics of people who request them including their motivation, prior trip experience, and demographic and socioeconomic factors.

Change in immediate sales has been the most widely used measure of the effectiveness of brochures. Evaluation of the effectiveness of brochures is often part of a basic conversion study whose primary purpose is to estimate the so-called 'conversion rate,' which is the ratio between people who call for information and people who actually visit the destination after requesting information. However, it does not adequately assess the full effects of brochures.

The issue of the relationship between effectiveness of brochures and the characteristics of brochure-inquirers has not received adequate attention in most brochure studies. Fesenmaier and Vogt (1993) indicated that there is a need to better understand the reasons why brochures are effective or not effective. If these underlying reasons can be identified, tourism destination marketers would be able to design strategies to maximize the effectiveness of brochures.

LITERATURE REVIEW

Tourism destination marketing studies that relate most closely to brochure evaluation can be generally classified into three categories: economic impact studies; conversion studies; and brochure studies. While this classification seems arbitrary, because of the overlapping of these three types of studies, it is also true that each of them has a different objective and central focus.

Studies of the economic impact of travel information provided at welcome centers can be found in the works of Tierney and Haas (1988) and Fesenmaier and Vogt (1993). These studies tend to conclude that information obtained in the information centers had an impact on tourists in terms of an increase of their trip spending and an extension of their length of stay. In these studies, tourism destination marketers are mainly interested in how much money is spent by tourists and how these expenditures affect local economies including employment. Although the studies of economic impact of travel information provided at welcome centers noted above provide a good deal of information about the relationship between users of such information and spending behavior, it is not known whether these findings can be generalized to information-inquirers who call to request travel information.

Conversion studies are probably the most popular approach to studying the effectiveness of tourism advertising (Woodside, 1990) and have been claimed to be the basis for evaluating the effectiveness of tourism advertising (Silberman & Klock, 1986). Conversion studies yield a conversion rate which is the percentage of inquirers who visit after being exposed to the direct response marketing campaign. This conversion ratio can be used to estimate effectiveness and efficiency ratios, economic impact, and return on investment (Burke & Lindblom, 1989). The controversy over the usefulness of the conversion rate has been well documented (Ballman, Burke, Blank & Korte, 1984; Burke & Gitelson, 1990; Davidson-Peterson Associates, 1990; Ellerbrock, 1981; Purdue, 1984; Ronkainen & Woodside, 1987; Schroeder & Kreul, 1986; Woodside, 1990).

A review of the literature in the area of tourism destination marketing reveals that only a few research studies have been conducted to directly assess the effectiveness of brochures in marketing tourism destinations (e.g., Etzel & Wahlers, 1985; Baas, Manfredo, Lee, & Allen, 1989; Wicks & Schuett, 1991). It is, therefore, not surprising that little is known about the overall effectiveness of brochures (Wicks & Schuett, 1991). Baas et al. (1989) undertook a study to assess the effectiveness of an informational brochure for increasing awareness, interest, and participation in charter boat trip opportunities along the Oregon Coast. They concluded that the brochure did not positively or negatively affect charter trip participation and appeared to be effective only in increasing awareness of charter trip opportunities. Using involvement and risk theory, Etzel and Wahlers

(1985) reported that respondents requesting the brochure and having no knowledge of the attraction were much more likely to visit than would otherwise be expected.

Other brochure studies focus on on-site behaviors of brochure users. Fesenmaier and Vogt (1993) used three major criteria to measure the effectiveness of travel information provided at Indiana welcome centers. These criteria included: extension of time spent in Indiana, selection of alternative attractions, and incremental expenditures produced by longer visits or visiting different places. They concluded that motorists were influenced to extend their stay and select alternative attractions. Lime and Lucas (1977) examined the effects of a brochure for redistributing Boundary Waters Canoe Area visitors to lesser used areas and found that 33% of the study participants visited a new area after receiving the brochure. Krumpe and Brown (1982) found that 37% of visitors who received a brochure on Yellowstone National Park backcountry trail selection took a lesser used trail, as compared to 14% of the visitors who did not receive a brochure. Roggenbuck and Berrier (1982) studied the effects of a brochure designed to disperse campers in the Shining Rock Wilderness Area. Significant differences were found between individuals receiving brochures and those not receiving brochures. Cherem (1982) compared newspapers, radio announcements, and brochures for redistributing use in a crowded developed recreation area. Brochures were found to have some effect on redistributing use.

Still other brochure effects studies deal with physical aspects of brochures. Gilbert and Houghton (1991) conducted a brochure study to investigate the process of selecting brochures displayed in travel agency offices. The chief objective of their study was to examine factors which may lead a consumer to choose one or more brochures in preference to others.

From the above discussions, it is clear that each of these studies examined part of the potential effects of brochures on travel destination choice and on-site behavior. The overall effectiveness of brochures may be assessed by combining the strengths of these studies, namely, the immediate sale effects (e.g., Baas et al., 1989), the relationship between travel decision and information seeking behavior (e.g., Etzel & Wahlers, 1985) and the on-site behaviors (e.g., Roggenbuck & Berrier, 1982; Fesenmaier & Vogt, 1993). In addition, due to the nature of mailed-out brochures, reading of the brochure received is considered to be one of the critical points in measurement of effectiveness.

MAJOR HYPOTHESES

The above literature review and discussion give rise to several research hypotheses. They are presented as follows:

H1: The more respondents use brochures, the more likely they are to report a higher level of trip satisfaction.

H2: Brochures are more likely to have an impact on those who have not visited the destination than on those with prior experience in terms of influencing the trip decision.

H3: There exists a significant linear relationship between effectiveness of brochures and the independent variables including: prior experience, income, perceived usefulness of information contained in brochures, whether or not respondents spent a night in the study area and age.

METHODS

The brochure tested in this study was designed to attract potential tourists to visit Frankenmuth, a small town in Southeastern Michigan. Frankenmuth was founded in 1845 by a group of fifteen German-Lutheran missionaries who came to the area for the purpose of teaching Christianity to the Chippewa Indians. Today, it is a thriving community of 4,400 residents who take pride in preserving their German heritage. Frankenmuth has long claimed to be the number one visitor attraction in Michigan. It is located 86 miles north of Detroit, Michigan, approximately a two-hour drive from Detroit. Each year over three million people visit Frankenmuth.

The sampling frame consisted of the list of people who requested brochures between September 1 and March 15 of the following year in 1992-93 and 1993-94 respectively. The 1992-93 sample frame consists of 3,512 inquirers and the 1993-94 sample frame consists of 6,113 inquires for a total of 9,625. Both of these sample frames were provided by the Frankenmuth Chamber of Commerce.

A systematic random sampling procedure was applied to both the 1992-93 and the 1993-94 lists. One-thousand-two-hundred respondents were selected for the 1992-93 sample and another 1,200 for 1993-94, achieving a total sample size of 2,400 for the study. Of the 1,200 respondents selected for the 1992-93 sample, 600 were sent the unaided questionnaire (the brochure under study was not enclosed); the other 600 were sent the aided questionnaire (the brochure under study was enclosed). The same procedure was applied to the 1993-94 sample. The questionnaires were sent out by certified mail and no reminder postcards were sent afterwards.

RESULTS

Basic Findings

Questionnaires were mailed out May 15, 1994, and, by September 1, 1994, a total of 1,192 completed questionnaires were received. Responses across the four subsamples were evenly distributed. The overall response rate was 49.7 percent. The demographic characteristics of the respondents are provided in Table 1.

It was found that 91 percent of the respondents received a brochure after requesting information from the Frankenmuth Chamber of Commerce (FCC). Fifty percent of respondents said they visited Frankenmuth following requesting information from FCC, of which 99 percent stated that they read the brochure that was sent to them. This fifty percent is what is commonly referred to as the gross conversion rate. Among the other half of respondents who said they did not visit Frankenmuth after requesting information, ninety-six percent claimed that they read the brochure that was sent to them. In addition, among those respondents who did not visit Frankenmuth after requesting information, 91 percent said that they were considering a visit to Frankenmuth in the near future.

When asked about the timing of their request for information, only 29 percent of the respondents said that, when they requested the information, a visit to Frankenmuth was already planned. This number seems to be considerably lower than figures reported in other studies. For instance, a study of the effectiveness of the 1990 Wisconsin tourism marketing program (Davidson-Peterson Associates, 1990) found that 80% of respondents had already decided to go to Wisconsin at the time of requesting information. If the number (29%) reported here can be verified, it means that seventy-one percent of the respondents had either not made their final decision where to go for their trip or were not even considering a trip at all when they requested information.

When asked "To what extent did the brochure decrease or increase your interest in visiting Frankenmuth?" on a scale from 1 to 7 with 1 representing "not at all" and 7 indicating "greatly increased my interest," the mean response was 5.65, which indicates that the brochure was very helpful in increasing respondents' interest in visiting Frankenmuth. How-

TABLE 1. Demographic and Socioeconomic Characteristics of Respondents

Variable	Year		Total	Total
	1992-93 (frequencies)	1993-94 (frequencies)		(Percent)
Gender				
male	162	169	331	28
female	431	421	852	72
Education				
elementary	9	8	17	2
high school	197	213	410	35
undergraduate	264	274	538	46
graduate	115	91	206	18
Employment				
full time	296	315	611	52
part time	68	74	142	12
unemployed	6	8	14	1
homemaker	71	72	143	12
retired	142	93	235	20
student	4	17	21	2
other	5	10	15	1
Age				
under 18	1	7	8	0.7
18-24	12	17	29	2.5
25-34	79	96	175	15
35-49	181	239	420	36
50-65	219	161	380	32.8
66 and over	92	63	155	13.3
Income				
under $25,000	22	22	44	4.2
$25,000-$34,999	20	23	43	4.1
$35,000-$49,999	30	31	61	5.9
$50,000-$74,999	74	76	150	14.4
$75,000-$104,999	150	126	276	26.5
$105,000-$119,999	139	155	294	28.3
$120,000 and over	56	60	116	11.2

ever, using a similar scale, when asked "To what extent did the brochure cause you to spend more money in Frankenmuth on this trip than you would have otherwise?" the mean was only 3, which means that basically the brochure had only a minimal effect on the total expenditure the respondents would have otherwise made on their trip.

Brochure Use and Trip Satisfaction

Hypothesis 1 states that the more respondents use brochures, the more likely they are to report a higher level of trip satisfaction. When asked the question whether they consulted the brochure while visiting Frankenmuth, 78 percent of the respondents answered yes. This suggests that their information needs did not end with the beginning of the trip but continued during the period of the visit. The usefulness of the brochure was, thus, greatly increased and consequently more likely to exert its expected effects. Consulting the brochure on-site was taken to represent frequent use of the brochure, since logic suggests that respondents who consulted the brochure on-site are likely to use the brochure more often than respondents who did not consult the brochure. The chi-square test shows that there was a significant difference between those who consulted the brochure on site and those who did not in terms of their trip experience. The result of the chi-square test suggests that if people consulted the brochure, they were more likely to report recommending a trip to Frankenmuth to someone else.

The Role of Prior Experience

One important question that this research was designed to explore was that of how prior experience with Frankenmuth is related to the importance of brochures in influencing the decision to choose Frankenmuth again as a destination. The issue of the influence of prior experience really touches upon two separate but related questions: (a) Was there any difference between those who had visited before and those who had not visited before? (b) What is the relation between having prior experience and the effect of the brochure? In other words, will prior experience make the brochure less important or more important in the decision-making process?

On a scale of 1 to 7 with 1 representing no influence and 7 strong influence, respondents who had visited Frankenmuth before reported a mean of 4.16 as compared to 4.8 for those who had no such experience. The results of the T-test show that there exists a significant difference between these two types of respondents in terms of the role of the brochure in the process of choosing Frankenmuth as a tourist destination. To be specific, brochures are likely to exert more influence on the travel decision of those who have not visited Frankenmuth before than upon those who have previously visited Frankenmuth. The hypothesis that prior experience reduces decision-making risk and consequently brochures will exert less impact on brochure-inquirers is therefore supported.

The finding that respondents without prior visit(s) to Frankenmuth were more likely to be influenced by the brochure conforms with Milman and Pizam's (1995) finding that respondents go through a process from awareness to familiarity to action. Familiarity is considered a critical stage in this process. Potential first-time visitors call for information (awareness) to gain familiarity (reading the brochure received) which may lead to action (visit to Frankenmuth). In this process, reading the brochure can be a necessary step to gain familiarity which, in turn, increases the likelihood of making a trip to the destination.

A Linear Multiple Regression Model of Effectiveness

The conceptual basis of the regression model developed for this study builds on the notion that effectiveness as discussed in the beginning of this paper is affected by various variables derived from literature review. These variables are represented by different questions employed in this study. Specifically, the independent variables were represented by: (1) respondents' annual household income; (2) prior experience in terms of whether respondents had visited the destination before the inquiry; (3) perceived usefulness of brochures, (4) whether or not respondents spent a night in Frankenmuth; and (5) age of respondents.

The reason for choosing income to represent socio-economic variables is that other variables such as education and employment status tend to be highly correlated with income. In order to keep the model as parsimonious and practical as possible, it was decided to include only the income variable in the model. In their regression model for assessing travel advertising effectiveness, Messmer and Johnson (1993), using a similar argument, selected income per capita to capture the socio-economic composition of their sample. The viability of using income as an independent variable in the regression model was also supported by Silberman and Klock's (1986) findings.

Prior experience was included in the model, because it was found to be independently related to brochure effectiveness as discussed in the previous section and in previous studies (e.g., Etzel & Wahlers, 1985). The inclusion of the variable "any night spent in Frankenmuth" is based on the hypothesis that the spending of one or more nights in Frankenmuth is associated with the degree of involvement and perceived risk. The reason for selecting the perceived usefulness of the brochure variable is intuitive: if the brochure was perceived to be useful, it would have more influence than if it were perceived not to be useful. The last variable, age of respondent, is included as an exploratory variable to see if age affects the perceived impact of the brochure.

To ensure that the regression model accurately reflects the effectiveness of brochures, respondents who had already made the decision to visit Frankenmuth were excluded from the analysis. The general linear multiple regression model can be expressed as follows:

$$Y_i = \beta_0 + \beta_1 X_{1i} + \beta_2 X_{2i} + \ldots + \beta_p X_{pi} + e_i \qquad (1)$$

where β_0 is the intercept and other β's are the slopes associated with the respective independent variables. The notation X_{pi} indicates the value of the pth independent variable for case i. Independent random variables or the population error term is represented by e_i, which is the difference between the actual Y and (Y') predicted by the regression model. The model assumes that there is a normal distribution of the dependent variable for every combination of the values of the independent variables in the model.

Specifically, the mathematical formula for the regression model used in this particular study can be written as:

$$E_i = \beta_0 + \beta_1 I_{1i} + \beta_2 P_{2i} + \beta_3 N_{3i} + \beta_4 U_{4i} + \beta_5 A_{5i} + e_i \qquad (2)$$

where, again, β_0 is the intercept and β's are the slopes. The symbols of this model are explained below:

E_i = *EFFECTIVENESS* (effectiveness of the brochure, represented here by the response to the question: "To what extent did the brochure influence your decision to visit Frankenmuth?"

I_{1i} = *INCOME* (a measure of total household income)

P_{2i} = *PRIOR EXPERIENCE* (Had the respondent visited Frankenmuth before?)

N_{3i} = *NIGHT SPENT* (whether or not staying overnight)

U_{4i} = *USEFULNESS* (perceived usefulness of the brochure)

A_{5i} = *AGE* (of respondents)

The full correlation matrix (Table 2) for the multiple regression model was computed to examine if the independent variables showed more than a weak correlation with other independent variables in the model. The result was that none of the coefficients exceeded 0.35 and so the issue of multicollinearity can be ruled out (Tull & Hawkins, 1990).

The next step is to derive the regression coefficients. The coefficients estimated for this model as well as the related goodness of fit estimates and analysis of variance results are shown in Table 3. There are several noteworthy findings contained in Table 3. First, the sign of the regression coefficient (B) for *PRIOR EXPERIENCE* is negative and the coefficient is

TABLE 2. Correlation Matrix for the Multiple Regression Model

	E_i	I_{1i}	P_{2i}	N_{3i}	U_{4i}	A_{5i}
E_i	1.000					
I_{1i}	−.111					
P_{2i}	−.212	−.026				
N_{3i}	.038	.033	.005			
U_{4i}	.334	−.097	.006	.020		
A_{5i}	−.046	−.212	.007	.050	−.029	1.000

TABLE 3. Regression Results for Effectiveness Model

Parameter Estimates					
Variable	B	SE B	Beta	T	Sig T
Constant	1.83	.73		2.51	.013
Prior experience	−.84	.19	−.22	−4.41	.000
Night spent	.14	.21	.03	.66	.510
Usefulness	.57	.09	.33	6.62	.000
Income	−.09	.06	−.08	−1.74	.102
Age	.01	.01	.02	.38	.707

Goodness of Fit Estimates

Variable	Value
Multiple R	.41
R^2	.17
Adjusted R^2	.15
Standard Error	1.79

Analysis of Variance Results

Source	Degrees of Freedom	Sum of Squares
Regression	5	221
Residual	347	1113
Total	352	
F-Statistic	13.81	
Significance of F	.0000	

Note:
$p = 0.05$
B = unstandardized partial regression coefficient (prc)
SE B = unstandardized prc standard error
Beta = standardized prc
T = T-test score, and Sig T = significance level of T-test

statistically significant. The negative relationship between prior experience and effectiveness means that respondents with prior experience with the destination were more likely to report that the brochure had less influence on their decision to make a trip to Frankenmuth. In other words, those respondents who had not visited Frankenmuth were more likely to rely on the brochure for information to make a decision. Prior experience is, thus, a significant predictor of brochure effectiveness.

Second, the predictor variable, perceived *USEFULNESS*, is significant and has a positive B. This suggests that the more a respondent thought that the information contained in the brochure was useful, the more likely the brochure was to influence the decision to visit Frankenmuth.

Third, it is interesting to find that the variable *night spent* is not statistically significant in this model. Risk and involvement theory would have predicted that if respondents spent one or more nights in Frankenmuth, their involvement would have been high and they would have spent more money and hence would face higher risk which they would want to reduce by obtaining more information. Results here suggest that perceived risk and respondent involvement were not high in the decision to visit Frankenmuth.

Fourth, age and income were not significantly related to effectiveness of the brochure. Information-seeking behavior appears not to be affected by how old or how rich respondents are.

The goodness of fit test shows that the model explains less than 20 percent ($R^2 = .17$) of the variation in the dependent variable EFFECTIVENESS, with a standard error of 1.75. The hypothesis that no linear relationship exits between the dependent variable and the set of independent variables, was rejected. In other words, the multiple regression model built for this study fits the data but only to a modest degree.

In summary, the multiple regression model presented above suggests that: (1) The perceived usefulness of the information contained in the brochure appears to be the best predictor of the effectiveness of the brochure; (2) Prior visit(s) to Frankenmuth also appears to be important; (3) Age, income and overnight staying were not significantly related to effectiveness of the brochure; and (4) The model was statistically significant and fits the data, although only about 17% of the variation in effectiveness was accounted for by the model.

CONCLUSIONS

The underlying premise of this paper was that the value or effectiveness of a brochure rests on its efficiency in reaching consumers and its saliency in addressing their needs and interests. Based on the definitions of the word "effectiveness" developed for this study, the brochure under study can be said to be very effective in the following areas: (1) Ninety-nine percent of respondents who visited Frankenmuth after requesting information read the brochure that was sent to them; (2) Of the other half of respondents who did not visit Frankenmuth after requesting information, 99% reported having read the brochure; (3) Fifty percent of respondents visited Frankenmuth following requesting information and (4) Seventy-eight percent of respondents who visited Frankenmuth consulted the brochure during their visit. However, the brochure appears to have had minimal to moderate effect on changing respondents' total trip spending and a moderate effect on influencing respondents' decision to visit Frankenmuth.

The brochure appears to produce other benefits as well. Respondents who consulted the brochure while visiting Frankenmuth reported a better-than-expected trip experience and were more likely to recommend a visit to Frankenmuth to others after their trip. Factors affecting effectiveness of the brochure include prior visit(s) and perceived usefulness of the brochure. Respondents with prior visit(s) to Frankenmuth tended to report that their decision to visit Frankenmuth was less influenced by the brochure. Respondents who perceived that information contained in the brochure was useful were more likely to state that the brochure was influential in their trip decision to Frankenmuth. Age, income and spending a night at Frankenmuth did not contribute significantly to the effectiveness of the brochure in the trip decision process.

Marketing Recommendations

Results of this study suggest that since nearly all recipients read the brochures they received, and the majority who decided to visit consulted them on-site during their visit, there is a need to design a brochure that is user-friendly. A brochure should not only convey promotional messages but also provide information such as maps, business hours, parking areas and regulations, and other information one would expect to find in a travel guidebook. Clearly, responding to requests for brochures is important because they are read—brochure inquirers are a most receptive audience for a destinations's marketing message. The strong tendency for inquirers to retain and bring brochures with them suggests an opportunity to use them not only as tools to influence destination choice but also as devices to influence on-site behavior. Maps and other destination information should be included to enhance the visitors' on-site experience and thereby the probabilities of longer stay, repeat visits and more favorable recommendations of the destination to friends and relatives.

According to the findings of this study, seventy-one percent of the respondents had not made their final decision where to go for their trips. The implication of this is that there is considerable opportunity for destination marketers to influence and attract this large portion of the undecided potential travel population. Additional measures such as offering coupons, on-site prize drawing, and follow-up contacts could persuade the inquirer to make a trip to the destination.

Finally, through their request for information, inquirers identify themselves as high potential customers and ideal targets for aggressive marketing efforts. Study results show that brochures have different influences on first-time and repeat visitors. Knowing this, a destination could design separate brochures to target the interests of these two market segments. Repeat visitors are likely to be more influenced by a brochure featuring new attractions. First-time visitors may be more responsive to messages featuring a destination's more long-standing and well-known attractions. By investing minimal resources, destinations can simply provide targeted messages via brochures to enhance their influence on both first-time and repeat visitors.

DISCUSSION

As was pointed out in the beginning of this paper, this research study dealt with only one type of brochure distribution, i.e., via mail to brochure-inquirers. These brochure-inquirers tend to be more motivated and therefore their responses to the questions may not represent situations in which brochures are acquired through other means such as those displayed in the lobbies of hotels, in convention centers, in rest areas, in travel agency offices, or in tourist information centers. Reasonable caution should, therefore, be exercised when applying the results to these different populations. Demographic, socioeconomic and motivational factors may be different from those of brochure-inquirers who call to request information.

The overall response rate obtained in this study was 49.7 percent, which is above average for a mail survey. Still, it is not known if respondents may differ significantly from non-respondents, and time and budget did not permit an assessment of the possibility of nonresponse bias.

As was discussed earlier, the methodology used in this study was designed to measure effectiveness of mailed brochures requested by inquirers, and it would need to be modified to accommodate other brochure distribution systems. For instance, readership was an essential and all important first step in measuring effectiveness for mailed brochures. However, in the case of displayed brochures, the definition of effectiveness would necessarily include some measures of a brochure's ability to attract enough interest to convince passersby to select the brochure from the display, especially when presented with brochures for other destinations. Studying the process of brochure selection may reveal much information about interest in the destination and the types of people who pick up brochures and this would need to be incorporated in a study of effectiveness of a displayed brochure.

REFERENCES

Baas, J.M., M.J. Manfredo, M.E. Lee, & D.J. Allen (1989). Evaluation of an informational brochure for promoting charter boat trip opportunities along the Oregon coast. *Journal of Travel Research*, 27(3), 35-37.

Ballman, G., J. Burke, U. Blank, & D. Korte (1984). Toward higher quality conversion studies: Refining the numbers game. *Journal of Travel Research*, 22(4), 28-33.

Burke, J.F. & L.A. Lindblom (1989). Strategies for evaluating direct response tourism marketing. *Journal of Travel Research*, 28(2), 33-37.

Burke, J.F. & R. Gitelson (1990). Conversion Studies: Assumptions, Applications, Accuracy and Abuse. *Journal of Travel Research*, 28(3), 46-51.

Cherem, G. (1982). *Shenango River Lake: Interpretation Strategies and Evaluation, Report for Waterways Experiment Station*, U.S. Corps of Army Engineers.

Davidson-Peterson Associates (1990). *A Study of the Effectiveness of the 1990 Wisconsin Tourism Marketing Program* (unpublished). Prepared for Frankenberry, Laughlin & Constable.

Ellerbrock, M.J. (1981). Improving coupon conversion studies. *Journal of Travel Research*, 19(4), 37-38.

Etzel, M.J. & R.G. Wahlers (1985). The use of requested promotional material by pleasure travelers. *Journal of Travel Research*, 23(4), 2-6.

Fesenmaier, D.R. & C.A. Vogt (1993). Evaluating the economic impact of travel information provided at Indiana welcome centers. *Journal of Travel Research*, 31(3), 33-39.

Fesenmaier, D.R., C.A. Vogt & W.P. Stewar (1993). Investigating the influence of welcome center information on travel behaviors. *Journal of Travel Research*, 31(3), 47-52.

Gilbert, D.C. & P. Houghton (1991). An exploratory investigation of format, design, and use of U.K. tour operators' brochures. *Journal of Travel Research*, 30(2), 20-25.

Krumpe, E.E. & P.J. Brown (1982). Using information to disperse wilderness hikers. *Journal of Forestry*, 79, 92-94.

Lime, D.W. & R.C. Lucas (1977). Good information improves the wilderness experience. *Naturalist*, 28, 18-20.

Messmer, D.J. & R.R. Johnson (1993). Inquiry conversion and travel advertising effectiveness. *Journal of Travel Research*, 31(4), 21.

Millman, A. & A. Pizam (1995). The role of awareness and familiarity with a destination: The Central Florida case. *Journal of Travel Research*, 33(3), 21-27.

Purdue, R. (1984). Segmenting state travel information inquirers by timing of the destination decision and previous experience. *Journal of Travel Research*, 23(3), 6-11.

Roggenbuck, J.W. & D.L. Berrier (1982). A comparison of the effectiveness of two communication strategies in dispersing wilderness campers. *Journal of Leisure Research*, 14, 77-89.

Ronkainen, I.A. & A.G. Woodside (1987). Advertising conversion studies, pp. 481-487. In J.R.B. Ritchie & C.R. Goeldner (eds.), *Travel, Tourism, and Hospitality Research*. New York: John Wiley & Son.

Schroeder, J.J & L.M. Kreul (1986). *The effectiveness of travel information in converting the "inquirer" into a "traveler" to Indiana* (unpublished). Purdue University. Prepared for Indiana Department of Commerce.

Silberman, J., & M. Klock (1986). An alternative to conversion studies for measuring the impact of travel ads. *Journal of Travel Research*, 24(4), 12-16.

Tierney, P., & G. Haas (1988). *Colorado welcome centers: Their users and influence on length of stay and expenditures*. Ft. Collins: Department of Recreation Resources and Landscape Architecture.

Tull, D.S. & D.I. Hawkins (1990). *Marketing Research: Measurement and Method*. New York: Macmillan.

U.S. Travel Data Center (1996). *Survey of State Travel Offices 1995-1996*. Washington, DC: USTDC.

Wicks, B.E., & M.A. Schuett (1991). Examining the role of tourism promotion through the use of brochures. *Tourism Management*, 12(4), 301-12.

Woodside, A.G. (1990). Measuring advertising effectiveness in destination marketing strategies. *Journal of Travel Research*, 29(2), 3-8.

Motivation, Participation, and Preference: A Multi-Segmentation Approach of the Australian Nature Travel Market

Cheng-Te Lang
Joseph T. O'Leary

SUMMARY. The purpose of this study was to develop a typology of nature travelers based on their motivations, activity participation, and destination preferences. A secondary analysis from the Pleasure Travel Market Survey for Australia (1994) was used. The results indicated that the proposed 'motivation-participation-preference' multi-segmentation bases could classify Australian nature travel market into six segments. They were 'Physical Challenge Seekers,' 'Family Vacationers,' 'Culture & Entertainment Seekers,' 'Nature Tourists,' 'Escape & Relax Vacationers,' and 'Indifferent Travelers.' Travelers among groups exhibited significant differences in terms of their sociodemographics, trip-related characteristics, and travel philosophies. Implications of the findings are discussed. *[Article copies available for a fee from The Haworth Document Delivery Service: 1-800-342-9678. E-mail address: getinfo@haworth.com]*

Cheng-Te Lang is Post-Doctoral Research Associate and Joseph T. O'Leary is Professor, Department of Forestry and Natural Resources, Purdue University, West Lafayette, IN 47907.

The data utilized in this paper were made available by the Canadian Tourism Commission (CTC). The data for Australia Pleasure Travel Market Survey, 1994 was originally prepared by Coopers and Lybrand Consulting. Neither the collector for the original data nor the CTC bear any responsibility for the analysis or interpretations presented here.

[Haworth co-indexing entry note]: "Motivation, Participation, and Preference: A Multi-Segmentation Approach of the Australian Nature Travel Market." Lang, Cheng-Te, and Joseph T. O'Leary. Co-published simultaneously in *Journal of Travel & Tourism Marketing* (The Haworth Press, Inc.) Vol. 6, No. 3/4, 1997, pp. 159-180; and: *Geography and Tourism Marketing* (ed: Martin Oppermann) The Haworth Press, Inc., 1997, pp. 159-180. Single or multiple copies of this article are available for a fee from The Haworth Document Delivery Service [1-800-342-9678, 9:00 a.m. - 5:00 p.m. (EST). E-mail address: getinfo@haworth.com].

159

INTRODUCTION

Study Background

The tourism industry has grown over the past several decades and has become one of the most important economic activities around the world. Along with the expansion of tourism, a significant trend is a growing volume of tourists to nature destinations. Broadly speaking, these tourists can be called 'nature travelers.'

'Nature traveler' is one of the fastest growing tourist markets. Many studies identify the characteristics of the travelers who take nature-oriented trips. Generally speaking, it is believed that nature travelers are well educated, relatively wealthy, and willing to spend more. In addition, they are more interested in nature, travel more frequently, go longer distances, and stay longer than other groups (Boo, 1991; Eagles, 1992; Lang and O'Leary, 1990, 1991, 1992; Whelan, 1991; Wilson, 1987).

Although nature travelers share similar interests in visiting nature areas, they are not a homogeneous group. Travelers visit natural areas for different reasons. They also participate in different activities and impose various impacts on the environment. In order to improve marketing efforts and develop management programs, it is necessary to differentiate nature travelers into groups that help to identify and target homogenous characteristics.

Problem Statement

Although a better understanding of different types of nature travelers can lead to more effective planning, management, and marketing strategies, only a few studies have examined this issue and those have provided limited information. Some researchers suggested that nature travelers could be classified into different groups based on dedicated or casual interest (Laarman and Durst, 1987), travel distance and primary purpose (Ashton, 1991), or destination types and visiting purposes (Lindberg, 1991). These studies either had no empirical studies to confirm their classifications through an analytic approach, or they only investigated visitors to a specific destination and the information could not be generalized and applied to other markets or destinations.

Searching for the most appropriate and effective market segmentation bases is always an important research task for tourism businesses. Many market segmentation bases have been suggested and applied. They can be categorized as four types: sociodemographic, product-related, psychographic, and geographic (Morrison, 1992; Stynes, 1983). However, travel behavior is multi-dimensional and influenced by all of these various factors. Therefore, a multiple segmentation approach should be employed in order to define submarkets. Activity, motivation, and product preference have been the most popular segmentation bases for the travel and tourism industry because each of them can provide important product-related or psychographic information to assist in developing tourism products and promotion strategies for selected markets (Bryant and Morrison, 1980; Cha, McCleary, and Uysal, 1995; Crompton, 1979; Goodrich, 1977; Hendee, Gale, and Catton, 1971; Jamrozy and Uysal, 1994; Lang, O'Leary, and Morrison, 1993 & 1996; McCool, 1979; Woodside and Jacobs, 1985). A review of the literature suggests that most studies focus on only one of these segmentation bases. It is believed that segmenting travelers by a combination of benefit pursued, activity participation, and destination preference can reveal the relationships between the psychographic backgrounds and actual behavior to better classify markets and provide more information to aid in the development of tourist products, promotion materials and channels, management programs, and marketing strategies. Therefore, this study aims to develop a motivation/participation/preference multiple segmentation approach to understand travel behavior and further examine whether this approach can statistically and substantively classify the nature travel market into distinct segments. Further, recommendations for marketing, management, and research applications based on the results would be provided.

The proposed motivation/participation/preference segmentation approach was performed on the Australian outbound nature travelers.

Australian Nature Travel Market

The economy of Australia has began to recover since 1992 after years of recession. The continuing economic recovery indicates a potential for increasing the number of pleasure trips taken by Australians (U.S. Travel Data Center, 1994; Waters, 1994).

Studies indicate that more than half of Australians visit nature destinations during their overseas trips and the numbers are increasing (Market Facts of Canada Limited, 1990; Lang and O'Leary, 1990; Coopers & Lybrand Consulting, 1995). In response to the expansion of the Australian outbound nature travel market, in-depth studies on travelers from Australia are necessary.

METHODS

Data Collection

Data from the 'Pleasure Travel Market Survey to North America' for Australia were collected in 1994, under the sponsorship of the Canadian

Tourism Commission (former Tourism Canada) and the United States Travel and Tourism Administration. A total of 1,500 personal in-home interviews were conducted with Australian international travelers who met the following target qualifications: 18 years of age or over; and took a vacation trip of four nights or longer by plane outside of Australia and New Zealand in the past three years, or intend to take such a trip in the next two years. Approximately 80% of interviews were conducted in the cities and the remaining 20% in rural regions of the six states and two mainland territories. The questionnaire collected information on socio-economic and demographic variables (age, gender, income, education, occupation, life cycle, etc.), trip-related characteristics (party size, length of stay and trip type, trip description, destination, activities engaged, etc.), and psychographic attributes (travel philosophy, trip-driven items, product preferences).

A total of 1,032 Australian nature travelers selected (from 1,500 respondents) in this study are those who visited 'national parks/forests (n = 785),' 'wilderness areas (n = 603),' 'protected land/areas (n = 555),' 'mountainous areas (n = 831),' *or* 'coastal area (n = 962)' during the most recent long-haul overseas trips.

Data Analysis Procedures

The analysis of data in this study consisted of four stages. First, 25 benefit pursued attributes, 36 activity items, 78 destination attributes, and 18 travel philosophy items were grouped separately by factor analysis to exhibit their underlying patterns. The factor model selected was principal component analysis with varimax rotation and the preselected eigen value was 1.00. Second, cluster analysis with "Ward's Minimum Variance Method" was used to segment travelers into groups based on their motivation, activity, and destination preference factor scores. Later, multiple discriminant analysis was applied to confirm the number of clusters selected, i.e., examine whether distinct differences of factors could be found among selected clusters. Finally, five sociodemographic variables (age, income, education, sex, and marital status), five trip-related variables (trip type, major destination, length of trip, number of trips taken, and party size), and travel philosophy factors for the Australians were analyzed by a chi-square test and analysis of variance (ANOVA) to profile the characteristics of travelers under each cluster and examine whether differences exist between travelers among clusters.

RESULTS

There were seven benefit factors formed by factor analysis with 59.6% of the total variance explained. According to the characteristics of representative items, these factors were named as 'New Experience,' 'Escape and Entertained,' 'Show and Tell,' 'Family Oriented,' 'Cultural Groups Interest,' 'Physical Challenge and Nature,' and 'Relax' (Table 1). In addition, ten activity factors were formed with a 50.6% explained variance. They were 'Historic-Related Activity,' 'Nature-Related Activity,' 'Culture-Related Activity,' 'Shopping/Sightseeing,' 'Water-Related Activity,' 'Villages/Countryside,' 'Visit Cultural Groups,' 'Amusement Park/City Activity,' 'Guided Tours,' and 'Dining/Nightclubs' (Table 2). There was 50.2% of the total variance of destination preferences explained by eleven factors which were 'Budget/Convenience/Environment,' 'Natural Attractions,' 'Cultural Attractions,' 'Change and Relax,' 'Water-Related,' 'Luxury Facilities,' 'Sports,' 'Casinos/Amusement Parks,' 'Family Together,' 'Show/Tell,' and 'Unique Cultural Groups' (Table 3).

Also, six travel philosophy factors were formed and explained 59.4% of the total variance. They were 'Package Travel,' 'Self-Arrangement Travel,' 'Budget/Value Travel,' 'Long-haul Travel,' 'Frequent Travel,' and Reluctant Travel' (Table 4).

Through the cluster analysis, there were six distinct motivation/activity/preference types formed based on 850 valid cases. According to the representative factors and attributes in the cluster, the descriptions of each type follow (Table 5):

1. Physical Challenge Seekers (Cluster 1, n = 82, 8% of Australian respondents)

   Travelers in this group were likely to pursue physical challenges from overseas trips. They usually engaged in nature or water-related activities and preferred destinations that provided sport and water-related activity opportunities.

2. Family Vacationers (Cluster 2, n = 275, 27% of Australian respondents)

   Being with their families was the major reason for this group of travelers to take overseas vacation trips. These travelers preferred to visit a village or countryside, go shopping, and go sightseeing at destinations. A destination which provided an opportunity for them to be with their families was important.

3. Culture and Entertainment Seekers (Cluster 3, n = 259, 25% of Australian respondents)

   To this group of travelers, getting a chance to be entertained and visiting cultural groups were major trip-driving forces. They enjoyed participating in guided tours, visiting cultural groups, and doing city sightseeing. They preferred casinos, amusement parks or nightlife types of destinations. However, they also were concerned whether destinations provided convenience and value.

4. Nature Tourists (Cluster 4, n = 83, 8% of Australian respondents)

Seeking new experiences was an important reason for this group of travelers to go overseas. They usually participated in nature or heritage related activities and preferred destinations which had good natural and cultural attractions.

5. Escape and Relax Vacationers (Cluster 5, n = 119, 12% of Australian respondents)

The major purpose of this group was to escape from their daily routines and be entertained. They preferred to engage in water-related activities, sightseeing in cities, or nightlife entertainment. To them, a destination which could provide opportunities to getaway, relax, and have fun is essential.

6. Indifferent Travelers (Cluster 6, n = 32, 3% of Australian respondents)

This group of travelers did not reveal particular benefits which they intended to seek from their trips. Historic-related activities and guided tours were the most popular activities they engaged in. However, they also preferred destinations with natural attractions and luxury facilities.

Results of Discriminant Analysis

In order to examine differences among the six clusters in terms of motivation, activity participation, and destination preference factors, discriminant analysis was employed. Table 6 summarized the univariate test statistics of 28 factors (from Table 1, 2, 3) for Australian nature travelers and indicated that all these factors were significantly different among six clusters. Since this was a six-group model, it was necessary to calculate five canonical discriminant functions in order to distinguish among the six groups (Hair, Anderson, Tatham, and Black, 1992). Table 7 contains the results for the canonical functions and the statistics suggesting that all of them were significant. To validate the discriminant functions, the classification matrices were constructed and analyzed. The results indicated that the discriminant functions correctly classified 72.2% of the respondents from the analysis group and 72.4% of the respondents from the holdout group (Table 8). According to the proportional chance criterion (used

TABLE 1. Benefit Pursued (Motivation) Factors for Australian Outbound Nature Travelers.

Factor/Item/Reliability	EV[a]	Variance Explained[b]	Factor Loading
New Experience (factor I, α = 0.75)	5.48	21.9%	
Opportunity to increase one's knowledge			0.73
Meeting new and different people			0.70
Going to places I haven't visited before			0.66
Experiencing new and different life			0.60
Escape and Entertained (factor II, α = 0.73)	2.63	10.5%	
Getting a change from a busy job			0.70
Getting away from the demands of home			0.67
Escaping from the ordinary			0.63
Finding thrills and excitement			0.47
Indulging in luxury			0.44
Having fun, being entertained			0.40
Show and Tell (factor III, α = 0.70)	1.88	7.5%	
Going places my friends have not been			0.82
Talking about the trip after I return			0.79
Experiencing a simpler lifestyle			0.51
Meeting people with similar interest			0.49
Family Oriented (factor IV, α = 0.69)	1.51	6.0%	
Being together as a family			0.79
Visiting places where my family came from			0.68
Visit friends and relatives			0.66
Activities for the whole family			0.64
Cultural Groups Interest (factor V, α = 0.67)	1.26	5.0%	
Unique immigrant cultural groups (e.g., Chinese in Canada)			0.68
Unique native cultural groups (e.g., Eskimos, Indians)			0.66
Physical Challenge and Nature (factor VI, α = 0.60)	1.14	4.6%	
Outdoor activities			0.74
Roughing it			0.64
Visits to appreciate natural ecological sites (forests, wetlands, animal reserves)			0.43
Relax (factor VII, α = 0.64)	1.02	4.1%	
Doing nothing at all			0.78
Just relaxing			0.78

[a]Eigenvalue
[b] Of the total variance, 59.6% was accounted for by the 7 factors.

TABLE 2. Activity Factors of Australian Outbound Nature Travelers

Factor/Item/Reliability	EV[a]	Variance Explained[b]	Factor Loading
Historic-Related Activity (factor I, α = 0.72)	5.34	14.4%	
Visiting places of historical interest			0.68
Visiting sites commemorating important people			0.66
Visiting places of archaeological interest			0.58
Visiting places of importance in military history			0.54
Visiting places with religious significance			
(e.g., temples, churches, missions)			0.54
Visiting scenic landmarks			0.51
Visiting museums/galleries			0.50
Nature-Related Activity (factor II, α = 0.60)	2.56	6.1%	
Visits to appreciate natural ecological sites			
(forests, wetlands, or animal reserves)			0.64
Outdoor activities such as climbing, hiking			0.61
Observing wildlife/bird watching			0.58
Taking a nature learning trip			0.53
Culture-Related Activity (factor III, α = 0.55)	1.94	5.3%	
Attending local festivals/fairs/other special events			0.67
Enjoying ethnic culture/events			
(e.g. festivals, music, neighborhoods, food)			0.64
Arts and cultural attractions			
(e.g. live theater, concerts, dance, opera, ballet)			0.45
Sampling local food			0.42
Shopping/Sightseeing (factor IV, α = 0.54)	1.64	4.4%	
Shopping			0.55
Sampling local food			0.53
Sightseeing in cities			0.53
Taking pictures or filming			0.46
Water-Related Activity (factor V, α = 0.78)	1.44	3.9%	
Sunbathing or other beach activities			0.79
Swimming			0.74
Villages/Countryside (factor VI, α = 0.49)	1.43	3.9%	
Visiting small towns and villages			0.67
Sightseeing in the countryside			0.64
Driving to scenic places			0.49
Visit Culture Groups (factor VII, α = 0.50)	1.33	3.6%	
Opportunity to see or experience unique or different			
native group (Indians, etc.)			0.72
Unique/different immigrant cultural groups			
(Chinese in Canada, etc.)			0.61
Local crafts and handiwork			0.35
Amusement Park/City Activity (factor VIII, α = 0.45)	1.18	3.2%	
Visiting amusement/theme parks			0.66
Dining in fast food restaurants			0.54
Seeing big modern cities			0.50

Factor/Item/Reliability	EV[a]	Explained[b]	Loading
Guided Tours (not VFR) (factor IX, $\alpha = 0.44$)	1.11	3.0%	
Short guided excursions/tours			0.70
Visiting friends and relatives			−0.55
Taking a day cruise			0.55
Dining/Nightclubs (factor X, $\alpha = 0.43$)	1.04	2.8%	
Dining in fine restaurants			0.67
Visiting nightclubs			0.50
Informal or casual dining with table service			0.49

[a] Eigenvalue
[b] Of the total variance; 50.6% was accounted for by the 10 factors.

when group sizes are unequal), 23.4% (C_{pro}) of the observations would have to be correctly classified to meet each criterion. Because the classification accuracy of the two discriminant functions (72.2% and 72.4%) exceeded this criterion substantially, we would conclude that the discriminant models were valid.

Profiles of Six Motivation/Activity/Preference Groups

Five sociodemographic items, five trip-related variables and six travel philosophy factors were analyzed to profile the characteristics of travelers in each group.

Sociodemographic Variables

Travelers across six groups presented significant differences in terms of their age, education background, sex, and marital status (Table 9). Generally speaking, the 'Indifferent Travelers' group was the oldest (average 61.5 years of age), followed by the 'Nature Tourists' (average 53.0 years of age). The 'Physical Challenge Seekers' described the youngest group (average 35.2 years of age).

The Chi-Square test for education levels between groups was statistically significant. Results showed that 'Physical Challenge Seekers' had the highest education background (40.2% of them with a university or higher degree) and the 'Culture and Entertainment Seekers' had comparatively the lowest education background (54.6% of them with a high school or less degree).

Income distributions did not show significant difference between travelers among clusters. In terms of gender distribution, significant differences existed among groups as well. The 'Indifferent Travelers' was the only group that was male dominated (71.9% were male). In addition, marital status was also different between travelers among groups. The majority of the 'Family Vacationers,' 'Culture and Entertainment Seek-

TABLE 3. Destination Preference Factors for Australian Outbound Nature Travelers

Factor/Item/Reliability	EV[a]	Variance Explained[b]	Factor Loading
Budget/Convenience/Environment (factor I, α = 0.91)	15.94	17.5%	
Advertised low cost excursions (i.e., special offers)			0.77
Ease of exchanging currency			0.74
Inexpensive travel within the country			0.65
Inexpensive travel to the country			0.65
Inexpensive restaurants			0.65
Destination that provides value for my holiday money			0.64
Ease of obtaining visa			0.64
Taking advantage of currency exchange rate			0.63
Good public transportation such as airlines and local transit system			0.58
Availability of package trips and all inclusive vacations			0.57
Availability of pre-trip tourist information			0.56
Personal safety. Even when traveling alone			0.56
Being able to communicate in English			0.53
Standards of hygiene and cleanliness			0.51
Budget accommodations			0.46
Variety of short excursions/tours			0.45
Environmental quality of water, air, and soil			0.44
Fast food restaurants			0.42
Natural Attractions (factor II, α = 0.87)	6.28	6.9%	
National parks/forests			0.77
Visits to appreciate natural ecological sites (animal reserves, wetlands, etc.)			0.73
Wilderness and undisturbed nature			0.70
Interesting rural countryside			0.68
Lakes and rivers			0.66
Mountainous areas			0.66
Chances to see wildlife and birds			0.58
Wilderness adventure			0.57
Outstanding scenery			0.55
Coastal areas			0.46
Going places I have not visited before			0.44
Cultural Attractions (factor II, α = 0.84)	5.71	6.3%	
Local festivals			0.61
Interesting and friendly local people			0.60
Arts and cultural attractions			0.59
Experiencing new and different lifestyles			0.59
Museums and art galleries			0.58
Local crafts and handiwork			0.56
Trying new food			0.55
Meeting new and different people			0.52

Factor/Item/Reliability	EV[a]	Variance Explained[b]	Factor Loading
Local cuisine			0.51
Interesting small towns and villages			0.48
Opportunities to increase knowledge			0.48
Change and Relax (factor IV, $\alpha = 0.77$)	3.48	3.8%	
Getting a change from a busy job			0.70
Getting away from daily routines			0.70
Doing nothing			0.58
Just relaxing			0.53
Escaping from the ordinary			0.50
Finding thrills and excitement			0.45
Exotic atmosphere			0.44
Having fun			0.43
Water-Related Attractions (factor V, $\alpha = 0.75$)	2.93	3.2%	
Scuba diving			0.68
Snorkeling			0.66
Water sports			0.65
Beaches for sunbathing and swimming			0.53
Fishing			0.46
Luxury Facilities (factor VI, $\alpha = 0.78$)	2.40	2.6%	
Indulging in luxury			0.74
First class hotel			0.74
High quality restaurants			0.66
Resort areas			0.48
Sports (factor VII, $\alpha = 0.76$)	2.11	2.3%	
Alpine skiing			0.68
Cross country skiing			0.67
Doing sports			0.61
Tennis			0.51
Exercises and fitness			0.49
Outdoor activities			0.48
Golf			0.43
Casinos/Amusement Parks (factor VIII, $\alpha = 0.73$)	1.92	2.1%	
Casinos			0.66
Other gambling			0.63
Theme parks or amusement parks			0.59
Big modern cities			0.47
Nightlife and entertainment			0.45

TABLE 3 (continued)

Factor/Item/Reliability	EV[a]	Variance Explained[b]	Factor Loading
Family together (factor IX, α = 0.73)	1.75	1.9%	
Being together as a family			0.75
Visiting friends and families			0.72
Visiting place my family came from			0.66
Activities for entire family			0.58
Show/Tell (factor X, α = 0.71)	1.62	1.8%	
Visiting places I can talk about when I return home			0.59
Going somewhere my friends have not been			0.56
Meet friends who have similar interests			0.51
Unique Cultural Groups (factor XI, α = 0.79)	1.53	1.7%	
Unique/different immigrant cultural groups			0.56
Unique/different native cultural groups			0.47

[a] Eigenvalue
[b] Of the total variance; 50.2% was accounted for by the 11 factors.

ers,' and 'Nature Tourists' were married (over 74%), while more than half of the 'Physical Challenge Seekers' were single, divorced, or widowed.

Trip-Related Variables

Statistical differences existed between groups when Australian nature travelers identified their trip types (see Table 10). The most common trip type for the 'Physical Challenge Seeker' was 'a touring trip organized by myself' (43.9%). The 'Family Vacationers' often traveled to visit their relatives (46.9%). The 'Nature Tourists' group demonstrated stronger interest in a 'package tour' (24.1%) than other groups.

As to major vacation destinations, there were no significant differences between travelers among groups. In general, United States destinations (including the mainland, Hawaii, Guam, and American Samoa) were the most popular.

Length of trip was different between groups. Compared with travelers in other clusters, the 'Physical Challenge Seekers' had the longest length of trip (mean = 69.9 nights), while the 'Escape and Relax Vacationers' and 'Culture and Entertainment Seekers' had comparatively shorter trip lengths (40.9 and 41.4 nights).

TABLE 4. Travel Philosophy Factors for Australian Outbound Travelers

Factor/Item/Reliability	EV[a]	Variance Explained[b]	Factor Loading
Package Travel (factor 1, α = 0.70)	2.92	16.2%	
I like to have all my travel arrangements made before I start out on holiday			0.72
I usually travel on all-inclusive package holidays			0.68
Once I get to my destination, I like to stay out			0.67
It is important that the people I encounter on a holiday trip speak my language			0.55
I prefer to go on guided tours when holidaying overseas			0.54
Self-arrangement Travel (factor 2, α = 0.59)	2.16	12.0%	
I like to be flexible on my overseas holiday going where and when it suits me			0.81
I enjoy making my own arrangements for my holiday			0.71
Budget/Value Travel (factor 3, α = 0.50)	1.79	9.9%	
Getting value for my holiday money is very important			0.80
Inexpensive travel to the destination country is important to me			0.79
I like to go to a different place on each new holiday trip			0.49
Long-haul Travel (factor 4, α = 0.68)	1.50	8.3%	
When traveling overseas I usually take holidays of two weeks or less			− 0.81
I don't consider overseas trips unless I have at least three weeks to travel			0.77
I prefer to travel long distances with only one person (vs. the whole family)			0.35
Frequent Travel (factor 5, α = 0.47)	1.32	7.4%	
I take long holidays overseas whenever I have the opportunity			0.70
For me, money spent on overseas travel is well spent			0.68
I take short holidays overseas whenever I have the opportunity			0.67
Reluctant Travel (factor 6, α = 0.51)	1.01	5.6%	
Overseas travel is more of a hassle than a holiday			0.80
I do not really like to travel			0.73

[a] Eigenvalue
[b] Of the total variance, 59.4% was accounted for by the 6 factors.

There were no significant differences in party size and number of trips taken before between travelers among clusters.

Travel Philosophy Factors

Travelers between groups demonstrated statistically different travel philosophies in terms of 'Package Travel,' 'Self-Arrangement Travel,' 'Budget/Value Travel,' 'Long-Haul Travel,' and 'Reluctant Travel' (see Table 10). In general, the 'Culture & Entertainment Seekers' is the only group that presented positive attitudes toward 'Package Travel' and 'Bud-

TABLE 5. Clusters of Motivation/Participation/Preference Factors for Australian Nature Travelers

Cluster	Representative Factor*	Mean Factor Score
Physical Challenge Seekers	Physical Challenge & Nature (M)	0.53
(n = 82, 8% of respondents)	Show & Tell (M)	0.35
	Nature-Related Activity (A)	0.81
	Water-Related Activity (A)	0.67
	Water-Related Attractions (P)	0.53
	Sports (P)	
Family Vacationers	Family Oriented (M)	0.31
(n = 275, 27% of respondents)	Village/Countryside (A)	0.14
	Shopping/Sightseeing (A)	0.13
	Family Together Opportunity (P)	0.39
Culture & Entertainment Seekers	Cultural Groups Interest (M)	0.31
(n = 259, 25% of respondents)	Escape & Entertained (M)	0.13
	Guided Tour (A)	0.49
	Amusement Park/City Activity (A)	0.42
	Visit Cultural Groups (A)	0.29
	Casinos/Amusement Park/Nightlife (P)	0.40
	Budget/Convenience/Environment (P)	0.29
Nature Tourists	New Experience (M)	0.66
(n = 83, 8% of respondents)	Cultural Groups Interest (M)	0.60
	Physical Challenge & Nature (M)	0.32
	Nature-Related Activity (A)	0.79
	Visit Cultural Groups (A)	0.68
	Natural Attractions (P)	0.61
	Unique Cultural Groups (P)	0.60
	Cultural Attractions (P)	0.50
Escape & Relax Vacationers	Escape & Entertained (M)	0.66
(n = 119, 12% of respondents)	Water-Related Activity (A)	0.72
	Amusement Park/City Activity (A)	0.54
	Dining/Nightclubs (A)	0.43
	Change/Relax/Having Fun (P)	0.40
	Casinos/Amusement Parks/Nightlife (P)	0.34
Indifferent Travelers	Historic-Related Activity (A)	0.50
(n = 32, 3% of respondents)	Guided Tours (A)	0.29
	Natural Attractions (P)	0.43
	Luxury Facilities (P)	0.12

*: (M): motivation; (A): activity participation; (P): destination preference

TABLE 6. Summary of Univariate Test Statistics for Nature Travelers from Australia

Variable	R^2	F-value	Pr > F
Motivation			
New Experience	0.10	19.09	0.00
Escape & Entertainment	0.15	24.66	0.00
Show and Tell	0.05	8.82	0.00
Family Oriented	0.12	20.68	0.00
Cultural Groups Interest	0.21	35.31	0.00
Physical Challenge & Nature	0.33	56.17	0.00
Relax	0.03	5.19	0.00
Activity Participation			
Historic-Related Activity	0.07	11.98	0.00
Nature-Related Activity	0.21	44.27	0.00
Culture-Related Activity	0.10	18.83	0.00
Shopping/Sightseeing	0.27	63.48	0.00
Water-Related Activity	0.14	28.18	0.00
Villages/Countryside	0.13	24.33	0.00
Visit Cultural Groups	0.12	22.79	0.00
Amusement Park/City Activity	0.13	25.36	0.00
Guided Tour	0.18	37.99	0.00
Dining/Nightclub	0.04	7.73	0.00
Destination Preference			
Budget/Convenience/Environment	0.08	14.14	0.00
Natural Attractions	0.16	32.26	0.00
Cultural Attractions	0.09	16.38	0.00
Change/Relax	0.08	15.60	0.00
Water-Related Attractions	0.11	20.63	0.00
Luxury Facilities	0.06	11.57	0.00
Sports	0.04	7.69	0.00
Casinos/Amusement Park	0.11	20.00	0.00
Family Together	0.18	36.19	0.00
Show/Tell	0.02	3.64	0.01
Unique Cultural Groups	0.06	11.17	0.00

get/Value Travel.' Both the 'Physical Challenge Seekers' and the 'Family Vacationers' identified interests in 'Self-Arrangement Travel.' The 'Escape and Relax Vacationers' is the only group that disliked 'Long-Haul Travel.' In addition, only the 'Indifferent Travelers' had a positive attitude toward 'Reluctant Travel.' 'Family Vacationers' did not prefer 'Frequent Travel.'

CONCLUSIONS AND IMPLICATIONS

The most important contribution of this study is that it provides an opportunity to combine three of the most important traveler information

TABLE 7. Summary of Discriminant Analysis Results for Nature Travelers from Australia

Variable	Discriminant Function				
	F1	F2	F3	F4	F5
Discriminant Statistics					
Canonical Correlation	0.71	0.69	0.61	0.60	0.39
Eigenvalue	1.01	0.93	0.58	0.56	0.18
Wilks' Lambda	0.09	0.18	0.34	0.54	0.85
Probability	0.00	0.00	0.00	0.00	0.00

categories (benefit pursued, activity participation, and destination preference) and utilize their interrelationships as a segmentation base. The findings not only agree with the discussion in the literature that travel behavior is strongly influenced by these three dimensions, but further prove that the proposed motivation/participation/preference tourist visit type is a theoretically and statistically feasible approach to understand and classify travelers.

This three-component typology suggests a new alternative to segment the international travel market and provides more useful information. It is also superior to previous classification methods in terms of the theories supported, statistical approach employed, and traveler information revealed. The results not only show the actual activity types one segment of Australian travelers engaged in, but also reveal the forces behind their behavior (motivation) and their preferences toward vacation destinations. This three-dimensional information allows tourism providers to better understand their target markets and develop more effective promotional strategies and tourism products.

According to the results, Australian nature travelers in each segment varied in terms of their sociodemographic profiles (age, education, gender, marital status), trip-related characteristics (length of trip and trip type), and travel philosophies ('Package Travel,' 'Self-Arrangement Travel,' 'Budget/Value Travel,' 'Long-Haul Travel,' and 'Reluctant Travel'). For a travel and tourism related organization or agency, this means that marketing efforts should be focused to take into account these factors. For example, 'Physical Challenge Seekers' visit nature areas to engage in physical and nature-related activities. However, a visit to a nature area is just an add-on activity for 'Family Vacationers' since they travel overseas to visit relatives or be together with their families and they prefer to engage in family-oriented activities. This information is important to organizations

TABLE 8. Classification Matrices for Nature Travelers from Australia

		Predicted Group Membership					
Actual Group	No. of cases	1	2	3	4	5	6
Results from Analysis Stage				%			
Cluster 1[a]	41	61.0	12.2	17.1	9.7	0.0	0.0
Cluster 2	138	2.9	76.8	11.6	3.6	2.9	2.2
Cluster 3	129	1.6	12.4	76.7	2.3	5.4	1.6
Cluster 4	42	4.8	19.0	9.5	61.9	2.4	2.4
Cluster 5	109	7.3	3.7	20.2	67.0	67.0	0.9
Cluster 6	16	0.0	6.2	6.2	0.0	0.0	87.5

** Percent of cases correctly classified: 72.21%

Results from Validation Stage (Holdout Sample)				%			
Cluster 1	41	58.5	12.2	14.6	9.7	0.0	4.9
Cluster 2	137	2.2	77.4	10.9	4.4	2.2	2.9
Cluster 3	130	2.3	13.1	76.9	2.6	4.6	1.5
Cluster 4	41	7.3	17.1	9.8	63.4	2.4	0.0
Cluster 5	110	7.3	3.6	20.0	0.9	66.4	1.8
Cluster 6	16	0.0	12.5	0.0	0.0	0.0	87.5

** Percent of cases correctly classified: 72.42%

Note: C_{pro} = Proportional chance criterion
$$= p_1^2 + p_2^2 + p_3^2 + p_4^2 + p_5^2 + p_6^2$$
$$= (.10)^2 + (.32)^2 + (.30)^2 + (.10)^2 + (.14)^2 + (.04)^2 = 23.36\%$$
[a]: cluster 1 = 'Physical Challenge Seekers'
  cluster 2 = 'Family Vacationers'
  cluster 3 = 'Culture & Entertainment Seekers'
  cluster 4 = 'Nature Tourists'
  cluster 5 = 'Escape & Relax Vacationers'
  cluster 6 = 'Indifferent Travelers'

for designing promotional materials and travel products that appeal to or entice these two different groups.

Tourism providers also should be aware of the differences between travelers among groups in terms of their trip-related characteristics and philosophies toward travel. Package tours with a low cost and about one month trip length will be an ideal arrangement for the 'Culture and Entertainment Seekers.' In contrast, different kinds of information about destination (such as accommodation, transportation, weather) and assistance

TABLE 9. Sociodemographic Characteristics of Clusters

Variable N	cls1 (82)	cls2 (275)	cls3 (259)	cls4 (83)	cls5 (119)	cls6[a] (32)
Age (df = 5, F-value = 31.12, p < = 0.00)*						
mean years (all = 46.1)	35.2	46.9	48.2	53.0	38.0	61.5
Education (df = 30, chi-sq. = 59.82, p < = 0.00)*			%			
Primary school (grades 1-7)	1.2	1.5	4.7	0.0	0.8	3.1
Some high school	20.7	18.6	33.0	12.2	26.9	28.1
High school graduated (grade 12)	19.5	19.7	15.9	20.7	25.2	15.6
Tech./Voca. school graduated	4.9	13.9	15.2	17.1	11.8	12.5
Some college or university	13.4	11.3	11.2	13.4	9.2	3.1
Graduated from university	32.9	27.0	14.7	26.8	18.5	25.0
Graduated w/ an advanced degree	7.3	8.0	5.4	9.8	7.6	12.5
Income (annual) (df = 15, chi-sq. = 19.51, p = 0.19)			%			
Less than AU$20,000	18.4	17.1	16.2	21.7	10.6	23.3
AU$20,000 - AU$39,999	25.0	24.0	30.7	22.9	21.2	33.3
AU$40,000 - AU$59,999	23.7	23.3	27.8	24.1	25.7	20.0
AU$60,000 or more	32.9	35.7	25.3	31.3	42.5	23.3
Sex (df = 5, chi-sq. = 13.89, p = 0.02)*			%			
Male	42.7	40.0	39.0	39.8	45.4	71.9
Female	57.3	60.0	61.0	60.2	54.6	28.1
Marital Status (df = 5, chi-sq. = 31.01, p < = 0.00)*			%			
Married	48.8	74.1	74.1	74.7	57.1	68.8
Single/Divorced/Widowed	51.2	25.9	25.9	25.3	42.9	31.2

*: significance level = 0.05
[a]: cls1 = 'Physical Challenge Seekers'
  cls2 = 'Family Vacationers'
  cls3 = 'Culture & Entertainment Seekers'
  cls4 = 'Nature Tourists'
  cls5 = 'Escape & Relax Vacationers'
  cls6 = 'Indifferent Travelers'

should be provided through various channels for the 'Physical Challenge Seekers' type of Australian nature traveler since they prefer to organize trips themselves.

An interesting question relates to the complexity of the segmentation. Many existing surveys limit the number of variables used and avoid areas like psychographics. But the survey employed in this paper is much more complex and multifaceted and part of a research program going on throughout the world. As survey research takes into account a broader

TABLE 10. Trip-Related Characteristics and Travel Philosophy of Clusters

Variable N	cls 1 (82)	cls2 (275)	cls3 (259)	cls4 (83)	cls5 (119)	cls6[a] (32)
Trip Type (df = 80, chi-sq. = 235.48, p < = 0.00)*			%			
A visit to friends	8.5	10.6	3.9	10.8	5.9	12.5
A visit to relatives	20.7	46.9	20.5	25.3	13.5	28.1
A package tour	6.1	4.4	23.9	24.1	16.8	9.4
A touring trip organized yourself	43.9	21.1	32.8	21.7	35.3	28.1
A city trip	1.2	0.0	0.0	0.0	0.0	0.0
An outdoor trip	1.2	0.0	0.0	1.2	0.8	0.0
A resort trip	1.2	0.7	1.2	1.2	1.7	0.0
Exhibition/event/theme park	0.0	0.7	1.9	0.0	3.4	3.1
A trip to a historical place	0.0	0.0	0.4	0.0	0.0	3.1
A business/pleasure combined trip	4.9	6.9	8.9	8.4	4.2	15.6
Honeymoon trip	1.2	1.8	1.2	0.0	8.4	0.0
Incentive travel	0.0	0.7	2.3	1.2	1.7	0.0
A working holiday	0.0	1.1	0.8	0.0	0.8	0.0
A conference/convention	8.5	1.1	0.0	1.2	4.2	0.0
Religious holiday/pilgrimage	1.2	0.7	0.0	1.2	0.0	0.0
Other	0.0	0.7	0.4	0.0	0.0	0.0
Major Destination (df = 90, chi-sq. = 87.77, p = 0.64)						
Mainland USA	39.0	38.6	36.3	27.7	32.8	28.1
Hawaii	23.2	22.9	26.6	22.9	19.3	31.3
Guam/American Samoa	15.9	16.7	14.3	22.9	22.7	21.9
Puerto Rico/US Virgin Islands	4.9	8.4	11.6	9.6	6.7	3.1
Other South Pacific	9.8	5.5	3.1	6.0	6.7	6.3
Canada	0.0	1.5	1.9	4.8	3.4	3.1
Mexico	3.7	2.2	1.5	1.2	2.5	3.1
Central/South America	0.0	1.5	0.8	1.2	1.7	0.0
The West Indies/Caribbean	1.2	0.4	1.2	1.2	0.8	3.1
SouthAfrica	0.0	1.1	0.8	0.0	0.0	0.0
Other Africa	0.0	0.4	0.4	0.0	0.0	0.0
UK	1.2	1.1	0.8	1.2	0.0	0.0
Japan	0.0	0.0	0.4	0.0	0.8	0.0
Former USSR (CIS)	0.0	0.0	0.0	0.0	0.8	0.0
Korea	0.0	0.0	0.0	0.0	0.8	0.0
Thailand	0.0	0.0	0.0	0.0	0.8	0.0
Singapore/Malaysia, Philippines	1.2	0.0	0.0	0.0	0.0	0.0
Taiwan (ROC)	0.0	0.0	0.4	0.0	0.0	0.0
Other	0.0	0.0	0.0	1.2	0.0	0.0

TABLE 10 (continued)

Variable N	cls 1 (82)	cls2 (275)	cls3 (259)	cls4 (83)	cls5 (119)	cls6[a] (32)
Length of Trip (df = 5, F-Value = 11.65, p < = 0.00)[*]						
mean nights (all = 50.6)	69.9	49.0	41.4	50.1	40.9	50.0
Number of trips taken (df = 5, F-Value = 0.73, p = 0.60)						
mean trips (all = 1.66)	1.7	1.6	1.5	1.8	1.6	1.7
Party Size (df = 5, F-Value = 1.21, p = 0.30)						
mean persons (all = 3.0)	3.5	2.4	3.3	2.9	3.2	2.2
Travel Philosophy Factor						
Package Travel (df = 5, F-Value = 7.96, p < = 0.00)[*]						
mean scores (all = -0.10)	-0.37	-0.21	0.19	-0.30	-0.11	-0.18
Self-Arrangement Travel (df = 5, F-Value = 9.45, p < = 0.00)[*]						
mean scores (all = -0.02)	0.15	0.27	-0.25	-0.27	-0.06	-0.30
Budget/Value Travel (df = 5, F-Value = 7.86, p < = 0.00)[*]						
mean scores (all = -0.15)	-0.07	-0.33	0.14	-0.21	-0.18	-0.73
Long-Haul Travel (df = 5, F-Value = 3.23,p < = .00)[*]						
mean scores (all = 0.09)	0.24	0.23	0.01	0.11	-0.17	0.05
Frequent Travel (df = 5, F-Value = 2.16, p = 0.06)[**]						
mean scores (all = 0.08)	0.17	-0.06	0.14	0.24	0.09	0.20
Reluctant Travel (df = 5, F-Value = 2.38, p = 0.04)[*]						
mean scores (all = -0.15)	-0.13	-0.06	-0.19	-0.36	-0.18	0.20

[*]: significance level = 0.05
[**]: significance level = 0.10
[a]: cls1 = 'Physical Challenge Seekers'
cls2 = 'Family Vacationers'
cls3 = 'Culture & Entertainment Seekers'
cls4 = 'Nature Tourists'
cls5 = 'Escape & Relax Vacationers'
cls6 = 'Indifferent Travelers'

array of important measures that appear to influence travel, the ability to develop "sharper" segments based on these multiple factors becomes possible. But in terms of application, do these become too complicated to be adapted to contemporary marketing and sales programs? Perhaps these questions need to be addressed through more aggressive education and training programs that show incorporation into successful commercial activity.

In addition, periodic surveys and research for repeat travelers should be conducted to monitor whether travel behavior and motivation/activity/

preference patterns change along with time before we can generalize the results. Further studies are also needed to better profile travelers, including questions like how the tourists can be reached and what information sources they need. Do travelers among clusters have different trip-planning horizons? Do travelers from different countries have similar travel patterns? The opportunities in this area of research are important and wide open with the increasing demand for global travel forecasted.

REFERENCES

Ashton, R.E. (1991). Defining the Ecotourist Based on Site Needs. In J.A. Kusler (Ed.), *Proceeding of the 2nd International Symposium: Ecotourism and Resource Conservation* (pp. 91-98). Florida.

Boo, E. (1991). *Ecotourism: the Potentials and Pitfalls* (2 Vols.), Washington, DC: World Wildlife Fund.

Bryant, B.E. & A.J. Morrison (1980). Travel Market Segmentation and the Implementation of Market Strategies. *Journal of Travel Research*, 18(3), 2-8.

Cha, S., McCleary, K.W. & M. Uysal (1995). Travel Motivations of Japanese Overseas Travelers: A Factor-Cluster Segmentation Approach. *Journal of Travel Research*, 34(1), 33-39.

Coopers and Lybrand Consulting (1995). Pleasure Travel Market Survey for Australia–Final Report. Canada.

Crompton, J.L. (1979). Motivations for Pleasure Vacation. *Annals of Tourism Research*, 6(4), 408-424.

Eagles, P.F.J. (1992). The Travel Motivations of Canadian Ecotourists. *Journal of Travel Research*, 31(2), 3-7.

Goodrich, J.N. (1977). The Relationship between Preferences for and Perceptions of Vacation Destinations: Application of a Choice Model. *Journal of Travel Research*, 17(1), 8-13.

Hair, J.F., R.E. Anderson, R.L. Tatham, & W.C. Black (1992). *Multivariate Data Analysis with Readings* (3rd ed.). New York: Macmillan Publishing Company.

Hendee, G.C., R.R. Gale, & W.R. Catton (1971). A Typology of Outdoor Recreation Activity Preference. *The Journal of Environmental Education*, 3(1), 28-34.

Jamrozy, U. & M. Uysal (1994). Travel Motivation Variations of Overseas German Visitors. *Journal of International Consumer Marketing*, 6(3/4), 135-160.

Laarman, J.G. & P.B. Durst (1987). Nature Travel in Tropics. *Journal of Forestry*, 8(5), 43-46.

Lang, C.T. & J.T. O'Leary (1990). *International Travel and Tourism: Analysis of Overseas Travelers to National Parks/Historic Sites–Australia*. A Report Prepared for U.S. National Park Service.

Lang, C.T. & J.T. O'Leary (1991). *International Travel and Tourism: Analysis of Overseas Travelers to National Parks/Historic Sites–Italy*. A Report Prepared for U.S. National Park Service.

Lang, C.T. & J.T. O'Leary (1992). *International Travel and Tourism: Analysis of Overseas Travelers to National Parks/Historic Sites–United Kingdom*. A Report Prepared for U.S. National Park Service.

Lang, C.T., J.T. O'Leary, & A.M. Morrison (1993). Activity Segmentation of Japanese Female Overseas Travelers. *Journal of Travel & Tourism Marketing*, 2(4), 1-22.

Lang, C.T., J.T. O'Leary, & A M. Morrison (1996). Trip-Driven Attribute Segmentation of Australian Outbound Nature Travelers. In *Proceedings of the Australian Tourism and Hospitality Research Conference*, Coffs Harbour, New South Wales, Australia.

Lindberg, K. (1991). *Policies for Maximizing Nature Tourism's Ecological and Economic Benefits*. Washington, DC: World Resources Institute.

McCool, S.F. (1979). Recreation Activity Packages at Water-Based Resources. In C.S. Van Doren, G.B. Priddle & L.E. Lewis (Eds.), *Land and Leisure*. Chicago, IL: Maaroufa Press.

Morrison, A. M. (1992). *Hospitality and Travel Marketing* (2nd). Albany, N.Y.: Delmar Publishers Inc.

Stynes, D.J. (1983). Marketing Tourism. *Journal of Physical Education and Dance*, 54(4), 21-23.

U.S. Travel Data Center (1994). *1995 Outlook for Travel and Tourism*. Washington DC: USTDC.

Waters, S.R. (1994). *Travel Industry World Yearbook: The Big Picture*. New York: Child and Waters Inc.

Whelan, T. (1991). Ecotourism and Its Role in Sustainable Development (pp. 3-22). In T. Whelan (Ed.), *Nature Tourism*. Washington, DC: Island Press.

Wilson, M.A. (1987). Nature-Oriented Tourism in Ecuador Assessment of Industry Structure and Development Needs. *Southeastern Center for Forest Economics Research, Research Triangle Park, NC. FPEI Working Paper*, No. 6.

Woodside, A.G. & L.W. Jacobs (1985). Step Two in Benefit Segmentation: Learning the Benefits Realized by Major Travel Markets. *Journal of Travel Research*, 24(1), 7-13.

Index

Page numbers followed by "t" indicate tables.

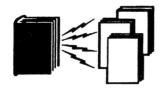

Haworth
DOCUMENT DELIVERY
SERVICE

This valuable service provides a single-article order form for any article from a Haworth journal.

- *Time Saving:* No running around from library to library to find a specific article.
- *Cost Effective:* All costs are kept down to a minimum.
- *Fast Delivery:* Choose from several options, including same-day FAX.
- *No Copyright Hassles:* You will be supplied by the original publisher.
- *Easy Payment:* Choose from several easy payment methods.

Open Accounts Welcome for . . .
- Library Interlibrary Loan Departments
- Library Network/Consortia Wishing to Provide Single-Article Services
- Indexing/Abstracting Services with Single Article Provision Services
- Document Provision Brokers and Freelance Information Service Providers

---

MAIL or *FAX* THIS ENTIRE ORDER FORM TO:

Haworth Document Delivery Service
The Haworth Press, Inc.
10 Alice Street
Binghamton, NY 13904-1580

or FAX: 1-800-895-0582
or CALL: 1-800-342-9678
9am-5pm EST

PLEASE SEND ME PHOTOCOPIES OF THE FOLLOWING SINGLE ARTICLES:
1) Journal Title: _____
   Vol/Issue/Year: _____ Starting & Ending Pages: _____
Article Title: _____
_____

2) Journal Title: _____
   Vol/Issue/Year: _____ Starting & Ending Pages: _____
Article Title: _____
_____

3) Journal Title: _____
   Vol/Issue/Year: _____ Starting & Ending Pages: _____
Article Title: _____
_____

4) Journal Title: _____
   Vol/Issue/Year: _____ Starting & Ending Pages: _____
Article Title: _____
_____

(See other side for Costs and Payment Information)

COSTS: Please figure your cost to order quality copies of an article.

1. Set-up charge per article: $8.00

   ($8.00 × number of separate articles)   _____

2. Photocopying charge for each article:

   1-10 pages: $1.00   _____

   11-19 pages: $3.00   _____

   20-29 pages: $5.00   _____

   30+ pages: $2.00/10 pages   _____

3. Flexicover (optional): $2.00/article   _____

4. Postage & Handling: US: $1.00 for the first article/

   $.50 each additional article   _____

   Federal Express: $25.00   _____

   Outside US: $2.00 for first article/

   $.50 each additional article _____

5. Same-day FAX service: $.35 per page   _____

   GRAND TOTAL: _____

METHOD OF PAYMENT: (please check one)

❏ Check enclosed   ❏ Please ship and bill. PO # _____

(sorry we can ship and bill to bookstores only! All others must pre-pay)

❏ Charge to my credit card: ❏ Visa; ❏ MasterCard; ❏ Discover;

❏ American Express;

Account Number:_____ Expiration date:_____

Signature: *X*_____

Name: _____ Institution: _____

Address: _____

_____

City: _____ State:_____ Zip:_____

Phone Number: _____ FAX Number: _____

MAIL or *FAX* THIS ENTIRE ORDER FORM TO:

Haworth Document Delivery Service	**or FAX:** 1-800-895-0582
The Haworth Press, Inc.	**or CALL:** 1-800-342-9678
10 Alice Street	9am-5pm EST)
Binghamton, NY 13904-1580